SOUTHEAST ASIA
A HISTORY IN OBJECTS

SOUTHEAST ASIA
ASIA
A HISTORY
IN OBJECTS

ALEXANDRA GREEN

Thames &Hudson   The British Museum

Contents

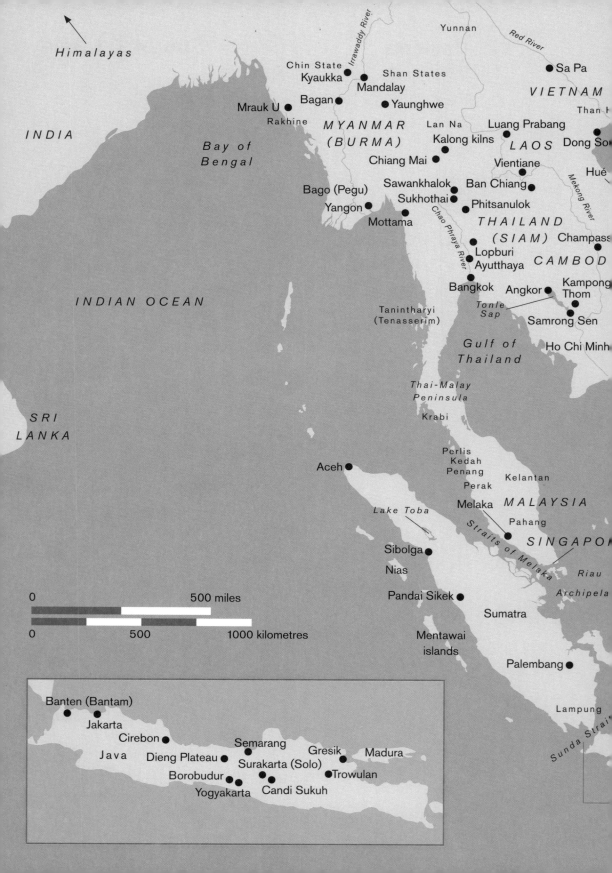

Himalayas

INDIA

Bay of
Bengal

Chin State
Kyaukka
Bagan
Mandalay
Mrauk U
Rakhine
MYANMAR
(BURMA)
Shan States
Yaunghwe
Lan Na
Kalong kilns
Chiang Mai

Yunnan
Red River
Sa Pa
VIETNAM
Than H
Luang Prabang
LAOS
Dong So
Vientiane
Huế

Bago (Pegu)
Yangon
Mottama
Sawankhalok
Sukhothai
Ban Chiang
Phitsanulok
THAILAND
(SIAM)
Mekong River
Champass
CAMBOD
Lopburi
Ayutthaya
Bangkok
Angkor
Kampong
Thom
Samrong Sen
Chao Phraya River
Tonle
Sap
Ho Chi Minh

INDIAN OCEAN

Tanintharyi
(Tenasserim)

Gulf of
Thailand

Thai-Malay
Peninsula

Krabi

SRI
LANKA

Aceh
Lake Toba
Perlis
Kedah
Penang
Perak
Kelantan
Melaka
MALAYSIA
Pahang
SINGAPO
Sibolga
Nias
Straits of Melaka
Riau
Archipela
Pandai Sikek
Sumatra
Mentawai
islands
Palembang

0   500 miles

0   500   1000 kilometres

Banten (Bantam)
Jakarta
Cirebon
Java
Semarang
Dieng Plateau
Surakarta (Solo)
Borobudur
Yogyakarta
Candi Sukuh
Gresik
Trowulan
Madura

Lampung
Sunda Strait

CHINA

Guangdong

Fujian

TAIWAN

Southeast Asia

South China
Sea

Cordillera
Region

Luzon

PACIFIC OCEAN

Da Nang

Hoi An

VIETNAM

Manila

Mindoro

PHILIPPINES

BRUNEI

Kelabit
Highlands

Sabah

Igan River

Sarawak

Baram River

Rejang River

Mindanao

Talaud islands

Sambas

Kalimantan

INDONESIA

Sulawesi

Mamasa

Maluku islands

Seram

Ambon

Makassar
(Ujung Pandang)

Ulu Leang

Kei islands

Ritabel

Tanimbar islands

Mount Sindoro

Mount
Agung

Tenganan Pageringsingan

Mount
Sumeru

Lombok

Solor

EAST TIMOR

Bali

Kamasan

Ubud

Sumba

Introduction

The concept of Southeast Asia as a distinct region emerged
after the Second World War, and it is today largely encapsulated
by the Association of Southeast Asian Nations (ASEAN),
formed in 1967. There are currently two distinct parts:
the mainland region, comprising Myanmar, Thailand,
Cambodia, Laos and Vietnam; and the island region of
Indonesia, Malaysia, Brunei, Singapore, East Timor and
the Philippines. Both are home to numerous ethnic and
linguistic groups, ranging even today from large and complex
societies to small communities of hunter-gatherers. There
has been substantial discussion about the usefulness of the
term 'Southeast Asia', given the linguistic, religious, social
and cultural diversity it encompasses, and also the existence
of strong cultural connections with the indigenous groups
of Taiwan, southwestern China and northeastern India,
as well as links with Sri Lanka and Madagascar. Yet, within
Southeast Asia there are clear lines of contact and strong
similarities culturally, historically and materially.

The multiplicity found in Southeast Asia emerged from
a geography characterized by rich river basins and shallow
seas (2) that enabled interaction and mountainous terrain and
highlands that hindered it (1). Rice became the staple crop
of people living in the lowlands (3), with other starches, such
as sago, tapioca and dry rice, grown by those living in the
highlands and in parts of island Southeast Asia (particularly
the eastern Indonesian islands) that were not suitable for wet
rice agriculture. The region is rich in resources, such as cloves
and sandalwood, many of which were once found nowhere
else, and Southeast Asians extracted and used them locally,
and also developed routes of exchange (5). Over time, these
networks expanded regionally and internationally, and the
region's location between the South Asian subcontinent and
China made it a trade hub. Because the annual monsoons
forced traders to stay in Southeast Asia while waiting for
favourable winds to take them onwards, cosmopolitan ports
and cities developed, notably Palembang, Melaka (Malacca),
Brunei, Mottama (Martaban), Ayutthaya, Hoi An and later

1. Mountainous terrain near the Thai-Myanmar border, Mae Hong Son Province, Thailand

Mainland Southeast Asia is divided by roughly north–south oriented rivers, with the Mekong, Red, Irrawaddy and Chao Phraya and their tributaries forming lowland riverine plains suitable for wet rice cultivation. Highland rivers, such as that seen here, along with dense tropical jungle, form major impediments to overland travel. These mountainous regions were unsuitable for large-scale agriculture, creating cultural distinctions between the coastal and riverine peoples and the upland and interior ones. Highland terrain supported smaller-scale, semi-nomadic societies and also provided a refuge from state control until quite recently.

Da Nang, Jakarta (Batavia) (**6**) and Singapore. There, Arabs, Tamils, Gujaratis, Chinese and Southeast Asians among many others, and later Westerners, interacted and intermingled (**7**). Southeast Asia's openness to the outside world meant that new ideas were constantly being integrated into local cultural frameworks, creating the myriad art forms of the region. The flows of ideas and information were reciprocal, however, and terminologies, technologies and art forms demonstrate that ideas circulated regionally and beyond.

To Southeast Asians, the world was inhabited by unseen spirits, ancestors, demons and deities, who became interwoven with the Hindu and Buddhist concepts and iconographies arriving from the Indian subcontinent, Islamic beliefs that came via Arabs and Muslim Indian traders, and eventually the values of various Christian denominations. Until recently, art was not considered a separate category from craft, performance or the everyday, and it was produced by and for all echelons of society. Nor were certain materials viewed as more representative of art than others; their durable or ephemeral qualities were channelled into different

purposes, ranging from stone temples for deities to wood sculptures enhancing the prestige of a clan house, lacquer vessels for daily use, woven leaf offerings, protective tattoos, basketry for use and display, and masks or puppets used in performance. It was the efficacy of objects – in displaying social rank and status, as well as making the environment more potent, communicating with the gods and the spirit world, or honouring ancestors to ensure the current and future well-being of family, community and the world – that was paramount. Southeast Asian artists did not usually sign their work, and many types of artifacts were produced collaboratively. Since the 19th century, there has been an increase in the production of art for art's sake. Art has recently been used to record particular events, such as the war against the United States in Vietnam as well as Vietnamese society at the time (**7**). Today, Southeast Asia has a burgeoning contemporary art scene.

Starting in the late 18th century, Europeans began to collect art from various Southeast Asian cultures, and over the course of the 19th and 20th centuries, these artworks were

2. View from Padar island, Komodo archipelago, East Nusa Tenggara, Indonesia
The peninsular and island regions combine lands that are geologically stable and those that lie along subduction zones, forming volcanic arcs from Sumatra to the Maluku islands (Moluccas), and from Sulawesi through the Philippines and further north. Some areas, such as Java, have fertile soils and monsoon climates, supporting high population densities; but outside volcanic zones, island areas often have poor soils and can only support sparse populations, such as in central Borneo. The shallow seas and mangroves were territories occupied by sea nomads, like the Orang Laut, who historically were sources of maritime commodities and naval forces.

3. Rice fields, Bali

Rice is the most widely cultivated staple crop in Southeast Asia, with thousands of varieties that can be grown in flooded fields, swampy areas and on terraces and mountain slopes. Although labour-intensive, it is highly productive, particularly as wet rice (*padi*) in the lowland areas. The surplus that rice farming generated enabled the emergence of stratified societies over 2,500 years ago and created the demand for workers that concerned local rulers prior to the 20th century.

increasingly donated to museums. The British Museum's Southeast Asian collection is organized according to national boundaries that emerged under colonial rule in the 19th and 20th centuries, and this is reflected in the structure of the present book. (Papua and West Papua, provinces of Indonesia since the 1960s, have been classified at the museum as culturally part of Oceania and so are not included in this volume.) The Southeast Asian collections thus follow colonial history quite closely, strongly representing areas where the British were present as colonizers or for trade: Myanmar, Malaysia, including Sabah and Sarawak, Java, Sumatra and Thailand. Inevitably, such collections reflect collectors' and curators' interests and ideas, rather than Southeast Asian priorities. Sir Stamford Raffles (an official of the East India Company in the early 19th century) amassed large numbers of Javanese metal figures of Hindu and Buddhist deities, as well as other small metal objects (**4**), both for their portability and their indication of a once-great civilization according to European standards, and applied contemporary European scientific principles of collecting to groups of cultural items. Likewise, the British colonial administrator Charles Hose was

4. Bowl with the zodiac and heavenly figures

Ritual bowls like this one are currently used to hold holy water during rituals in the Tengger region of east Java and on Bali, but it is not possible to say how they were used when first produced in the 1300s. The bowls usually display two rows of figures, comprising the twelve signs of the zodiac from Aquarius to Capricorn in the lower row and possibly divine figures representing heavenly constellations in the upper. Many early bowls include a date in the upper row, suggesting their use at particular events; here it is above the bird.

1329
East Java, Indonesia
Bronze
Diameter 14.5 cm, height 11.4 cm
Donated by William Raffles Flint, collected by Stamford Raffles, 1859,1228.139

involved with the suppression of headhunting on Borneo (he endeavoured to replace it with rowing competitions), and so was able to gather quantities of headhunting equipment in the late 19th and early 20th centuries. The later 20th century saw acquisitions of shadow puppets from the Malay puppeteer Tok Awang Lah, and of Vietnamese ceramics as an adjunct to the museum's extensive Chinese ceramic collection. Because many of the Southeast Asian objects were gathered at specific moments, rather than collected systematically over time, they often present snapshots of Southeast Asia's numerous cultures, rather than fully documenting change.

Nevertheless, the objects discussed here give a rich sampling of the diverse peoples, cultures, materials and techniques found in the region from the earliest times through to the present day. Although it is hardly possible to be comprehensive, the topics touch upon the major themes running through Southeast Asian history: mountains and water, geography, trade and exchange networks, cross-cultural interactions, spirits and ancestors, religious adaptations and social and political structures. Chapter 1 explores the ancient past of Southeast Asia, looking at changing social structures, the use of materials and emergence of technologies, and

5. Clove boat
Cloves originated in the Maluku
islands (Moluccas) and were
a major impetus for the spice
trade. Miniature boats like this
one, constructed of threaded
cloves, have been made for
several hundred years as gifts.
Whether they were ritual
objects locally is not known.
Boats have been of great
significance to Southeast
Asia, where they provided
livelihoods ranging from fishing
to slave trading and were a
part of social and belief systems.

19th century
Maluku islands, Indonesia
Cloves, fibre
Length 58 cm, height 30 cm
As 1972,Q.1944

also specific sites, in order to understand common trends,
some of which persisted into the 20th century. As discussed
in Chapter 2, the rise and efflorescence of kingdoms and
early empires saw Southeast Asian peoples participating in
the wide-ranging worlds of Hinduism and Buddhism and
adapting new ideas to suit local political and religious needs.
Islam made its appearance, developing along trade routes.
Chapters 3, 4, 5 and 6 are less straightforwardly chronological,
as all four look at different aspects of Southeast Asia from
about 1500 through to the present. This is not to suggest that
Southeast Asian cultures were timeless and unchanging over
several hundred years; rather, it reflects the ephemerality of
objects in tropical climates and the consequent difficulty in
using objects to tell full histories. Chapter 3 addresses the
themes of empire, diplomacy and trade in terms of goods,
communities, commodities and art. The customs, practices,
belief systems and methods of cultural expression – some of
which survive in the 21st century, while others became obsolete
as Southeast Asia modernized – are explored in Chapter 4.
Chapters 5 and 6 focus upon art forms of great importance:
narrative, performance, textiles and basketry. Evidence for the
representation of stories extends back more than 1,500 years.

The City of BATAVIA in the Island of Java and Capital of all   I   La Ville de BATAVIA en l'Isle de Java et Capitale de tous les
the Dutch Factories & Settlements in the East Indies. — Published at Ponted by I.WHITTLE and R.H.LAURIE, N°53, Fleet Street London. — Comptoirs et Etablissements Hollandois dans les Indes Orientales.

Because of its ephemerality, the history of performance is less clear, but regional texts and descriptions by visitors starting in the 15th century, as well as stone reliefs, reveal its prevalence. Diverse and innovative textile production is one of the great achievements of the region; less well known is basketry, a relatively neglected area, but one of practical and symbolic use to Southeast Asians. Finally, Chapter 7 explores a few of the many trends that occurred after the Second World War, particularly the end of colonialism and the often troubled emergence of modern nation states. Participation in global trends has affected the region through a burgeoning tourism industry and the development of modern and contemporary art movements, as well as the loss of knowledge of many traditional crafts and the adoption of new materials. Modern trends, however, are still being shaped and adapted in ways that suit Southeast Asians and their conceptual frameworks, in the same way that has occurred over many millennia.

All the objects in this book represent occasions when a set of ideas, materials, beliefs and techniques coalesced to enable people to produce magnificent cultural works. Over time these

6. Jan van Ryne, *The city of Batavia in the Island of Java and Capital of all the Dutch Factories and Settlements in the East Indies*
The Dutch East India Company (VOC) established a port on the north coast of Java in 1619, naming it Batavia. The city became the capital of the Dutch East Indies, composed of parts of present-day Indonesia, as the Netherlands consolidated their hold in the 19th century, when this engraving was made. The marshy port area was laid out on a grid with canals and agriculture on the outskirts. In 1949, the city was renamed Jakarta, becoming the capital of the newly formed Indonesia.

1818
London
Engraving on paper
Height 30 cm, length 42.5 cm
Donated by E. E. Leggatt,
1916,0411.60

7. Quang Tho, *Corner of Dong Khanh Street, Da Nang*
An important port in Vietnam in the 19th century, Da Nang was also where the United States began to land ground troops in 1965. Artists enlisted in the army were encouraged to record contemporary Vietnamese life, rather than the fighting, during the wars of independence in the mid-20th century. Colonel Quang Tho (1929–2001) was awarded numerous prizes for his art, and his work has been acquired by several museums.

1967
Vietnam
Watercolour sketch on paper
Height 27.5 cm, width 39 cm
1999,0630,0.66

were reformulated to accommodate new arrivals, producing change that has not always been recorded owing to myriad forces from environmental to human. For ease of access, objects are frequently identified in this volume in association with specific nation states, many of which only emerged in their current form during the 20th century.

While Southeast Asia's kaleidoscopic array of cultures defies easy categorization and description, it is hoped that this book will lead to a greater awareness and understanding of the region and its wonderful material cultures, and inspire readers to take another look, especially as the area is en route to becoming the world's fourth largest economy and is already home to a large percentage of its people.

Timeline

c. 1.5 million years ago	Early hominid occupation of Southeast Asia
c. 26,000 years ago	Evidence of first rock paintings
c. 10,000 years ago	Evidence of flaked stone technology
c. 10,000–8,000 years ago	Sea levels rise, creating the island region
c. 8,000 years ago	Ceramic production begins
c. 5000–2500 years ago	Austronesian people, probably from Taiwan, settle initially in the Philippines and then across many parts of island Southeast Asia
c. 3600 BCE–200 CE	Ban Chiang cultural complex in Thailand
c. 3000–2000 BCE	Evidence of substantial population movements
	Connections with Yangzi River valley in China
	Rice cultivation emerges on the mainland
	Development of maritime exchange networks
	Flourishing of Toalean cultural complex with Maros points
c. 3000–300 BCE	Evidence of habitation at Samrong Sen, Cambodia
c. 2500–1500 BCE	Phung Nguyen culture flourishes in northern Vietnam
c. 2000–1000 BCE	Use of bronze begins in mainland Southeast Asia
c. 500 BCE–1st century CE	Flourishing of the metalworking Dian peoples in Yunnan, China
c. 500–300 BCE	Earliest production of Dong Son bronze drums in northern Vietnam
c. 500–200 BCE	Major migrations between the islands and the mainland
	Emerging rice cultivation in the island region
	Bronzeworking emerges in island Southeast Asia
	Iron Age begins in island and mainland Southeast Asia
	Rapid expansion of trade within the region, with South Asia and with China
	Village-like fortified settlements appear in the archaeological record
111 BCE	Han China invades northern Vietnam
1st–5th centuries CE	Transition from metalworking phases to the historic period

1 Early cultures

c. 26,000 years ago to *c.* 500 CE

There is evidence of early hominid occupation of what is now Southeast Asia from about 1.5 million years ago, but the archaeological record becomes more plentiful and varied within the past 50,000 years. Much evidence of human occupation has been lost, as around 10,000 years ago sea levels began to rise at the end of the last glacial period, inundating low-lying regions in Southeast Asia and making Sumatra, Java, Bali, Borneo and other parts of modern Indonesia into the islands they are today. When the sea settled at the current level, it created two distinct regions – mainland and island Southeast Asia. The landscapes of both are characterized by tremendous diversity, ranging from mountain peaks (**1**), upland plateaus and narrow river valleys to lowland flood plains, estuaries and extensive coastlines. Difficult terrain made the rivers and the sea the easiest paths of travel, and the earliest sea crossings by humans took place in Southeast Asia (**4**).

While much of Southeast Asia is tropical, there is great variability in rainfall, ranging from the semi-aridity of central Myanmar to the regular rains of the eastern Philippines. Many areas have distinct wet and dry seasons produced by the northeastern and southwestern monsoon winds. Because of the array of climates and geographical conditions, there is a

1. Mount Sumeru, Java
Sumeru is the most sacred mountain on Java. During the prehistoric period, caves and mountains were important, not only physically, but also as part of ritual and beliefs in Southeast Asia. That spiritual aspect has persisted up to the present day.

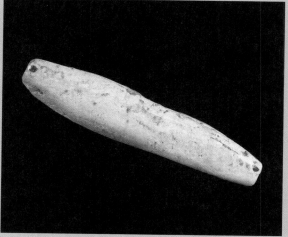

2. Lingling-o

Lingling-o are a form of double-headed slit earring made of valuable stones, metal or shell, and found across a wide region. Their distribution is associated with the migration of Austronesian language speakers. Made from about 500 BCE until around 500 CE, some jade examples were produced with stone imported from Taiwan.

1st–5th century CE
South or central Vietnam
Jade
Height 2.6 cm
Asian Civilisations Museum,
2007-56435

3. Bead

Artifacts from Samrong Sen in modern Cambodia indicate a lengthy occupation of the site and connections to the Mekong Delta and northeastern Thailand. While these and similar finds often lack archaeological context, fish hooks, net weights and shell ornaments, such as this one, show a substantial reliance on water resources.

c. 3000–300 BCE
Samrong Sen, Cambodia
Shell
Length 5.6 cm, height 1.4 cm
1890,0208.48

great variety of animals and plants, but owing to the niche environments, there are relatively few individuals of any particular species. Early humans, therefore, had to exploit numerous food sources, leading to nomadic and semi-nomadic lifestyles as they moved between known sites. Groups developed specializations in the extraction of resources, and over time, in order to obtain a broader range of materials, began trading with one another. This was a pattern of interaction that persisted into the 20th century and contributed to the development of the extensive exchange networks that came to characterize Southeast Asia.

Excavations have revealed that there was a period of substantial population movement within and from outside the region starting about 5,000 years ago. Austronesian peoples initially travelled from what is now Taiwan to the Philippines and, eventually, further on to the Indonesian archipelago and southern Vietnam. On the mainland, there were connections with the first agriculturalists in the Yangzi River valley via Yunnan in southwestern China and the settlements in northern Vietnam. Further migrations between the islands and mainland Southeast Asia occurred about 2,500 years ago.

Initially, people settled on the coasts, usually around the mouths of rivers, and along inland rivers and streams, to gain access to shellfish and other water resources, and for ease of travel and transportation. The adoption of farming and wet rice cultivation in Southeast Asia was gradual, occurring on

4. Outrigger canoes
The outrigger, a stabilizing projecting structure on one or both sides of a boat, was probably invented in Southeast Asia between 1000 and 500 BCE, along with other sailing technologies that facilitated the movement of peoples. There is evidence of Southeast Asian knowledge of boat construction, navigation and trade products in South Asia as early as about 2000 BCE and in Africa between 1000 and 500 BCE. Southeast Asians also migrated to Madagascar more than 1,000 years ago. Outriggers were employed on both large and small boats, as seen here, and are still in common use today.

1934–35
Sulawesi, Indonesia
Photograph probably by Vera Delves Broughton
Gelatin silver print on paper
Height 21.4 cm, width 29.1 cm
Donated by Walter Guinness, 1st Baron Moyne, Oc,B57.15

the mainland from between 3000 and 2000 BCE and in the island region from about 500 BCE. From this period also comes the first evidence of village-like settlements. Many sites, such as Samrong Sen, Ban Chiang and Ulu Leang, show evidence of habitation over very long periods of time (**3**). While some communities became sedentary rice farmers, others remained as hunter-gatherers, a configuration that in a few cases still exists today. Patterns of tooth wear show that these two groups interacted, with some individuals living for parts of their lives in both types of community.

Because of the diversity of landscapes in Southeast Asia, the adoption of new stone technologies and bronze- and ironworking, as well as the development of agriculture, occurred at different times across the region; nor did the arrival of new technologies necessarily have an immediate impact on social structures. The technology used by the early hunter-gatherers included heated stones for cooking, ochre for pigment and flaked stone tools. Over the next several millennia, communities started to grind and polish their stone tools to make them more effective, manufacture fired ceramic vessels and work with other media, such as shell, to make personal adornments and grave goods, indicating a belief in an afterlife. Bronze began to be used on the mainland between 2000 and 1000 BCE. Current evidence indicates that the production of both bronze and iron started around 500 BCE in island Southeast Asia, but excavations on the Malay peninsula suggest that further investigation may revise this assessment. Increasing social complexity is indicated by expanding arrays of goods found in graves. Excavations have uncovered rice, adzes, jewelry, beads, shells, glass, ceramics, textiles ranging from barkcloth to silk, semi-precious stones (such as carnelian, serpentine and jade) and weapons. While some of these were made of local materials, there were also objects fashioned locally from imported raw materials as well as finished pieces produced elsewhere. The fact that some graves contained hundreds or even thousands of objects demonstrates the importance of access to foreign goods, personal adornment and aesthetics in Southeast Asia's developing hierarchies.

The distribution of prehistoric objects, such as jade *lingling-o* earrings (**2**) and pottery covered with a reddish-coloured liquid clay before firing, around the islands of the South China Sea indicates that maritime exchange networks emerged in Southeast Asia over 3,000 years ago. Early exchanges also occurred between people living inland and coastal communities, evolving into symbiotic relationships where goods were sent upstream in exchange for raw materials and forest products which were then exported from a coastal port. Exotic precious items are consequently found in graves far inland.

Trade between India, Southeast Asia and China expanded rapidly from about 2,500 years ago, which, in conjunction with wealth from agriculture and salt production, enabled the emergence of trading polities and the sharing of political, social and cultural configurations. This ushered in a period of significant change, including expanding social structures that developed into the chiefdoms and kingdoms of the first centuries CE. The connection of these Asian maritime and inland networks with other ones from around 500 BCE created an interactive landscape that stretched from the Mediterranean to the Indian subcontinent, Southeast Asia and China. Not only was Southeast Asia centrally located between India and China, but its products, such as cloves and nutmeg, were highly valued and known as far afield as Rome. The movement of people and goods stimulated artistic production, and foreign artisans also settled in Southeast Asia.

1 | 1 Hunter-gatherer societies and Neolithic communities

In Southeast Asia, remains of prehistoric hunter-gatherer societies exist along the coasts, especially in estuaries, and close to the rivers and forests of the interior. Access to water was important for resource extraction, which included finding the pebbles and stones needed to make tools (**2**). The archaeological record suggests that early Southeast Asians moved frequently across a range of landscapes, following seasonal food sources and settling temporarily at sites to which they returned regularly as they hunted and fished (**5**), collected fruits and vegetables and processed food. Rock paintings appear to have been a way of marking the landscape and may also have connected with beliefs (**1**). Because the resources were diverse but limited in quantity, early Southeast Asians required tools that could be used flexibly for a variety of tasks. Examples made of bone, stone and shell are known, and usage patterns indicate that stone tools were also used to fashion bamboo and wood implements (**3**, **4**). The occupation of sites for long periods of time allows technological changes to be traced. At locations in modern Thailand, such as Khok Phanom Di, the increasing domestication of plants is indicated by the presence of such specialized tools as hoes and reaping knives; clay figurines found at Ban Na Di suggest the importance of domesticated animals, such as pigs and buffalo.

1. Rock paintings on the cliffs at Pha Taem, Luang Prabang Province, Laos
Red ochre pigment was used for the rock paintings that are found in large quantities on cliff faces and in caves and rockshelters used as burial sites or for temporary occupation across Southeast Asia. Painting dates range from approximately 26,000 years ago through to the 20th century. At Pha Taem on the Ou River in Laos, there are images of bovines, figures, dogs, boats and hand-prints. Water buffalo were domesticated about 5,000 years ago, but dogs were only domesticated about 2000 BCE, indicating that the paintings were made after that date.

2. Pebble hammer

Such naturally shaped objects were used to strike other rocks to make flaked tools. This type of hammer is associated with early technologies.

3000–1000 BCE
Found at Samrong Sen, Cambodia
Buff granite
Height 6.1 cm, diameter 6.3 cm
1890,0208.25

3. Adze preform

An adze preform is an unfinished axe-like tool. Over time, tools developed from simple flaked examples to more effective polished, bevelled and edge-ground types.

c. 2000–1000 BCE
Found in Kelantan, Malaysia
Stone
Length 23.8 cm
Donated by H. Ridley,
1951,0725.6

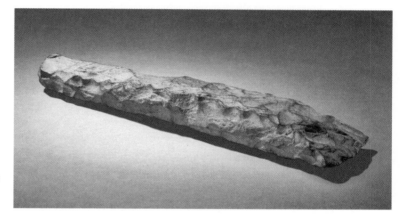

4. Adze

Polished adzes in a regular, usually quadrangular, shape were a technological improvement on flaked stone tools. Although the stone's beauty suggests a ceremonial object, the wear on the piece indicates that it was actually used.

c. 2000–1000 BCE
Padang Lalang, Penang, Malaysia
Stone, possibly jasper
Length 7.4 cm
Donated by Adelaide Lister,
As1914,1012.52

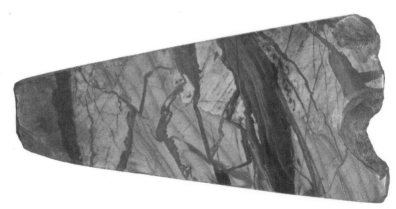

5. Weight for a fishing net

Fishing was an important source of food in prehistoric Southeast Asia, and early archaeological finds from the region include fishing equipment. This stone would have been tied to the edge of a fibre net to weight it for catching fish.

c. 3000–500 BCE
Found at Samrong Sen, Cambodia
Stone
Diameter 2.4 cm
1890,0208.42

1 | 2 Ulu Leang and Leang Burung, Sulawesi, Indonesia

Owing to semi-nomadic lifestyles and the movements of people into and around Southeast Asia, archaeological sites display substantial interconnections within the region and beyond it. However, the geography of the region also produced significant local traditions that are found only in small areas. One such place is in southwest Sulawesi, an island in present-day Indonesia where there is evidence of human habitation for at least 30,000 years. Excavated in the late 1960s and 1970s, the Ulu Leang mortuary site and the Leang Burung rockshelter revealed, among others, a hunter-gatherer society with a distinctive technological complex, named Toalean by archaeologists.

The earliest tools from these two sites were numerous varieties of blade-like stone flakes and microliths (small shaped stone tools), typical island Southeast Asian technologies that later expanded to include pointed bone tools (2), shell scrapers and serrated and hollow-based stone points, usually of chert stone (1). Stone objects resembling arrowheads with serrated edges, so-called Maros points, identify the Toalean culture as unique in Southeast Asia (3). Rock art was also produced. While shellfish, wild animals (such as monkeys, wild pigs, civet cats and pygmy buffalo) and wild seeds and nuts formed the early diet of the people from these sites, in later times they also collected wild grains, possibly including rice. Glass beads, which are associated with iron use in Indonesia from about the 3rd century BCE, have also been excavated, as well as locally produced ceramics (4). Imported Chinese glazed ceramics indicate that the sites continued to be occupied within the past thousand years.

1. Stone flake tools
Excavations at Ulu Leang have revealed many small stone flake tools, an early technology. Some were not resharpened after use, suggesting that they were disposable, while others display a gloss that came not from polishing but from residue left after cutting plant material.

c. 4000–2500 BCE
Ulu Leang I
Chert
Length 3.8–4.7 cm
Donated by Ian Glover and the Government of the Republic of Indonesia, 2000,1209.1–3

2. Bone implements
Ulu Leang has revealed the largest group of bone tools produced by early Southeast Asian cultures. Stone, wood and bamboo were more commonly used elsewhere in the region. Mostly cut from the bones of large mammals, there are three main types at Ulu Leang: solid, symmetrical examples with a point at each end, solid implements with a thick and a pointed end, and points with a hollow section. Their specific uses are as yet unknown, but in keeping with other Southeast Asian societies they probably had multiple functions.

c. 4000–2500 BCE
Ulu Leang I
Bone
Length 3.1–6.7 cm
Donated by Ian Glover and the Government of the Republic of Indonesia, 2000,1209.11–15

3. Maros points

Unique to southern Sulawesi, Maros points became particularly common after the emergence of pottery decorated by burnishing, painting, incising and impressing. This suggests the development of a series of new technologies; whether these arose independently on Sulawesi or in concert with the movement of peoples is not yet known. The hollow Maros points are characterized by saw-toothed edges worked on both sides that converge in a sharp point.

c. 4000–2500 BCE
Ulu Leang I
Chert stone
Length about 1 cm
Donated by Ian Glover and the Government of the Republic of Indonesia, 2000,1209.4

4. Painted ceramic sherd

This sherd is from a vessel with an incised pattern and polychrome painted decoration consisting of black, red and white chevrons. Only a small proportion of the sparse ceramics excavated at Ulu Leang were embellished, though numerous decorative techniques such as painting, impressing, incising and appliqué were used on such pieces. Decorative shapes included shell impressions, chevrons, meanders, herringbone patterning and geometric forms.

1st–8th century CE
Ulu Leang II
Earthenware and pigment
Width 9.3 cm
Donated by Ian Glover and the Government of the Republic of Indonesia, 2000,1209.16

1 | 3 Ceramic production

Ceramics are an important part of the archaeological record as they survive well over time. They were clearly highly valued by prehistoric peoples in Southeast Asia, as substantial quantities have been found buried in graves. In addition to independent invention, ceramic technology travelled across Southeast Asia through periodic human migrations and trade, including the early migration of Austronesian language speakers from Taiwan to island Southeast Asia about 5,000 years ago.

It was originally thought that ceramic production first occurred around the time that humans became more settled and began farming, but this is now known to be inaccurate. In Southeast Asia, even before farming commenced, people were producing ceramics in the locations where they stayed temporarily while exploiting seasonal resources. This was happening as early as about 8,000 years ago, as indicated by the finds from Spirit Cave in northwestern Thailand. Decoration initially included simple cord- or basket-marking, incising and burnishing (rubbing to smooth the surface and make it shiny) (**2**). Some of the earliest pottery from Southeast Asia, dating to about 4,500 years ago, was found on the island of Timor. Shortly after this, ceramics were embellished with a red slip (a thin, liquified clay) and impressed patterns such as circles. Such pieces have been found over a wide area from Taiwan to the Philippines, some Indonesian islands and even Micronesia. The fact that decoration became common soon after ceramic production began reveals the importance of aesthetics to early Southeast Asians (**1**). Later ceramics were also stamped, painted and incised, often with complex geometric and curving designs (**4**). Besides pots and vessels, prehistoric peoples made clay pellets for slingshots, weights to hold nets for fishing, spindle-whorls (**3**) and, eventually, moulds for bronze casting.

1. Beaker

One of the earliest settlements in the Red River region of present-day Vietnam belonged to the peoples of the Phung Nguyen culture that flourished from about 2500–1500 BCE. They initially made pottery with incised parallel lines filled with S shapes. Later, incised bands were filled with speckled impressions, and later still, curvilinear patterning emerged. On this vessel, speckled impressions combine with curving lines. Ceramics were produced along with bone, stone and bronze artifacts.

2500–1500 BCE
Vietnam
Pottery
Diameter 14.7 cm, height 21 cm
Donated by A. W. Franks,
Franks.3100

2. Trumpet-mouthed vessel

Earthenware vessels have been found at several Neolithic sites along the Malay peninsula. Striations indicate that they were made on the slow wheel (the earliest form of potter's wheel), and they were burnished on the upper surface and cord-marked around the body. Shapes vary from beakers on splayed feet to trumpet-mouthed pieces like this one. There has been little research on these wares, but they were probably used for cooking, as water containers, and possibly for ritual and mortuary purposes.

c. 2000–500 BCE
Bukit Tengku Lembu, Perlis,
Malaya
Earthenware
Diameter 24.9 cm (mouth),
height 16 cm
Donated by the National Museum
of the Federation of Malaya,
1956,1118.14

3. Spindle-whorl

Found in many parts of Southeast Asia, spindle-whorls are used as weights for spindles when making yarn for weaving. This example is incised and impressed with geometric patterns, suggesting a later production date. It comes from Kampong Thom, located on the Tonle Sap lake, which is connected to the Mekong River. While textiles have not survived, impressions on clay and patterned residues in archaeological excavations provide evidence of early production.

500 BCE–500 CE
Kampong Thom, Cambodia
Terracotta
Diameter 3.8 cm, height 4.2 cm
Donated by H. Ridley,
1951,0725.74

4. Mortuary vessel

Mortuary vessels such as this one have been found in the graves of high-ranking individuals, showing the emphasis on conspicuous display that emerged as a major element of many Southeast Asian societies. The site of Ban Chiang, in present-day Thailand, dates from about 3600 BCE to 200 CE. This pot comes from its later phases, and displays the typical everted rim and distinctive red-painted decoration in curvilinear and spiral forms on a buff ground. The high foot was also a common feature.

3rd–1st century BCE
Ban Chiang, Thailand
Pottery
Diameter 18.6 cm (mouth),
height 25.4 cm
1972,0919.1

1 | 4 Bronzeworking

Copper and bronze technology may have come to mainland Southeast Asia from northern China over 4,000 years ago, via trade networks for the exchange of jade. Island Southeast Asia followed a different trajectory, with bronze and iron technology apparently both arriving around 2,500 years ago, though further archaeological work may change this understanding. Bronze was an important trade item and was exchanged – as ingots and finished objects – around the region, and bronze grave goods indicate growing social complexity.

Bronze was used for ceremonial ornaments and implements, as well as for weapons and other equipment (**1**). Large, complex bronzes, requiring great skill to produce, appeared between 1000 and 500 BCE. Southeast Asian smiths used both bivalve moulds, where two halves are held together while filled with molten metal, and lost-wax casting. For the latter, a mould is shaped around a wax model, the wax is melted away and molten bronze poured in. The most impressive bronze objects are the drums and bells. The earliest of these were produced with low-relief, stylized figural and geometric motifs in northern Vietnam by the Dong Son culture between 500 and 300 BCE. The scale of production was large, and many drums were exchanged as prestige goods around Southeast Asia and southern China following established trade routes. The drum tradition was adopted by a number of cultures in the region (**2**); they were made and used in southwestern China, the highlands of eastern Myanmar and northern Vietnam, in some cases into the 20th century. Drums with elongated bodies were produced during prehistoric times in Indonesia. The purpose of these instruments has varied over time and in different places. As well as being sounded, they have been used as funerary urns, utensils in agricultural rituals and bride price payments.

Bronze urns and bells are also found in Southeast Asia, but none has been excavated in a controlled fashion and their production locations are unknown, so they are little understood (**3**, **4**). How the bells were used remains unknown.

1. Spearheads

Although the Dong Son culture of the Red River valley in northern Vietnam is often associated with the production of drums, smiths also produced large quantities of spearheads, knives and daggers, bracelets, agricultural implements, bells and axes. In Southeast Asia, it was often the case that beads and bracelets rather than tools and weapons were the first bronze (and later iron) objects. Yet, implements like these spearheads could also function ritually, and many apparently functional objects were buried as grave goods.

1st century CE
Dong Son, Vietnam
Bronze
Length 9 cm, length 10.5 cm
Donated by the Musée des Arts Asiatiques Guimet, 1950,1215.43–44

2. Drum

Over 2,000 years ago, the Dian culture in what is now southwestern China began to make drums like those produced by the Dong Son culture. Their motifs range from geometric shapes, stars and animals to warriors on boats and scenes of food preparation, religious ceremonies and musical performances. Continuity of patterning with other drum-producing cultures suggests that the motifs had great symbolic power. On this drum, the frogs around the edge and the star at the centre of the tympanum became imagery that lasted regionally into the 19th century.

c. 100 BCE–500 CE
Southwestern China
Bronze
Diameter 85.3 cm, height 59.3 cm
Donated by the Government of the United Kingdom (War Office), 1903,0327.6

Below left
3. Bell
Several bronze bells have been found in peninsular Malaya and one in Cambodia. It is possible that they all originated from the same centre, which was not necessarily Dong Son, as there were numerous bronze-casting sites in Southeast Asia by the 2nd century BCE. This example is decorated with a saw-tooth motif that edges double zig-zag lines emerging from tight S-shaped designs. Within the latter are tear-drop shapes.

c. 2nd century BCE
Found in Malaysia
Bronze
Diameter 31.3 cm, height 58 cm
1949,0715.1

Above
4. Bell with spiral motifs
All early Southeast Asian bells, small and large, display decorative S-curves and spirals across their entire external surfaces.

500 BCE–500 CE
Found in Thailand
Bronze
Height 5.8 cm
Donated by Johannes Schmitt and Mareta Meade, 1992,1214.128

1 | 5 The Iron Age

The introduction of iron to Southeast Asia heralded major cultural changes and increasing social hierarchies, including the development of locally powerful chiefdoms. Ironworking arrived in the region about 2,500 years ago, probably from Indian sources. Initially, like bronze, iron was reserved mostly for personal ornaments, but it quickly became used for tools for agriculture, hunting and fishing, as well as knives, spindle-whorls (for textile production) and weapons (**1**).

The tremendously expanded trade networks of this time brought a whole variety of goods to Southeast Asia. Metal ingots were traded, as well as finished goods, and there is evidence for itinerant craftsmen. Inland communities had access to new materials and techniques via overland trade routes that linked with maritime ones. There was trade in cotton from India and silk from China and also in such raw materials as hemp and abacá fibre. Glass, carnelian and agate were exchanged either as unfinished materials to be used for local production, or in the form of beads and other ornaments (**2**, **3**). Objects from as far afield as the Mediterranean included stone intaglios, glass bowls and coins, some of which were imitated in pendant form in Southeast Asia. In turn, the region exported forest products, including spices, ores such as tin (which was scarce in India) and salt, particularly from the central mainland area. There were also technological transfers, such as the adoption of Han Chinese ceramic glazing techniques in northern Vietnam while it was under Chinese control in the first centuries CE (**4**).

The large number of weapons excavated from this period reveals growing competition and conflict, enhanced by the production of iron. Large moats and earth banks were constructed around settlements, probably for defence and facilitated by iron tools. Between 200 and 500 CE, the metalworking phases transitioned into the historic period, with the production of stone inscriptions and buildings that utilized concepts also emerging on the Indian subcontinent.

1. Axe
This is a socketed axe, one of the many tools whose efficiency was increased through the use of iron rather than the softer bronze. Iron-smelting and forging were common across Southeast Asia by 400–200 BCE.

2nd–1st century BCE
Perak, Malay peninsula
Iron
Length 29.8 cm
1880.1166

2. Carnelian bead
Between 400 and 200 BCE, beads of semi-precious stone were among the high-prestige goods that travelled via the expanding trade networks across the South China Sea and the Indian Ocean. These exchanges, which also included new technologies, brought about increasing social stratification and profound economic and political changes in both South and Southeast Asia. Orange- and red-hued carnelian beads are found across the region from this time and well into the historic period.

c. 400 BCE–c. 1000 CE
Found in Borneo
Carnelian
Diameter 1.1 cm, height 4.5 cm
Donated by Margaret
Brooke, Ranee of Sarawak,
As1896,0317.43.b

3. Glass beads

As a prestige good, glass was an important commodity, particularly in the form of beads. These were initially produced in India, but between the 4th and 2nd centuries BCE production centres developed in Southeast Asia.

c. 300 BCE–500 CE
Ulu Leang 2, Sulawesi, Indonesia
Glass
Length 39.6 cm
Donated by Ian Glover and the Government of the Republic of Indonesia, 2000,1209.19

4. Jar

This clear-glazed, buff-coloured pottery jar was excavated from a tomb at Lach Truong, a major mortuary site in Than Hoa province (Vietnam) located near a river estuary. The glaze technique was brought by Chinese colonizers to northern Vietnam, where it was adapted for local usage.

1st–2nd century CE
Than Hoa, Vietnam
Pottery
Height 20.3 cm
Donated by the Musée des Arts Asiatiques Guimet, 1950,1215.8

Timeline

c. 2nd century BCE–6th century CE	Flourishing of the port of Oc Eo in the Mekong Delta region
c. 1st century BCE–10th century CE	Pyu culture in central Myanmar
c. 1st–4th centuries CE	Buddhism develops among the Pyu and peoples of southern Myanmar
c. 6th–11th centuries	Buddhist Dvaravati cultures flourish in central and northeastern Thailand
c. 7th–13th centuries	Emergence and prominence of Srivijaya-Malayu
732	First records of the Hindu Sanjaya dynasty on Java
778	The Buddhist Sailendra dynasty on Java emerges
c. 8th century	Muslim traders arrive in Southeast Asia
8th–10th centuries	Artistic flourishing of the Cham cultures in southern Vietnam
802	Founding of Angkor in central Cambodia
900	Laguna copperplate inscription from Luzon in the Philippines documents several polities in the island region
929	Central Javanese court moves to east Java, where it remains until the 1500s, during which time many long narrative poems are written
938	Independence of northern Vietnam from control by Han China
1009–1225	Ly dynasty of Dai Viet (northern Vietnam)
1025	Srivijaya attacked by Chola dynasty of southern India
c. 11th–13th centuries	Khmer period of the Lopburi kingdom, central Thailand
	Tai peoples sweep into mainland Southeast Asia, becoming politically ascendant but merging with local populations
11th–late 13th centuries	Bagan kingdom flourishes in Myanmar
1222–92	Singasari dynasty in east Java
1225–1400	Tran dynasty in Dai Viet
Early 13th to mid-15th centuries	Sukhothai kingdom in central Thailand
Mid-13th century	Rise of the kingdom of Lan Na in northern Thailand
1292	Earliest date of a Muslim sultanate at Samudera Pasai in northeast Sumatra
c. 1293–1527	Majapahit empire of island Southeast Asia
End of the 13th century	Kingdom of Ayutthaya emerges in central Thailand
Mid-14th century	Kingdom of Lan Xang arises in Laos
14th–16th centuries	Efflorescence of export ceramic production in Thailand and Vietnam
Early 15th century	Founding of the Demak sultanate on the north coast of Java
1430s	Mrauk-U becomes capital of Rakhine
1431	Defeat of Angkor by the kingdom of Ayutthaya

2 Kingdoms

c. 300–1500 CE

Huge changes swept Southeast Asia between the early first millennium CE and the middle of the second. Part of what drove the artistic changes was increasing social stratification and the development of major polities able to muster substantial resources, including human labour. In what is now Myanmar, early cultures such as the Pyu were followed by the Bagan kingdom, and in the region of present-day Thailand, the Dvaravati polities were succeeded by the Sukhothai and then Ayutthaya kingdoms. Khmer kingdoms emerged in the Mekong Delta, but eventually moved inland to the Angkor plain, where the Khmer empire was centred; it is famous for such great monuments as Angkor Wat. Several Cham polities developed in present-day southern Vietnam, known today primarily through brick architecture and stone and metal sculpture (1), and Dai Viet established itself in the north. Maritime Southeast Asia was dominated for a long time by the empire of Srivijaya-Malayu, which controlled the Straits of Melaka (Malacca) through which most east–west trade passed. There were various kingdoms centred on the island of Java, including the Sailendra, Sanjaya, Singasari and

1. Rampant lion
Rampant animals were a common image in South and Southeast Asia during this time. Sculptures of animals, such as this lion, and dancing figures were produced by the Cham to decorate Hindu and Buddhist altars and pedestals. Cham artistic production reached its zenith between the 8th and the 10th centuries, with stone and metal sculptures and religious architecture surviving best.

10th–11th century
Cham culture, southern Vietnam
Sandstone
Height 30 cm
1981,0304.1

2. Captain G. P. Baker, S.E View of two of the Temples of Bhimo, Gunung Prao, Java

Once home to hundreds of temples, the Dieng Plateau on Gunung (Mount) Prahu was a pilgrimage centre from the mid-7th to early 13th centuries. The two temples of the Bima group (illustrated here) share some features with northern Indian buildings, indicating Java's participation in a cultural sphere reaching beyond political boundaries. Europeans assumed that Indians had colonized Java and built temples, which helped to justify European colonization.

1815
Java
Ink and wash on paper
Height 43.8 cm, width 56.9 cm
Donated by J. H. Drake, collected by Stamford Raffles, 1939,0311,0.4.2

Majapahit, the latter another substantial maritime empire. Found on Luzon, the Laguna copperplate inscription from 900 CE provides evidence of polities on the Philippine islands, as well as connections with Java. There were also numerous smaller political units across Southeast Asia, many of which are known today only as names in Chinese historical records. Trade was important for the island polities and empires, while the major states on the mainland emphasized the control of agricultural and associated human resources. Both mainland and island regions relied on inland communities for products and resources from the forests.

The profound impact of Hinduism and Buddhism on many parts of Southeast Asia started about 2,000 years ago. Merchants, artisans and religious persons travelled between South and Southeast Asia, moving technologies, techniques and ideas around the region. Tamils from southern India were one of the earliest groups present in island Southeast Asia, as demonstrated by inscriptions using southern Indian scripts

3. Head of the Hindu female deity Parvati

It can be difficult to classify such female figures as this one, made before the founding of the Khmer kingdom at Angkor in 802 CE, since most have lost their identifying features, usually objects held in the hand. The stylized treatment of the hairlocks seen on this head from Cambodia exists on other sculptures of the time, as do the slightly arched eyebrows, clearly incised eyes with a staring gaze, and thick lips, features also seen on some early stone sculpture found in the peninsular region of Southeast Asia.

7th–early 8th century
Cambodia
Sandstone
Height 25.4 cm
1968,0213.1

found along maritime trade routes. Modified local versions of the Indian scripts were developed to write local languages around the 7th to 9th centuries. Hinduism and Buddhism gained acceptance as foreign communities settled in Southeast Asia and sponsored the establishment of monasteries and other religious institutions. Southeast Asian elites engaged with the emerging religious cultures and utilized their ideas and imagery to promote the development of states and entrench their own positions. Worship of the Hindu deity Vishnu, who is associated with kingship, played a major role in early state formation, while the other major Hindu deity, Shiva, primarily emerged as a political force in Southeast Asia in the 8th century. Buddhism appeared as the predominant religion in the Pyu kingdom in Myanmar by the 4th century, and with the Sailendra on Java in the 7th century. Southeast Asians amalgamated Hindu and Buddhist ideas with local concepts, such as the symbolic role of mountains and the importance of the sea, forming belief systems that were unique to the region.

While religious concepts legitimized the ruler, the political structures that developed among the lowland, agricultural cultures were based on the idea of the man of prowess, a charismatic person able to acquire the loyalty of followers through his (or rarely her) extraordinary abilities, including military might, access to supernatural power and possession of sacred objects. Kinship connections and gifts (such as exotic and precious items, political positions and agricultural produce) also played a role in attracting and retaining followers, as well as maintaining legitimacy. Political power consequently corresponded more to a leader's network of relationships, rather than territorial possessions.

Maritime polities, which were primarily ocean-based and relied on trade, rather than agriculture, emerged in parts of the island region, and these empires, such as Srivijaya, linked large areas across seas. Their centres were based near the coast and routes into the interior that supplied agricultural and forest products for exchange. They lasted while able to control trade and to ensure the use of their ports. Sea nomads and piracy also played a role in either strengthening or weakening maritime polities.

This period also saw the gradual arrival of new peoples, primarily those who migrated along river routes and valleys from the southwestern area of China, including the Burman and Tai groups in the 9th and 11th–13th centuries, respectively. Traders from the Middle East arrived soon after the emergence of Islam. Muslim enclaves gradually developed in the coastal areas, but it was not until the 14th and 15th centuries that Islam became a major religion in Southeast Asia. Chinese peoples also emigrated from the southern coastal regions and settled in Southeast Asia. Interactions with China through exchange networks began in the prehistoric period; the early kingdoms sent tribute missions and emissaries with local products to the Chinese court, a form of diplomatic activity that lasted intermittently into the 19th century. Many sites, such as a port at the mouth of the Santubong River on Borneo and polities on the Malay peninsula, were sufficiently important to be mentioned in early Chinese historical annals. Excavations at port sites have uncovered Chinese ceramics, as well as the remains of industries exporting iron to China.

Art provides substantial information about some Southeast Asian societies between 300 and 1500 CE. Late 19th- and early 20th-century Western scholars assumed that Southeast Asian artists first copied Indian art forms, and only later developed local styles (2). This is now known not to be the case. Art forms in Southeast Asia often arose around the same time as in South Asia, indicating that both regions participated in overlapping cultural landscapes, and while there are similarities in the art of both areas, neither is a direct copy of the other. Southeast Asia had connections with particular South Asian regions, particularly the Gupta kingdom (4th–6th centuries CE) in northern India and the Pallava (4th–9th centuries CE) in the south, as indicated by sculptural and architectural remains. The exception was northern Vietnam, which was colonized by the Chinese. However, the strongest artistic relationships occurred within Southeast Asia itself, with stone carvings and metal sculpture displaying consistency of style across the region around the 4th to 7th centuries CE, harking back to the shared artistic vocabularies of prehistoric art (3). It was only from about

4. Relief from the inner wall, first terrace, Borobudur
This is part of the series of reliefs narrating the story of the Buddha's life at the temple site of Borobudur in Java. The depictions of people paying homage to the Buddha in the upper register and of a wealthy person and his followers in the lower display examples of contemporary material culture, including symbols of rank such as umbrellas, thrones and offerings, as well as jewelry and headdresses.

Late 8th–early 9th century
Borobudur, central Java
Volcanic stone (andesite)

the 8th century that distinct regional styles emerged in order to suit new local political requirements.

Owing to the climate, time, theft and other destructive forces, the Southeast Asian art that remains from this early time is the most durable – stone, ceramic, metal, stucco and paintings inside temples. Images that portray everyday activities, such as cooking and weaving, religious rituals and major events including royal ceremonies and warfare, are found on stone relief sculptures at such religious sites as Borobudur on Java (**4**) and Angkor Wat in Cambodia, or in painted imagery, like that found at Bagan. Such imagery provides important evidence of perishable materials used in Southeast Asian societies, such as textiles, baskets and wooden architecture, which no longer remain.

2 | 1 The Thai-Malay peninsula, Srivijaya empire and Malayu

The Thai-Malay peninsula and eastern Sumatra were long part of early trade routes because of their strategic location. Srivijaya and Malayu for a time appear to have been one and the same polity based on the east coast of Sumatra. From the 7th century, both were mentioned in Chinese records, and their influence over the seas as far north as peninsular Thailand and the major trading sites along the coasts of western Java and Borneo lasted into the 13th century. Srivijaya-Malayu was a major Buddhist centre where numerous students and monks came to study, as is known from the writings of the Chinese monk Yijing who made lengthy visits in the 7th century. Inscriptions at Indian religious sites record that Srivijayan kings funded construction projects in various places, including Nalanda, a major Buddhist centre in northeast India that flourished from around the 4th to the early 13th centuries. The oldest inscription in Old Malay tells of a king who took a ship to make a profit, ending with the salute 'Great Sriwijaya. Magical powers and riches' (Guy 2014, 21). Excavations in Kedah in modern peninsular Malaysia have uncovered the earliest Buddhist scriptures in Southeast Asia, as well as easily portable religious clay tablets, of which numerous other examples have been found around the region (**2, 3**). Other artistic remains include representations of the *bodhisattva* Avalokitesvara, a figure of compassion who was believed to assist mariners (**4**).

Testifying to the region's extensive trading interactions are gold coins minted in the Khlong Thom region on the peninsula (**1**) and objects such as glass cups and bowls from the Persian Gulf area, glass and stone beads from India, iron from nearby areas and Persian, South Asian and Chinese Tang dynasty pottery. In exchange, Srivijaya-Malayu offered inland goods, such as spices, resins, gold, tin and camphor.

1. Coin

Khlong Thom was a maritime trade hub during the early first millennium CE, and the gold coins found there indicate wide-ranging contacts, even though there is evidence they were produced locally. The coins draw upon India for the script, weight standard and conch imagery, while the profile head seen on some of them is a derivation from Indo-Greek and Roman coins transmitted via Indian coin traditions. The Khlong Thom coins have also been found at the port site of Oc Eo (now southern Vietnam), indicating Khlong Thom's role in trans-Gulf of Thailand trade.

Probably 2nd–5th century CE
Khlong Thom, Krabi, Thai peninsula
Gold
Diameter 0.8 cm
1983,0530.4

2. Religious tablet with inscription

Some of the earliest evidence of Buddhism in Southeast Asia comes from moulded clay offering tablets. Small, lightweight and inexpensive to produce, they enabled people from all classes to participate in this form of religious practice. Used as a protective formula, the inscription on this tablet honouring the Buddha is called the *Bodhigarbhalamkaralaksa dharani*. Reproducing such texts and chanting them aloud were believed to help purify devotees and enable better rebirths in the future.

c. 11th century
Penang island, off the Thai-Malay peninsula
Terracotta
Height 12.5 cm, width 9.5 cm
Donated by W. Jevons,
As1864,1201.4

**3. Religious tablet with the
bodhisattva Avalokitesvara**

Made of sun-dried clay, this
tablet depicts the four-armed
bodhisattva Avalokitesvara.
Bodhisattvas are spiritually
advanced beings who remain
in the world to assist others.
Here he is shown with a high
headdress, seated on a lotus
throne that indicates purity.
As is typical, he holds a rosary
in his upper right hand and a
lotus flower in the upper left.
The lower left hand rests in his
lap, while the right is on his knee.
In the upper left section of the
plaque is a stupa (relic mound).
Small, light objects like tablets
were transported around the
region in large quantities.

8th–11th century
Peninsular Thailand
Terracotta
Height 9 cm, width 7.5 cm
Donated by W. Graham, 1907,-.39

**4. Standing figure of the
bodhisattva Avalokitesvara**

Avalokitesvara is a *bodhisattva*
who became popular in
Southeast Asia around the
7th century CE, as testified by
numerous archaeological remains
along the Thai-Malay peninsula,
on Sumatra and Java and as
far as Borneo. The four-armed
manifestation of Avalokitesvara,
typically dressed in a skirt-cloth
tied with a sash below the waist,
was called Lokanatha, Lord of
the World. Early depictions,
as seen here, showed him as
an ascetic, indicated by the
matted locks. The facial features
resemble other sculptures
produced around the same time
from mainland Southeast Asia,
particularly Dvaravati, including
full lips and broad nose.

c. 8th–9th century
Thailand
Gilded silver
Height 10.6 cm
1981,0704.1

1. Silver coin with throne and *srivatsa* motif

Associated with the Pyu peoples of early Myanmar, this is one of four main types of coin dating to the 7th to 9th centuries that display imagery such as an auspicious *srivatsa* symbol, a conch or wheel associated with the spread of Buddhist teachings, a throne, or a rising sun. The coin is marked on one side with a *srivatsa* with a conch inside it. On the other, there is a waisted throne that narrows in the centre, a form honouring the Buddha that persists today. Such coins were also made in gold.

8th–9th century
Pyu cultures, Myanmar
Silver
Diameter 2.2 cm
Donated by Spink & Son Ltd,
1921,1014.144

2. Silver coin issued by the ruler Nitichandra

This Rakhine coin was minted with the auspicious *srivatsa* symbol with the sun and the moon on one side, and an image of the Hindu god Shiva's mount, Nandi the bull, on the other. The inscription gives the name of the issuing ruler, Nitichandra (r. 6th century), in Brahmi script. The beaded border was a popular decorative device used across a vast swathe of land from the Sassanian empire to mainland Southeast Asia. Although the design of this coin was based on those from neighbouring Bengal, the design itself originated on Nepalese coinage of the 6th–7th centuries.

6th century
Rakhine, Myanmar
Silver
Diameter 3.2 cm
Donated by Grindlay, 1884,0510.1

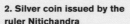

3. Silver coin with conch and *srivatsa* motif

Found in southern Myanmar, this coin displays a conch surrounded by beading, a method of emphasizing imagery that was repeated on numerous art forms into the 20th century. The back features the auspicious *srivatsa* symbol.

8th–9th century
Lower Myanmar
Silver
Diameter 3.3 cm
Donated by Arthur Phayre,
1882,0508.41

4. Silver *masa* lump coin

The *masa* was a major coin denomination in Java, equivalent to about 2.4 grams. Regularization of weights seems to have developed in the 9th century.

9th–10th century
Java, Indonesia
Silver
Diameter 1.2 cm
Donated by Spink & Son Ltd,
1982,0624.2

5. Gold lump coin

One side of this coin has been decorated with a square impression divided in half by a vertical line and flanking dots, while the other displays the letter 'ta' inscribed in Nagari Indian script. 'Ta' is short for *tahil*, the denomination equivalent to sixteen *masas*, despite the fact that the coins weigh about the same as one *masa*. This one comes from Java, but such coins were also found on Sumatra and in the Philippines.

9th century
Java, Indonesia
Gold
Height 0.7 cm, width 0.65 cm
Donated by Spink & Son Ltd,
CH.399

Coinage

The Pyu peoples dominated the central region of present-day Myanmar from approximately the 1st century BCE until the 9th–10th centuries CE. They expanded Iron Age sites into some of the earliest cities in Southeast Asia, including Sri Ksetra, Beikthano and Halin. To the west was the Rakhine kingdom ruled initially by the Buddhist Chandra dynasty at Dhanyawadi and then Vesali. Later the Mrauk-U kingdom arose. Southwards were peoples who shared cultural features with both the Pyu to the north and Dvaravati kingdoms located in present-day Thailand. All three areas produced coinage with various uses, primarily as currency for tribute, taxes and ceremonial functions, rather than for everyday transactions.

Made in varying denominations from the 8th to 9th centuries, Pyu silver coins display conches, wheels, thrones, rising suns and *srivatsas*, an auspicious design representing divinity or greatness and associated with the Hindu god Vishnu (**1**). The imagery is closely related to Rakhine silver coins of the 7th and 8th centuries that were decorated with bulls, conch shells and *srivatsas* and inscribed with the name of the king in Indian Brahmi script (**2**). Rakhine coin production ceased in the 9th century for unclear reasons. Similar coinage was produced in Myanmar's southern region (**3**). Gold and silver coinage disappeared on the mainland by around the 10th century CE and was not reintroduced until more than 500 years later.

In island Southeast Asia, coins were not produced continuously, although they remained in circulation. Early examples have been found on the Malay peninsula, where goods were transported by land across the narrow isthmus. Some coins resembled Pyu and southern examples. Given the standardized weights, they were probably for exchange, rather than ritual purposes. On Java, the earliest locally produced coins – gold and silver lumps stamped with religious designs, floral motifs or Indian script letters indicating their weight – date from about the 9th century (**4, 5**). Similar examples have been found in the Philippines, dating from the 10th–12th centuries, and on Bali. They were probably used for high-value transactions and administrative payments only and may also have been a symbol of kingship. On Java and Bali, coinage ceased being made before the late 13th century, when Chinese bronze *cash* was adopted as currency by the Majapahit empire. Despite the presence of coinage, lump silver, metal objects, cowrie shells, textiles and ceramics played substantial roles as currency in many parts of Southeast Asia, and barter was a major form of exchange.

2 | 2 Dvaravati imagery

Dvaravati is still a largely unknown entity. Was it a unified kingdom? A series of culturally related city-states? A socio-cultural area? The name is used for the artistic and structural remains sharing some, but not all, stylistic features found in central, eastern and northeastern Thailand that date between the 6th and 11th centuries. While some evidence of early Hinduism is visible, Buddhism became dominant in the mid-7th century. Initially, Dvaravati shared stylistic features with early Cambodian art, but then connections with southern and northern India, as well as with the Pyu and other peoples in southern Myanmar, grew stronger. Towards the end of Dvaravati, links with Champa in present-day southern Vietnam emerged.

Dvaravati art is known primarily from its sculpture in stone, terracotta and stucco (**1**). Buildings were produced in brick, but were decorated with terracotta and stucco imagery in high relief. There are also religious plaques with figural imagery (**2**). In stone, standing figures of the Buddha with both hands making the gesture of instruction, *vitarka mudra*, were prevalent. The facial features of these Buddhas included a broad mouth and full lips, large hair curls and a prominent, but unadorned, *ushnisha* (the cranial bump representing wisdom) (**3**). The downcast eyes enhance the impression of complete serenity. Some elements of Dvaravati styling lasted into the 13th and 14th centuries, often in combination with new features, such as those from the Khmer kingdom at Angkor.

1. Head of the Buddha
Characteristics of Dvaravati images include pendant earlobes that nearly reach the shoulders and a slight smile, as seen here, although the lips of this head are thinner than usual. Besides the stone Buddha images and boundary markers that remain from Dvaravati, many stucco objects like this one have been found or excavated. These added to the sanctity of stupas (architectural mounds housing relics of the Buddha) and temples through the representation of the Buddha and Buddhist imagery.

9th–10th century
Thailand
Stucco
Height 15.8 cm, width 12.9 cm
Donated by P. T. Brooke Sewell, 1957,0726.4

2. Religious plaque
This plaque features an image of the Buddha seated in *dhyana mudra*, the gesture of meditation, under a tree surrounded by numerous celestial figures. The remains of an inscription are incised into the back, and the whole piece has been covered with a brown slip. Similar types of religious plaques, in a rectangular format with representations of the Buddha or religious narratives, and dating to the 7th and 8th centuries, have been found in Thailand, Myanmar and as far as west Java.

c. 8th century
Found at Angkor, Cambodia
Pottery
Height 14 cm, width 11 cm
Donated by A. W. Franks, 1894,0926.19

3. Head of the Buddha

Dvaravati images such as this head share similar features like the emphasis on symmetry, the large hair curls, arched eyebrows that meet at the bridge of the nose and the full lips. Because of the number of centres associated with Dvaravati, however, images were not uniform and varied in proportion. A dark limestone, as used here, was one of the favoured materials.

8th–10th century
Thailand
Limestone
Height 33 cm
Donated by the heirs of Louise
Samson, 1963,1016.1

2 | 3 The Khmer empire

Viewed as beginning with the consecration of King Jayavarman II in 802 (r. 802–35) and lasting into the 1400s, the Khmer empire was centred at Angkor, the largest city in the world at the time and known widely for its wealth. Zhou Daguan, Chinese envoy from 1296 to 1297, wrote of a royal procession: 'Last came the king, standing on an elephant, the gold sword in his hand and the tusks of his elephant encased in gold. He had more than twenty white parasols decorated with gold filigree, their handles all made of gold' (Harris 2007, 82–3).

Over time, the empire produced huge water management dams and reservoirs, and numerous stone religious temple complexes, including the famous Angkor Wat. The fertile lands around the Tonle Sap lake provided the wealth and access to human resources necessary for these constructions. Symbolically, the architecture followed cosmological principles, including the five peaks of Meru (the universe's central mountain, according to Hindu and Buddhist thought) and the mountain ranges and oceans that surround it (**1**). Sites were dedicated with stone inscriptions detailing the resources, including land and slaves, provided for maintenance.

Angkorian society is known for its production of free-standing and relief stone sculpture, metalwork and ceramics. Khmer sculpture is characterized by exceptional precision, with the shapes and sizes dictated by strict conventions. Although aesthetically beautiful, Khmer sculpture was primarily produced by the elite to honour the gods (**2, 3**). Khmer ceramics have a limited repertoire of shapes and glazes, including roof tiles, urns, ewers, bowls, bottles and jars in a greenish or brown colour or even unglazed (**4**). Ceramics were sometimes buried under temples and religious foundations.

1. Louis Godefroy,
Le sanctuaire au soleil couchant (Angkor)
Associated with the Hindu god Vishnu, the temple of Angkor Wat was built by King Suryavarman II (1113–c. 1150) in the early 12th century. Each Khmer ruler constructed temples primarily in sandstone over laterite, to honour his ancestors and patron deity – Vishnu or Shiva or the Buddha. Single-storeyed, the temples are constructed on layered platforms, with several towers of tiered roofs arranged symmetrically around a central structure. The whole was surrounded by a moat. In post-Angkor Cambodia, Angkor Wat was used by Buddhists, and later captured the imagination of Europeans who sketched, photographed and illustrated the site extensively. Today it is a major tourist destination.

1921
Angkor, Cambodia
Etching
Height 26.9 cm, width 36.5 cm
Donated by Louis Godefroy,
1930,0211.6

2. Figure of a heavenly being
Minor deities such as represented here had stylized and idealized faces and bodies, representing the perfection of the gods. Despite this, many of the figures' details were individualized, creating complex assemblages populating the walls of buildings. While three-dimensional figures were produced from a single block, relief sculptures were part of a building's structure and comprised several pieces of stone.

12th century
Cambodia
Sandstone
Height 100 cm, width 30 cm,
depth 20 cm
2002,0330.1

3. The *bodhisattva* Avalokitesvara

Avalokitesvara in his multi-headed form was important to Mahayana and Vajrayana (Tantric) Buddhism, which became prevalent at Angkor during the reign of the Buddhist King Jayavarman VII (r. 1181–1218). The numerous heads indicate the *bodhisattva's* virtues, used to overcome the obstructions to enlightenment, and he is known for his ability to assist devotees because of his infinite compassion. The small figure in his headdress is the Buddha Amitabha, with whom he is associated.

12th century
Cambodia
Sandstone
Height 38.7 cm, width 21.8 cm
1933,0407.1

4. Glazed stoneware jars

Glazed stoneware was used in court rituals and religious rites by the Khmer elite, as demonstrated by images in relief sculpture. Most examples were wheel-thrown with minimal incised or moulded decoration. Glazes ranged from green hues to a thick brownish-black colour (as here) from an iron oxide ash compound. There are similarities between the decoration on ceramics and lathe-turned wood objects, and some of the shapes are also found in metal. Such jars were not exported but were retained for local consumption. There are no remaining texts that provide information on how ceramics were used specifically.

11th–12th century
Cambodia
Stoneware
Height 48.4 cm, height 36 cm, height 24 cm
1993,0417.1, 1993,0417.2, 1993,0417.3

2 | 4 The spread of Khmer art forms

Khmer artistic remains stretch over a wide area from present-day Cambodia to northeastern Thailand, southern Laos and southern Vietnam, indicating the extent of the Khmer empire and its sphere of influence. Some areas were important centres, such as Phimai in northeastern Thailand, which played major administrative and religious roles between the 11th and 13th centuries. Other places were outposts of Khmer influence. Lopburi in central Thailand was also intermittently dominated by the Khmer in the 11th to 13th centuries, such as when King Jayavarman VII (r. 1181–1218) installed one of his sons as governor of the region. Whether the Lopburi elite were Khmer, or locals adopting Khmer ideas for political purposes (a common practice across Southeast Asia), is not clear.

Following on from earlier Buddhist traditions in the area, the art that was produced in Lopburi during the Khmer period combined elements from Dvaravati and the Khmer, revealing the cultural and artistic ideas that developed with political interaction (**2**). The incorporation of Khmer-style crowns and jewelry on stone and metal religious images, as well as representations of the Buddha seated under a *naga* (mythical serpent), are examples of Lopburi artists using Khmer ideas (**3**, **4**). Similar bronze objects were made in Cambodia and Lopburi, such as palanquin hooks, and Khmer motifs and patterning are also visible on these (**1**). Towards the end of the Khmer period in central Thailand, art forms also displayed elements associated with Myanmar.

1. Khmer-style palanquin hook

People of high status were carried in palanquins adorned in ways that indicated their rank. This hook, decorated with rearing horses wearing an animal headdress, geometric patterns and flame motifs, would have been attached to a pole from which a hammock was hung, as recorded by a Chinese envoy to Angkor in the late 13th century.

12th–13th century
Possibly Lopburi, Thailand
Bronze
Height 33.7 cm, width 17.8 cm
1946,1015.1–2

2. Head of the Buddha

The Dvaravati qualities of wide and full lips and broad brow of this head, as well as its elegant face with gently downcast eyes and slightly arched eyebrows, are typical facial features associated with images produced in the Lopburi region of central Thailand during the 13th century.

Early 13th century
Central Thailand
Limestone
Height 32.5 cm
Donated by P. T. Brooke Sewell,
1957,0726.2

3. Head and torso of the Buddha

Although increasing connections with Buddhist Myanmar to the west as well as the movement of bronze images around the region encouraged artists to move away from Khmer-style imagery in central Thailand during the 13th century, this image retains strong links with Cambodia in the design of the jewelry and the tiered *ushnisha* (cranial bump).

13th century
Central Thailand
Sandstone
Height 39.4 cm
1931,0724.1

4. Head of the Buddha

This head of the Buddha has a slight smile, softening the face, and the headdress is embellished with two types of lotus petals that can also be seen on the browband. The pattern over the front of the hair curls links the band with the *ushnisha*, something seen on metal images from Lopburi, but less commonly on stone examples. The square brow and band across the forehead were common on Khmer sculpture, but here they have been changed into a reduced form that remained popular on Thai Buddha images into the 19th century.

13th century
Central Thailand
Sandstone
Height 40 cm
Donated by Colonel Earle, 1951,1112.1

2 | 5 Buddhist sculpture from Myanmar

With the rise of the Bagan kingdom (*c*. 11th to 13th centuries) in present-day central Myanmar and the first historic king, Anawrahta (r. 1044–77), there developed an energetic campaign of constructing temples, monasteries and other religious buildings over an area of some 65 square kilometres. Over the course of nearly three centuries, devout Buddhists donated several thousand brick structures, many of which still stand today. The buildings housed Buddha images and paintings, and in some cases religious tablets filled the walls, adding sanctity to the structures. Stylistic elements that developed during this time persisted after Bagan's decline (**3**). Religiously, the kingdom was eclectic with different forms of Buddhism present (**6**), as well as Hinduism and spirit beliefs. Over time, however, the Theravada tradition prevailed, in part through religious exchanges with Sri Lanka.

Religious buildings and objects were produced to make merit for the donor, function as reminders of the Buddha, and ensure the continuation of the tradition. Part of a king's duties was to protect the religion, and therefore missions were sent to help repair the temple at Bodhgaya, the site of the Buddha's awakening, during the reigns of King Kyanzittha (r. 1084–1113) and King Htilominlo (r. 1211–35). The Bodhgaya temple was replicated at Bagan under Htilominlo and in other art forms, such as tablets (**1**). Indian artists worked at Bagan, and there were strong artistic links with northeast India (**2**, **4**, **5**).

1. Religious tablet with the Buddha seated with legs pendant
Here, the Buddha makes the teaching gesture, spreading the Buddhist law to assist others to escape the torturous cycles of rebirth, and he sits with legs pendant, indicating his supremacy. Excavations have uncovered many hundreds of thousands of such religious offering tablets around temple compounds, in temple walls and in caves. Imagery ranges from lines of sacred texts and protective chants to stupas (relic mounds) and representations of the historic Buddha and previous Buddhas.

13th century
Myanmar
Terracotta
Height 15.5 cm, width 12.5 cm
Donated by A. W. Franks, collected by Rodway C. J. Swinhoe, 1896,0314.15

2. Religious tablet with scenes from the Buddha's life

On this tablet the Buddha is surrounded by depictions of eight of the most important events of his life, a religious and artistic theme popular in northeast India and Bagan between the 9th and 13th centuries. The events were his birth, enlightenment when he became a Buddha, his first sermon, the Parileyyakka retreat to the forest, the taming of the maddened Nalagiri elephant sent by the Buddha's enemies, his descent from Tavatimsa Heaven after preaching to his mother, his performance of miracles at Srivasti, and the Parinirvana, his final escape from the cycles of rebirth.

11th–12th centuries
Myanmar
Terracotta
Height 16.5 cm, width 11.7 cm
Donated by Lieutenant Dobson,
1899,1016.1

3. The Buddha making the gesture of enlightenment

The Buddha sits on a lotus throne, indicating purity, with one hand over the knee in the gesture of enlightenment. A finial emerges from a cranial bump (*ushnisha*) representing wisdom and is set with amber, which has been mined from prehistoric times in the northern hills. The 'fish-tail' robe design appeared during the Bagan period, a feature also found on images from northeastern India, but the attenuated appearance of this image suggests a later date. The base has been scratched with the name of the donor and records the merit generated by the gift.

15th–16th century
Myanmar
Bronze, amber
Height 23.7 cm, width 15.7 cm
Donated by P. T. Brooke Sewell,
1957,1015.3

4. The Buddha seated in *bhumisparsa mudra*

Seated and making the gesture of enlightenment, *bhumisparsa mudra*, this figure displays characteristic features from the Bagan period, many of which are also seen in the art of northeast India and the Himalayas at this time. These include broad shoulders and narrow waist, a broad forehead tapering down to the pointed chin, arched eyebrows and pursed lips. The clinging robes, with their plain lines, as well as the space for a jewel in the finial, also indicate connections with contemporaneous international Buddhist styles.

12th century
Myanmar
Bronze
Height 34 cm, width 25.5 cm
1971,0727.1

5. Standing crowned Buddha

Although the Buddha was most often represented in a seated position, some wooden standing images, including this one, were made during the Bagan period and later. They were usually shown crowned. While the tall, leaf-like forms of the crown resemble those seen in northeastern India, the elaborate ribbons to each side were a local innovation that became a standard format lasting through to the late 18th century.

14th–15th century
Myanmar
Wood, gold, lacquer
Height 114 cm
1981,0611.1

6. The Buddha Akshobhya

The multiplicity of religious ideas circulating in Myanmar during the Bagan period are expressed in this bronze figure of a seated Buddha. While Theravada Buddhism eventually came to dominate, during this time varying forms of Buddhism were present and were illustrated in sculpture and painting. Akshobhya, identified by the *vajra* thunderbolt lying in front and his gesture of enlightenment, is one of the cosmic Buddhas of Mahayana and Vajrayana (Tantric) Buddhism. He is shown seated upon a lotus throne atop a waisted plinth to honour him.

13th century
Myanmar
Bronze
Height 16.7 cm, width 10.8 cm
1971,0125.1

2 | 6 The sculpture of Sukhothai

Tai ethno-linguistic groups moved down into present-day Myanmar, Thailand and Laos from southwestern China and began establishing principalities in northern and north-central Thailand in the 11th and 12th centuries. The most famous king of the Buddhist Sukhothai kingdom was Ram Khamhaeng (r. 1279–98), who expanded the kingdom to its furthest extent. After his death it slowly shrank until it was absorbed into the kingdom of Ayutthaya in the early 15th century.

In 1331 in lower Myanmar monks from Sukhothai were ordained in the Mahavihara tradition that originated in Sri Lanka, and in the 1340s the monk Si Sattha travelled to Sri Lanka. After his return, Sri Lankan imagery appears in Sukhothai art.

Sukhothai is known for its religious buildings, bronze, stone and stucco work (**4**), and ceramics. Its sculpture is particularly famous for its innovative use of the four postures of meditation – seated, standing, reclining and walking – in reproducing images of the Buddha (**1, 2**). In an elegant new style, Buddha images were represented with a flame-like finial (found also in Sri Lanka and Nagapattinam in India), broad shoulders, robes that reveal the body, an oval face, slight smile and limbs that appear almost boneless (**3**). Other features, such as the oval face and the incised chin, indicate links with Sri Lankan art, and there were also strong connections with northern Thailand.

1. The Buddha in *dhyana mudra*, the gesture of meditation
Many of the Sukhothai features seen here, such as a prominent chest like a lion's, sinuous arms like an elephant's trunk, curved nose like a parrot's beak, long fingers and level feet, are associated with a canonical list of thirty-two physical characteristics of a great man. They indicate the Buddha's exceptional nature and his spirituality. Sitting is one of the four main postures of the Buddha that was represented regularly during the Sukhothai period. The gesture of meditation (*dhyana mudra*) is indicated by the hands in the lap, one of top of each other, with the palms facing up

14th–15th century
Thailand
Bronze
Height 46.5 cm
Donated by Clementina Tottenham, 1954,0219.4

2. Walking Buddha
Images of the Buddha walking with his right hand held in the gesture of reassurance (*abhaya mudra*) were an innovation of the Sukhothai period. Indicating the practice of walking meditation, the sculptures linked with the homage of the Buddha's footprints that developed around the same time. The Buddha was thought to have made an impression of his footprint after descending from Tavatimsa Heaven, where he had been preaching to his mother and the gods, but he also left a footprint for the devout *nagas* (mythical serpents) to worship.

14th century
Thailand
Bronze
Height 28 cm
1947,0514.1

4. Bronze, gilded *naga* terminal

Composed of a five-headed *naga* (mythical serpent) emerging from the mouth of a mythical sea creature (*makara*), this terminal would have formed the end of a temple balustrade. *Makara* are composite aquatic animals depicted as guardians, often of thresholds and entrances. Serpents are found in temples because they are associated with rainbows that function as bridges between the watery earth and the airy heavens. The heads would have faced visitors as they started to mount a temple's stairs. The use of *naga* imagery linked Sukhothai art with that of Angkor and the Khmer.

1460–90
Said to be from Wat Phra Sri Rattana Mahathat, Phitsanulok, Thailand
Bronze, gold
Height 95.4 cm, width 51 cm
Donated by Ernest Mason Satow, 1887,0714.1

3. Head of the Buddha

Once part of a very large bronze image, this Buddha head displays Sukhothai characteristics including a flame finial, tight hair curls meeting in a point on the forehead, arched eyebrows, curved, downcast eyes, slight smile and a double line around the lips that harks back to Khmer iconography.

14th–15th century
Thailand
Bronze
Height 54 cm
1880.1002

2 | 7 Dai Viet

In 111 BCE, the Han dynasty of China invaded what is today northern Vietnam, establishing control over the area that, despite intermittent rebellions, lasted until 938 CE when Ngo Quyen defeated the Chinese at the battle of Bach Dang River. The Ly and Tran dynasties ruled Dai Viet in northern Vietnam from 1009 until 1400, and the Ming emperor Yongle of China regained control in 1406, ruling until the 1420s. After this, there were a number of subsequent invasions, but the Chinese forces were no longer able to colonize Dai Viet for long.

The periods of Chinese occupation had profound impacts on all aspects of Vietnamese life, from administrative and political structures to script, culture and the arts. Potting technology expanded to include glazing, complex moulds, refinement of clay and the fast wheel that enabled pots to be shaped quickly; these techniques came from China but Vietnamese ceramicists used them innovatively (**1**). Designs often followed Chinese arrangements. After independence, new ceramic shapes and decoration emerged, some for domestic consumption, and others for the developing export market (**2**). Blue-and-white wares with brown bases first emerged in the 14th century, rapidly becoming a popular export item as evidenced by finds at Fustat in Cairo. The heyday of such exports was the 15th century, when kilns sold ceramics to other parts of Southeast Asia, the Middle East and Africa (**2**, **3**).

Coinage initially came from China during the Han (206 BCE–220 CE) and Tang (618–907) dynasties, with the first Vietnamese-issued example appearing in 970 (**4**). Production ceased in around 1050, when Chinese coins were used again, but resumed in 1205 (**5**). Later in the 13th century, Vietnamese kings began producing paper money in order to retain copper supplies for weaponry.

Shared religious traditions with China included Buddhism, Confucianism and Taoism, though few sculptures from Dai Viet relating to these traditions survive from before the 1500s.

1. Jar and cover

This covered jar, with a domed lid, stands on a pierced foot and has been covered with a cream glaze. Before firing but after glazing, the pattern was scraped into the clay and filled with an iron brown glaze, creating an inlaid effect. For local consumption rather than export, the piece relates to Chinese Cizhou-type wares technically, but the wide body and the design are Vietnamese adaptations.

11th–12th century
Thanh Hoa, northern Vietnam
Stoneware
Height 26 cm
1931,0320.1

2. Water pourer with fitting

Found in Syria, this ritual water pourer (*kendi*) is a type made primarily for the Southeast Asian market, although such pourers were also eventually exported to Europe and the Middle East. The decoration consists of stylized lotus motifs encircling the neck and lower edge, Indian trade textile patterns around the middle of the neck, and two Chinese mythical creatures, *qilin*, on the sides, demonstrating the international networks in which northern Vietnam participated.

1440–60
Chu Dau, northern Vietnam
Stoneware, bronze
Height 28 cm, width 30.4 cm
2009,3014.2

3. Dish with an elephant-fish

Vietnamese kilns made dishes such as this one in large quantities for export. Painted with designs in cobalt blue and covered with a clear glaze prior to firing, this dish depicts an elephant-fish, a mythical composite creature in Southeast Asia that is a form of the *makara* seen in sculpture. In some areas, such as central Java, *makara* with elephant trunks and associations with water formed the terminals of temple balustrades. In Myanmar, the *makara* came to represent the zodiac sign Capricorn.

1430–80
Vietnam
Stoneware
Diameter 36.5 cm
2002,1011.1

5. Coins with calligraphy

Coin issues during the Tran dynasty (1225–1400) tended to be small and still used the Chinese format. Calligraphy identifying the reign of Tran Du Tong, the seventh emperor of the dynasty, is represented on these coins in the regular, seal and cursive scripts.

1358–69
Vietnam
Copper alloy
Diameter 2.3–2.4 cm
1884,0511.2194, 1884,0511.2203,
1884,0511.2193

4. Coin

Issues of coins after Dai Viet won independence from China in 938 CE followed the Chinese round format with a square central hole. As seen here, the Vietnamese language was written using Chinese or Chinese-style characters until the 20th century.

980–89
Vietnam
Copper alloy
Diameter 2.5 cm
1884,0511.2166

1. Early photographic print of Borobudur

One of the world's largest Buddhist sites, Borobudur was built between the late 8th and early 9th century. This photograph shows the temple in 1913. It comprises a series of square terraces lined with niches containing the five cosmic Buddhas associated with Mahayana and Vajrayana (Tantric) Buddhism, as well as narrative relief panels illustrating Buddhist texts. There are stupas (relic mounds) containing Buddha images on the round terraces at the top of the building. As with other central Javanese buildings, Borobudur is organized around a central ritual point.

1913
Java
Gelatin silver print
Height 19.3 cm, width 26.2 cm
Oc,B122.39

2. G. P. Baker, *Remains of two of the three temples at Pringapus in the Kedu district Java from the S.W.*

Although three temples in various states of collapse were recorded at the time this drawing was made (in the early 19th century), only one reconstructed structure remains today. It is a Hindu temple dedicated to the god Shiva, currently containing a sculpture of his mount, the bull Nandi. The 20th century saw numerous reconstruction projects around Indonesia, including at major sites like Borobudur, but smaller sites like this one also received attention.

c. 1815
On the slopes of Mount Sindoro, Java
Ink and wash on paper
Height 44 cm, width 56.1 cm
Donated by J. H. Drake, collected by Stamford Raffles, 1939,0311,0.4.16

3. J. W. B. Wardenaar, Watercolour of Candi Bajang Ratu

This painting shows a mountain-like brick structure at Trowulan, once the gateway into a temple complex. After the capital moved to east Java, a new sacred building layout developed, reflecting new religious ideas and rituals. The holiest area was placed at the rear of the temple, nearest a mountain peak, rather than at the centre of the compound as had been the tradition in central Java. This orientation was similar to Balinese temple organization, and resulted from connections between Bali and east Java from royal intermarriage and Majapahit hegemony. Stamford Raffles, Lieutenant-Governor of Java, charged Wardenaar (a Dutch captain who, like many other Dutch people, stayed on in Java after the British seized it) with excavating Trowulan to clarify Javanese history and artistic achievements.

1815
Trowulan, Java
Watercolour on paper
Height 29.4 cm, width 23.1 cm
Donated by J. H. Drake, collected by Stamford Raffles, 1939,0311,0.5.31

Mountains and water on Java

Mountains and water played a major role in belief systems and cosmology in Southeast Asia, from the mountain abode of the *nat* spirits venerated in Myanmar, to the great *barays* (artificial bodies of water) and mountain-shaped temples of Cambodia and the ubiquitous seaward and mountainward orientation of space on Bali. On Java, mountains were believed to be sites for meditation, the abode of gods and spiritual places often associated with ancestors. From around the 7th century CE, about 400 small Hindu temples with little decorative carving were built on the Dieng Plateau (see p. 35), with other groups on nearby mountains (**2**). Down on the plains, the Sailendra (8th–9th centuries) and then Sanjaya (8th–10th centuries) dynasties built such massive, heavily decorated structures as Borobudur and Prambanan (**1**). The buildings and sculpture were produced using andesite, a local volcanic stone, and the varying forms all symbolically represent a mountain – the sacred Meru, the centre of the Hindu and Buddhist universes – but also mountains generally.

The court moved to east Java in 929, for reasons that are not clear. Between then and the early 1500s, there were three dynasties – Kediri, Singasari and Majapahit – with the capital moving with each change. Under King Rajasanagara, also known as Hayam Wuruk (r. 1350–89), and his prime minister Gajah Madah, Majapahit became a substantial trading empire that controlled much of present-day Indonesia and the Malay peninsula. After a period of strife and decline, it was finally defeated by the Javanese Islamic kingdom of Demak in 1527, whereupon many court members fled to Bali.

Architecture in east Java was initially produced in stone, but later brick became the main medium (**3**). While some religious sites were built near urban centres, many, including ritual bathing places, were constructed in the mountains, which were linked with the cult of holy water and mountain worship through the myth of the elixir of life, *amerta*. Water vessels replicating the shape of Meru were used in the ritual recreation of this myth (**4**).

4. Ritual water vessel

Hindus on Java once believed that *amerta*, the elixir of life, was made by the gods churning the ocean of milk with the cosmic Mount Meru, using the cosmic *naga* (mythical serpent) Basuki as the turning cord. Although the exact ritual purpose of this vessel is unknown, it must be associated with *amerta* because the tapering neck, with lotus petal forms at the base, represents Meru and the spout is in the form of a *naga*.

13th century
Java
Bronze
Height 27.3 cm
1976,0406.1

2 | 8 Religious objects in western maritime Southeast Asia

Areas that now form part of Indonesia were once kingdoms that played major roles in the ancient Buddhist world, as the monuments and sculptures from Sumatra, Java, Bali and Borneo indicate. Images from southern and eastern India were imported, but many were also produced in Southeast Asia.

Hindu and Buddhist religious buildings on Java were embellished with statuary of deities and relief sculptures that included celestial beings, animals and floral, textile and geometric motifs, as well as sacred narratives. Metal sculptures and utensils were also used in the ritual practices that occurred within the compounds of these sacred sites.

Sculpted and relief images were made of local andesite rock or carved in brick. Buddhist temples and stupas contained numerous representations of the five cosmic Buddhas (Vairocana, Akshobhya, Ratnasambhava, Amitabha and Amoghasiddhi) and *bodhisattvas*, and relief carvings displayed stories from the previous lives of the historic Buddha and from Buddhist texts circulating on Java. Hindu sites contained a main image – usually Shiva, occasionally Vishnu, and rarely Brahma – surrounded by associated deities (**3**) and sometimes episodes from the Ramayana and Mahabharata epics. At both Hindu and Buddhist sites, guardian figures and animals often stand to either side of entrances and stairways. In east Java, rulers also commissioned deification sculptures of themselves in which they were represented as ancestors paired with a deity (**4**).

Metal religious sculptures were produced on Java between about 600 and 1500 CE (**1, 2**). Many Hindu and Buddhist images were made in bronze, but silver and gold examples also exist. During the central Javanese period (600s–929), figural sculptures predominated, but by the east Javanese period (929–1500s) ritual objects and utensils were the main products (**5**). Contemporary texts provide no information about how the figures and objects were used.

1. Seated female *bodhisattva*
This female *bodhisattva* wears elaborate jewelry that is typical of Buddhist metal imagery of the period, particularly the five points of the crown around a central headdress. She holds a conch shell, representing the spread of Buddhist teachings, and sits upon a lotus, a symbol of purity and a common iconographic element across the Buddhist world.

9th–11th century
Java
Bronze
Height 15.2 cm
Donated by Berkeley Galleries,
1960,1213.1

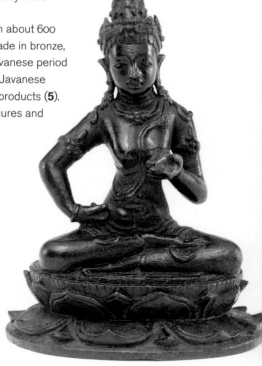

2. Buddha images from the Sambas hoard

A hoard consisting of small Buddhist statues, an incense burner and an inscription on silver foil was found by the Sambas River in west Borneo. The Old Javanese writing of the inscription presents verses from several different Buddhist texts, and mentions an unknown king, Candravarman. The varying features of the images indicate that some were made on the Indian subcontinent, but most were probably made on Java, using styles and ideas circulating regionally, such as the clinging clothing that originated with Gupta art forms in India, elaborate mandorlas (oval frames) surrounding the figures, lotus thrones and the presence of the *bodhisattva* Avalokitesvara.

9th–10th century
Made in Java and India
Bronze, gold, silver
Heights from 5.7–27.8 cm
Donated by P. T. Brooke Sewell,
1956,0725.1–9

3. Sculpture of Ganesha

In an arrangement unique to Java, the central shrine of a Hindu temple dedicated to Shiva contains an image of the god, and surrounding niches in temple walls hold sculptures of his consort Durga on the north side, the sage Agastya on the south side, and his son Ganesha on the west side. This image of Ganesha sits upon a double lotus throne with the soles of his feet pressed together, a typical Javanese characteristic, as are the tiered headdress and jewelry.

11th–12th century
Java
Volcanic stone (andesite)
Height 62 cm, width 41 cm
Donated by Charles Millet,
1861,1010.2

4. Ancestor figures as Shiva and Parvati

Considered to be incarnations of a god, the rulers and nobles of the Singasari dynasty (1222–92) and the Majapahit empire (c. 1293–1527) commissioned deification images that showed themselves as royal ancestors reunited with their chosen god – Shiva, Vishnu or the Buddha – after death. Here a couple are depicted as Shiva and his consort Parvati. The figures stand with eyes cast down to screen out the world and with their hands in meditation.

14th–15th century
Java
Volcanic stone (andesite)
Height 49 cm, width 25 cm;
height 48 cm, width 23 cm
1880.290, 1880.291

5. Incense burner

Incense is an important part of Buddhist and Hindu ritual practices. This cast bronze burner stands on four feet and has a tiered roof, the latter a common feature of Southeast Asian architecture. In many parts of the region, birds are associated with the heavens and are believed to act as messengers to the gods. Their presence on the roof of the burner connects with the smoke of the incense wafting upwards in honour of the Buddha.

10th century
Found in Sambas, Borneo
Bronze
Height 19.7 cm, width 16.1 cm
Donated by P. T. Brooke Sewell,
1956,0725.10

2 | 9 Gold rings and earrings from Java

On Java there are few gold deposits, and the metal appears to have been imported from Sumatra and Borneo, and possibly Sulawesi. There is substantial evidence of extensive and technologically advanced Sumatran mines, but there have been few archaeological investigations of the sites.

Gold played an important role in Javanese religious life, and its glitter had symbolic connections with the aura of royalty and spirituality. Hoards of gold objects have been found buried in the mountains of central Java, as well as beneath temple foundations, and rings were given away during temple-founding ceremonies.

Aside from its religious and political links, gold was also used for adornment. Gold jewelry items are some of the most numerous remains of early Java, indicating their widespread relevance to pre-Islamic society. Slit earrings come in numerous varieties (**1**), and rings were worn on fingers, toes, on chains around the neck and attached to clothing, not only as a means of adornment, but probably also for personal identification, protection and good fortune. The rings were made of cast or shaped sheet gold, though the two techniques could be combined. Embellishments were cast, incised or soldered, as well as made through the process of granulation (**3**). Some inscribed rings were seals for use in trade (**4**), while others bore names or imagery associated with the god Vishnu (**2**). Further imagery, such as a fish or a vase, was associated with protection, good luck and wealth, and the uncut stones in some of the rings were supposed to affect fate too (**2, 3**).

1. Ear ornament
This slit earring (the slit is just visible on the left) is in the shape of Mount Meru, shown as a spiral surrounded by foliage and cloud-like motifs. On Java and Bali mountains were considered to be sites of spiritual power, being the abode of gods and ancestors and places of meditation and spirituality.

c. 700–1000
Central Java, Indonesia
Gold
Diameter 3.4 cm
Bequeathed by A. W. Franks,
Af.2402

2. Three gold rings
These rings have differently shaped bezels – ovoid, hexagonal and circular – but all are flat; they also have stirrup-shaped hoops, which is typical of early examples from central Java. They are embellished with motifs associated with abundance and the god Vishnu. All have been cast.

Ring with an image of the vase of plenty
c. 700–1000
Central Java, Indonesia
Gold
Diameter 2.3 cm
Bequeathed by A. W. Franks,
Af.2384

Ring with a fish, symbol of the Hindu god Vishnu
c. 700–1000
Central Java, Indonesia
Gold
Diameter 3 cm
Bequeathed by A. W. Franks,
Af.2381

Ring with foliage springing from a bowl
c. 700–1000
Central Java, Indonesia
Gold
Diameter 2.7 cm
Bequeathed by A. W. Franks,
Af.2382

3. Three rings with gemstones

Rings were often decorated with precious and semi-precious gemstones. Most gems were smoothed and polished but left in irregular shapes, although they were occasionally incised with designs. There were various setting methods. The red carnelian stone with an intaglio design of a lion-like mythical creature has been sunk into a recess in the ring. The crystals, garnet and sapphire of the other rings have been fastened by raised metal collars. Additional decoration includes groups of tiny gold beads (granulation) and fine bands of twisted wires.

Finger-ring
c. 700–1000
Central Java, Indonesia
Gold and carnelian
Diameter 1.9 cm
Bequeathed by A. W. Franks,
Af.2380

Finger-ring
c. 1000–1400
Java, Indonesia
Gold, sapphire, garnet, rock crystal
Diameter 3.4 cm
Bequeathed by A. W. Franks,
Af.2401

Finger-ring
c. 1000–1400
Java, Indonesia
Gold and mineral
Diameter 3.5 cm
Bequeathed by A. W. Franks,
Af.2400

4. Signet ring

The oval bezel of this ring is inscribed in Kawi (Old Javanese) script with words for good luck and profit in the Sanskrit language that originated in India. Such rings were used as personal seals.

c. 1000–1400
Java, Indonesia
Gold
Diameter 2.1 cm
Bequeathed by A. W. Franks,
Af.2375

2 | 10 The arrival of Islam

Muslim traders arrived in Southeast Asia, travelling along maritime trade routes connecting the Middle East to South Asia and China, as early as the 8th century. Over the centuries that followed, some settled in the commercial centres of the region, where they appear to have commanded a certain prestige and were often granted positions of authority. These deepening local connections enabled the creation of new networks of exchange. Other people involved in the spread of Islam included teachers, and eventually kings. By the end of the 13th century, Samudera Pasai, the first sultanate of the region, was established in northeastern Sumatra. Melaka (Malacca), on the west coast of present-day peninsular Malaysia, became a major commercial centre in the early 15th century, and its rulers converted to Islam in the 1430s. Further royal conversions continued across the region after that, including on Sumatra and in southern Thailand. On Java, the spread of Islam is credited to nine saints (*wali songo*), the first of whom, Maulana Malik Ibrahim, is thought to have been of Persian origin and to have arrived from Gujarat, India. Upon his death in 1419, he was buried at Gresik, northeast Java, in a stone tomb that remains a pilgrimage site today (**1**). Carved tombstones are some of the earliest instances of Islamic art in Southeast Asia. Early mosques followed Southeast Asian architectural forms, including concentric, receding roof layers and a square format (**2**).

1. Drawing of the tomb of the Muslim saint Maulana Malik Ibrahim
Located in the Gapuro Wetan mosque in Gresik, northeast Java, this tomb is in a Gujarati Indian style. There was a substantial trade in marble Islamic tombstones around the Indonesian archipelago in the 15th century. Inscriptions were the main decoration, but the lamp motif seen on the tomb cover, representing the light of God, was also ubiquitous.

c. 1815
Java
Ink, wash and colour on paper
Height 52.7 cm, width 70 cm
Donated by J. H. Drake, collected by Stamford Raffles, 1939,0311,0.5.55

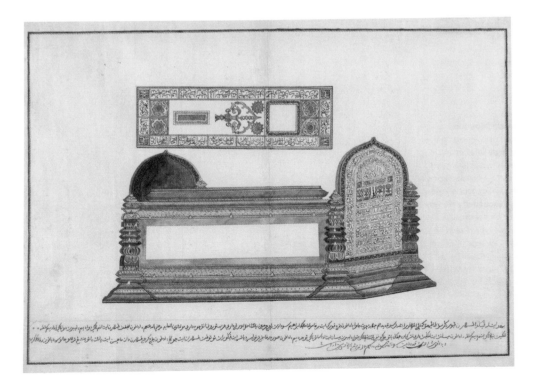

2. Wapauwe Mosque

This mosque, on Ambon in the Maluku islands (Moluccas), is one of the oldest in Indonesia. Dating from *c.* 1414, it retains its original wooden form with a tiered roof supported internally by four columns and no minaret. This is a style typical of early mosques in the region, which followed local architectural traditions. It was only in the 19th century that the domes and minarets common in Middle Eastern and South Asian mosques began to appear in Southeast Asia.

Timeline

15th–18th centuries	Theravada increasingly becomes the dominant form of Buddhism on the mainland, except for present-day Vietnam
Early 16th century	Founding of the Aceh Sultanate in northern Sumatra that later absorbed the Samudera Pasai Sultanate
16th century–1669	Kingdom then Sultanate of Gowa in southern Sulawesi, eventually defeated by the Dutch East India Company (VOC) and Bugis forces
16th–17th centuries	Brunei comes to prominence as a centre of trade after the decline of Melaka
1511	Portuguese conquer Melaka
1527–1813	Banten (Bantam), a trading kingdom based in west Java
c. 1527	Fall of the Majapahit empire to the Muslim kingdom of Demak on Java
1558	Nguyen dynasty expands control into southern Vietnam
1565	First Spanish settlement in the Philippines on the island of Cebu
1568–1815	Galleon trade between China, the Philippines and Mexico
1571	Spanish make Manila their capital after seizing it from its Muslim ruler
1578–1774	Toungoo and early Konbaung dynasties in Myanmar control the Lan Na kingdoms in northern Thailand
Late 16th–early 19th centuries	Cambodia alternates between periods of vassalage to Siam and Vietnam
Late 16th to mid-18th centuries	Mataram kingdom on Java
1619	Batavia (Jakarta) founded as VOC headquarters on Java
1641	VOC captures Melaka with help from the Johor Sultanate
1675–1823/5	Sultanate of Palembang on Sumatra
1707	End of the Lao kingdom of Lan Xang, which is divided into smaller kingdoms
1749	VOC gains control of part of Timor, setting the stage for late 20th-century conflict
1752–1885	Konbaung dynasty in Myanmar with its capital variously at Ava (Inwa), Amarapura and Mandalay
1767	Konbaung destruction of Ayutthaya and deportation of its people
1779	Anti-VOC rebellion in the eastern archipelago
1782–present	Chakri dynasty established in Thailand with the capital at Bangkok
1784	Konbaung Myanmar under King Bodawpaya annexes the Rakhine kingdom
Late 18th–19th centuries	Lan Na is absorbed by the Kingdom of Siam (Thailand) based in Bangkok
1802–1945	Nguyen dynasty with its capital at Hue
1819–26	Konbaung forces raid and depopulate Manipur, relocating people to the Myanmar heartland
1824	Anglo–Dutch treaty divides most of island Southeast Asia into a British region of Singapore, the Malay peninsula and northern Borneo and a Dutch area of the remaining islands, except the Philippines
1824–26, 1852, 1885	The three Anglo-Burmese Wars leading to the complete annexation of Myanmar by the British
1840s	Brunei grants territory to James Brooke, who established the Brooke Raj in the Sarawak region of the north coast of Borneo
1850s onwards	Gradual acquisition of Vietnamese territory by the French
1855	Bowring treaty between Thailand and Britain
1863	Cambodia becomes a French protectorate
1887	Establishment of French Indochina, comprising present-day Cambodia, Laos and Vietnam
1888	Brunei becomes a British protectorate
1904	Aceh falls to the Dutch

3 Trade, diplomacy and empire

c. 1400–1940

The major mainland Southeast Asian kingdoms that centred on Angkor in Cambodia, Bagan in Myanmar, Sukhothai in Thailand and My Son among the Cham polities, as well as the island polities of Srivijaya and Malayu, had all declined in political clout by 1400. Other kingdoms, empires and sultanates now dominated, including the Toungoo dynasty in central Myanmar, Ayutthaya in central Thailand and Lan Na to the north, Lan Xang in Laos, Dai Viet in Vietnam, the Majapahit empire in the island region, the important trading port of Melaka on the western side of the Malay peninsula and Islamic sultanates such as Samudera Pasai and Aceh in northern Sumatra. These entities retained many of the values, beliefs, customs and structures of their predecessors.

The kingdoms of the mainland progressively became more centralized administratively (4), despite numerous dynastic changes and wars. Toungoo under King Bayinnaung (r. 1551–81) extended control into Lan Na in northern Thailand in the late 16th century, and in the late 18th century, Ayutthaya was sacked and the population relocated to central Myanmar. Similarly, Rakhine and Manipur were also brought under Myanmar control in the late 18th century. King Rama I (r. 1782–1809) established the Chakri dynasty in central Thailand with its capital at Bangkok. From the late 18th through to the 19th century, Thailand slowly absorbed the polities of Lan Na in the north and relocated peoples from Laos into the northeast. Vietnam was ruled by the Nguyen and Trinh factions in the 17th and 18th centuries, and the northern and southern regions were consolidated in 1802 under the Nguyen dynasty. The kingdom also expanded to encompass parts of present-day Laos and Cambodia.

In island Southeast Asia, the political situation was fragmented under numerous courts, many of which converted to Islam (5). Often they were centred around a major port city with connections to the hinterlands; many were expansionary, fighting for control of trade and resources. Some were long-lived, such as Aceh, which only fell to the Dutch in 1904. Others existed for shorter periods, such as the kingdom of Demak on Java, which emerged in the 1470s, defeated the Majapahit empire in the 1520s, and was subsumed under the Javanese

1. John Oliver, *His Excellency Pungearon Nia Paria Ambassador Extraordinary from the King of Bantam to his Ma(jes)tie of Great Brittain in the year 1682 exactly drawn after the life*
From the 17th century, Southeast Asian kingdoms sent diplomats to European courts, as they had been doing within the region and to China for more than 1,000 years. Banten (Bantam) was an Islamic sultanate and a prominent trading kingdom based in northwestern Java from the 1500s until annexed by the Dutch in the early 1800s. The ruler may have sent the embassy and the ambassador represented in this engraving to seek British support against the Dutch VOC, who later in 1682 deposed him and placed his son on the throne as a puppet.

1682
London
Engraving on paper
Height 32.3 cm, width 21.2 cm
1849,0315.100

2. Tin coin of Manuel I, King of Portugal

The Portuguese, under the governor of Portuguese India, Afonso de Albuquerque, developed Melaka as a colonial city from 1511 by constructing a fortress and issuing currency. The use of tin took advantage of the plentiful local supply. The sphere on one side of this coin represents the king of Portugal's emblem; on the other side is a Christian cross. The Portuguese strongly promoted Catholicism as part of their colonial activities.

1511–21
Minted in Melaka, Malay peninsula
Tin
Diameter 4.1 cm
Donated by Ogilvy, 1861,0507.20

kingdom of Mataram in the 1560s. The major entrepôt Melaka was conquered by the Portuguese in 1511 (**2**).

Between 1400 and 1900, the religions of Southeast Asia also changed substantially. The Theravada branch of Buddhism gradually came to dominate the mainland, and connections with Sri Lanka, home of what was believed to be a pure form of Buddhism, continued. Islam came to dominate the island region as rulers converted, engaging with the Muslim heartland in the Middle East through diplomacy. The Islamic kingdoms and trading hubs of Southeast Asia, such as Melaka, Gowa on Sulawesi and Brunei on Borneo, became centres for the expansion of the religion. Christianity arrived with the Europeans in the early 16th century but did not gain converts where Islam and Buddhism were strong, becoming successful primarily in the eastern and highland parts of the Indonesian archipelago, the northern Philippines and the highland regions of the mainland. Rulers promoted specific religions, but ordinary people adapted new beliefs to suit local requirements.

Southeast Asia's location on busy trading routes as well as its unique resources encouraged the emergence of new commercial classes in growing multicultural and cosmopolitan regional centres and cities. Numerous Chinese settled in Southeast Asia. With them came the Chinese copper *cash*, which was used for low-value transactions and was often an important form of currency. Cowrie shells and other objects as currency and barter also remained widespread (**3**). Also settling in the region were Muslims from Gujarat, Bengal and southern India, who acted as the primary Indian merchants in Southeast Asia at this time,

3. Tin ingot in the shape of a crocodile

From about the 15th century, tin ingots in animal shapes or in 'square hat' forms were commonly produced on the Malay peninsula, particularly the state of Perak on the west coast, which had been mined for tin for several millennia. The ingots were used as currency, though little else is known about them. Initially tin mining on the Malay peninsula was small-scale and sporadic, but production increased hugely in the 19th century and by 1900 half the world's supply originated there. Numerous migrants from other areas, especially China, came to work in the mines.

c. 16th–19th century
Malay peninsula
Tin
Length 37.4 cm
Donated by Cecil Wray,
As 1933,1104.2

trading a wide variety of goods, including textiles, many of which became prized heirlooms, and other luxuries. Southeast Asian groups were, consequently, amalgamations of people from various areas, and while diversity is a characteristic of the region and different peoples were recognized, the categories were not fixed and incomers often integrated successfully. The movement of people was part of what made this flexibility possible, and this period saw intensified mobility – some involuntary. People were enslaved in warfare, or sold themselves to resolve debts. Their status was different from that of slaves in the Atlantic region; depending on their skills and abilities, they might take positions at court or continue as artisans, soldiers, merchants or farmers. Over time, many assimilated as non-slaves or bought their freedom. Only in the late 18th and 19th centuries did Southeast Asian rulers start to emphasize allegiance based on custom or belief, setting the scene for future rivalries.

Increased prosperity brought about by trade saw a rise in population and an expansion of cultivatable land. Early trade focused on spices and products unique to Southeast Asia, but by the 18th century, environmental issues from overharvesting the hinterlands emerged, causing conflict between lowlanders and groups living in the interior. Later, as Europeans acquired a hegemonic position through new scientific and military technology, such cash crops as sugar, tea, coffee and opium became the primary commodities. In the Philippines, Manila was a hub for the exchange of silver from the Americas and silk and ceramics from China, as well as other luxury goods.

4. Seal

Thailand's seals, usually made of ivory, took the shape of a Buddhist stupa (*chedi* in Thai). Monks and governmental administrators used the seals to stamp official paperwork or mark sacred texts as belonging to a particular monastery. The design on the base represents the specific bureaucratic department or monastery.

1800s
Thailand
Ivory
Height 9.2 cm, diameter (stamp face) 4.8 cm
Donated by F. Ward,
As 1919,1104.55

5. Grain measure (*gantang*)

Gantang were standardized grain measures for rice. The inscription in Arabic script gives the date and establishes that the measure was officially approved by the Sultan of Brunei. The large handle is necessary, because each *gantang* holds nearly 4 litres.

1899–1900
Sultanate of Brunei
Brass
Height 16.8 cm, diameter 21.5 cm
2020,3002.1

Europeans arrived at the end of the 1400s in search of highly valuable spices. First were the Portuguese, who captured Melaka in 1511 and established numerous fortified ports across the island region. The Spanish occupied the northern parts of the Philippines, including Manila, from the 1570s. The Dutch East India Company (VOC) emerged as the major European power on the Southeast Asian seas in the 17th century, and the British East India Company increasingly acquired authority in the 18th. Initially, Southeast Asians treated Europeans as yet another group of traders and even sent diplomatic missions to Europe (**1**), but by the late 19th century, most of Southeast Asia had come under colonial control. The Spanish controlled the Philippines, the Portuguese East Timor, the Dutch Indonesia, the French Indochina and the British Myanmar, Malaya, Singapore and northern Borneo. All instituted colonial bureaucracies that were radically different from previous forms of social organization; sometimes local rulers were installed as figureheads. Political control was exerted to extract the raw materials and harness the labour necessary for industrial expansion, and whole areas were converted into plantations and mines. The French, Spanish and Portuguese also heavily promoted religious conversion. Only Thailand remained independent, in part because it made concessions to the Europeans, but also because it functioned as a buffer zone between the British and French.

1. Seated Buddha image

Theravada Buddhism gradually became prevalent in Cambodia from the early 15th century, and by the 19th, it was dominant. Overshadowed by Khmer sculpture and architecture from Angkor, Cambodian Buddhist objects from later periods are less well preserved and less often represented in collections. This is a rare example of a lacquered and gilded stone Buddha wearing jewelry similar to that of earlier periods, including the broad collar and tiered crown and finial.

17th–19th century
Cambodia
Stone, gold, lacquer
Height 49.9 cm
1992,0707.1

2. Two standing monks

Sariputta and Moggallana became Gotama Buddha's foremost disciples on the day they were ordained as monks, because of their efforts throughout countless previous lives. Sariputta was known for his wisdom and ability as a teacher, while Moggallana had mastery over supranormal powers, a result of his advanced spiritual knowledge. Here, both monks stand in *anjali mudra*, the gesture of homage. Decorated robes became popular on Buddhist images in Thailand in the early 19th century.

Early to mid-19th century
Siam (Thailand)
Bronze, gold
Height 109 cm; height 106.2 cm
Donated by the Doris Duke Charitable Foundation, 2004,0628.20–21

Theravada Buddhist empires on the mainland

Starting around the 11th century, the Theravada branch of Buddhism gradually became predominant in Myanmar, Thailand, Laos and Cambodia through the travels of monks, exchanges between monasteries, and royal patronage and purification. There were strong links with Sri Lanka as the island was considered to be the source of an orthodox form of Buddhism, and rulers sent monks to be reordained there to ensure the purity of the local Sangha's (community of monks) practices. For example, King Dhammaceti (r. 1471–92) of the Hanthawaddy (Bago/Pegu) kingdom in lower Myanmar recorded such a reformation in the Kalyani inscriptions of 1476–79, and monks from surrounding regions came to be reordained in Hanthawaddy. Monks also brought the Sri Lankan tradition to Chiang Mai and Cambodia in 1423. In the 17th century, VOC ships facilitated monastic exchanges between Sri Lanka and the kingdom of Rakhine to undermine Portuguese influence, and in 1799 a group of Sri Lankan monks came to Myanmar for reordination.

In Theravada Buddhism, the Buddha's teachings (Dhamma) are presented in the 'three baskets' of the Canon that is preserved and interpreted by the Sangha. Texts of the Buddha's words are important in ritual and as symbols of the religion, and the language of the Canon, Pali, is considered to be sacred. Major practices involve chanting and reciting texts, praying, making offerings to the Buddha and donating food, clothes, daily necessities and labour to the Sangha to generate merit and ensure good rebirths in the future. Sponsoring the creation of Buddha images, manuscripts, religious buildings and monasteries is also highly meritorious.

The historic Buddha, Gotama or Sakyamuni, is the fourth of five Buddhas who will become awakened during the current cycle of time (**1**). The next is Metteyya (Maitreya in Sanskrit). Other important personages are the Buddha's main disciples. The foremost are Sariputta and Moggallana (**2**), but others were noted for their special skills, such as Kaccayana. Prior to his final

3. 'Curled worm' bullet coin
The kingdom of Ayutthaya and the early Chakri dynasty issued coins called 'curled worm' in Thai. These were small shaped balls of silver that were stamped with Buddhist symbols, such as elephants, wheels and conch shells. The image of the wheel (*cakka*) on this coin refers to the Buddha's teachings, known as the wheel of the law, and was also a symbol of the *cakkavatti*, the ideal universal emperor of Buddhism.

18th century
Late Ayutthaya or Siam (Thailand)
Silver
Diameter 1.5 cm
Donated by Reginald Le May, 1931,0505.13

life, Gotama endured innumerable previous lives (*jatakas*) in which he perfected the ten virtues necessary for Buddhahood. Upon becoming a Buddha, he entered a long lineage of previous Buddhas, many of whom he had encountered over his earlier lives. Besides Buddhas and monks, there are deities, also extant in Hinduism (**4**), that occupy the heavens of the Buddhist universe, including Sakka (Indra), the lord of Tavatimsa Heaven. These images and narratives were represented in numerous art forms that became important aspects of ritual activity, functioning as reminders of the Triple Gem – the Buddha, the Dhamma and the Sangha – and providing a focus for ritual activity.

Generating merit for the entire kingdom, the ideal Buddhist monarch ruled in accordance with the Buddha's teachings and displayed the ten royal qualities – charity, good conduct, non-attachment, straightforwardness, gentleness, austerity, non-anger, non-injury, patience and tolerance. As Buddhists believe in rebirth, the king's luxurious palace and lifestyle indicated the extent of his meritorious behaviour in previous lives. A Jesuit priest in the kingdom of Ayutthaya in the mid-17th century commented that 'there is nothing to be seen but gold... one single idol is richer than all... the Churches of Europe' (Baker & Phongpaichit 2009, 14). Believed to exhibit the thirty-two physical marks of a great man that are present on the bodies of Buddhas, the king was viewed as a future Buddha, and he supported and ensured the purity of the Sangha.

Rulers justified warfare in Buddhist terms, particularly that of instituting the Dhamma in areas ruled unjustly, but also to demonstrate their status as a Buddhist world emperor, a *cakkavatti* (*chakravartin* in Sanskrit), whose accession heralds the arrival of the eagerly awaited future Buddha, Metteyya. For instance, the Toungoo and later Konbaung courts of Myanmar attacked Ayutthaya in the 1560s and 1767, on the grounds of spreading a better form of Buddhism. Ayutthayan kings attacked Myanmar without much success, but brought the kingdom of Angkor under their sway in the 1430s. In the 1770s and 1780s, Thai kings subdued the Lao kingdoms of Viantiane, Luang Prabang and Champassak, capturing the important Emerald Buddha and installing it in the Thai capital, where it remains today. Likewise, Myanmar King Bodawpaya (r. 1782–1819) transported the Mahamuni Buddha image from Rakhine to Amarapura in 1784. Besides warfare, the Buddha's tooth relics could be diplomatic tools, being given or loaned between kingdoms. Myanmar's King Bayinnaung (r. 1551–81) received a tooth relic from Sri Lanka in the late 16th century, and recently, China sent its tooth relic to Myanmar for tours in 1955, 1994, 1996 and 2011.

In connection with the close relationship between kings and Buddhism, crowned images of the Buddha, indicating these links and also the Buddha's spiritual superiority in material form, became prevalent in the 14th and 15th centuries across the region. Coinage was often issued with Buddhist symbols into the 19th century (**3**).

4. The god Shiva riding on a bull with the Buddha atop his headdress
In a contest of superiority, the god Shiva challenged the Buddha to a game of hide and seek. The Buddha found Shiva easily, but Shiva was unable to find the Buddha hiding in his headdress. King Rama I ordered the Buddhist text, *Trailokavinicchayakatha*, from which this story is taken to be translated from Pali into Thai in 1802, and sculptures like this one became popular from that time. Included in Buddhism as protective figures and denizens of the heavens, deities associated with Hinduism have been part of Southeast Asian royal rituals administered by Indian Brahmins for hundreds of years.

Early to mid-1800s
Siam (Thailand)
Bronze with gilding
Height 68.8 cm
Donated by A. W. Franks,
1894,0926.11

3 | 1 Buddhist imagery in Myanmar

In the 1500s the Toungoo dynasty in Myanmar successfully expanded the regions under its political sway. Under King Bayinnaung (r. 1551–81), it incorporated the southern Hanthawaddy (Mon) kingdom and later absorbed the Shan States, Lan Na in present-day northern Thailand and parts of present-day Laos. King Hsinbyushin (r. 1763–76) of the new Konbaung dynasty ordered the attack on the kingdom of Ayutthaya (Thailand) that led to its destruction in 1767, and under King Bodawpaya (r. 1782–1819), Rakhine was annexed to Myanmar, of which it remains part today. Konbaung kings also fought wars with China and expanded westward into Manipur and Assam in what is now northeast India. As Konbaung Myanmar enlarged its sphere of influence, it resettled people from conquered areas into its heartland. At the same time, land and sea trade routes grew, and Buddhist monks travelled between monasteries around the region.

The movements and interactions just described resulted in innovative features in the Buddhist art of Myanmar. Materials for Buddha images expanded beyond the usual marble, wood and bronze to include other metals and glass. Clay offering tablets and plaques displayed new types of images or were covered with differently coloured glazes (**1**). Paintings and architecture showed connections with central Siam (Thailand) and Lan Na (northern Thailand). Traditionally, the emphasis was upon the Buddha seated in *bhumisparsa mudra*, the gesture of enlightenment, but in the 19th century, this was supplemented with reclining figures and the reintroduction of standing images, as well as innovative forms of dress and jewelry (**2**). Drawing on changes occurring across the Theravada Buddhist world, these new forms look more naturalistic than those of earlier times (**4**). The importance of generating merit was reinforced by depictions of the god Sakka (Indra) recording people's deeds starting around the 18th century (**3**).

1. Architectural religious plaque
Attached to the outside of a stupa or temple, glazed religious plaques were used from the Bagan period (11th–13th centuries) into the 19th century to beautify and enhance the sanctity of buildings. They depict scenes of the Buddha's life, his previous rebirths and prominent events of the Sangha (community of monks): here is a scene from the Third Buddhist Council in 247 BCE when monks from many regions gathered to maintain the purity of the Buddha's teachings by checking the texts. Acting as an exemplary Buddhist king, Mindon (r. 1853–78) convened the Fifth Council in 1871.

Early 19th century
Wuntho, Konbaung Myanmar
Glazed ceramic
Height 24 cm, width 24 cm
Donated by Richard Carnac-Temple, 1894,0719.4

2. Buddha image with Thai-style crown
Crowned Buddha images, in part indicating the Buddha's supreme spirituality, became common in the 17th and 18th centuries. Earlier images had crowns with large bunches of ribbons, but with the forced relocation of Thai artists into Konbaung Myanmar after the sack of Ayutthaya in 1767, Thai-style crowns with narrow finials and pointed flanges became common.

Early to mid-19th century
Konbaung Myanmar
Wood, glass, gold, lacquer
Height 82.5 cm
1919,0717.1

3. The god Sakka (Indra)

The god Sakka is lord of Tavatimsa Heaven in the Buddhist universe. Seen here holding a pen and writing tablet, he keeps records of people's merits and demerits that will determine the quality of future rebirths. This role became popular in the 18th century and still plays a part in Buddhist practices in Myanmar today. The clothing that the figure wears reflects a style of Konbaung court dress influenced by the costumes of Thai theatrical troupes brought from Ayutthaya in 1767.

Late 18th–early 19th century
Konbaung Myanmar
Sandstone, lacquer, gold leaf, glass inlays
Height 79 cm
1880.256

4. Standing Buddha

In keeping with changes within the Theravada world, mid- to late 19th-century Buddha images from Myanmar became more naturalistic looking, with more rounded faces and the loss of the finial, although the cranial bump representing the Buddha's wisdom remained. Robes also folded around the body, instead of covering it like a skin. A decorated band stretched across the forehead. Many of these figures, including this one (in his right hand), also showed the Buddha offering the *myrobalan,* a medicinal fruit, to devotees to resolve their spiritual woes.

Mid-19th century
Konbaung Myanmar
Wood, glass, gold leaf, lacquer
Height 100 cm
Donated by Mrs Ballantine, 1923,0305.1

3 | 2 Myanmar manuscripts

There were once three main types of manuscript in Myanmar: paper, lacquer and palm-leaf. The black and white paper manuscripts were used as copy books and information manuals (**1**); the former could be erased and reused. There were also illustrated white paper *parabaik* depicting the Buddha's life and previous lives, sumptuary laws regulating the use of goods by different levels of society, court activities, and Buddhist cosmology (**3**). Made using different base materials ranging from cloth and metal to ivory, lacquered and gilded *kammawasa* manuscripts record the Buddhist monastic code of discipline (**2**). They were donated to monasteries upon the ordination of monks. Most Pali and Myanmar language manuscripts are written in standardized script, but *kammawasas* use a different script called tamarind seed (*magyizi*), which requires special training to read. Palm leaf manuscripts (*pei-za*) were rarely illustrated and were used for religious texts. To produce these, the writing was incised into the leaf, which was then rubbed with ink and wiped clean, leaving the black colour in the incisions to reveal the text (**4**).

Commissioning and donating manuscripts were highly important methods of generating merit and ensuring the continuation of the Buddhist religion. Monastery libraries stored large numbers of manuscripts in special boxes called *sadaik*.

1. Tattoo manual
Tattoo masters produced white or black paper manuscripts for reference. Tattoo motifs were once believed to provide protection, bring power or good fortune and charm others. The powers of Buddhist texts, sacred numbers and animals, such as tigers (as here) or sweetly singing birds, were transferred to the individual through tattooing onto the thighs, chest, arms and neck. Once common, the practice declined in the 20th century.

Late 19th–early 20th century
Myanmar
Pigment on paper
Length 43 cm, width 29 cm
2005,0623,0.1

2. *Kammawasa* manuscript
Donated to a monastery in 1929 by U Myat Htun Aung of Peinzalok and his two daughters, this manuscript's pages are flexible, indicating that they are made of lacquered cloth, possibly a monk's discarded robes, which are considered to be sacred. During production, the liquid lacquer was combined with the ashes of U Myat Htun Aung's wife, a common practice, believed to generate merit for the deceased. The donor and his daughters would also have accrued merit since the donation of religious texts was considered to be a way of perpetuating Buddhist teachings and slowing what was believed to be a decline in the religion.

1929
Myanmar
Lacquer, textile, teak, gold
Length 58 cm, width 13.9 cm
Donated by Ralph and Ruth
Isaacs, 1998,0723.172

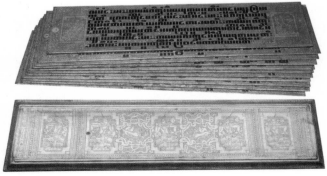

3. Cosmological *parabaik* (detail)

Manuscripts displaying the thirty-one levels of the Buddhist universe – the heavens, the hells and the earthly realms – are not particularly common. In the scenes shown here, the pillars represent Mount Meru, the universe's central axis, and its surrounding seven mountain ranges. Ananda the cosmic fish encircles the base of Meru in the surrounding ocean. On Meru's peak is the heavenly home of the god Sakka (Indra), where the Buddha was thought to have preached to his mother, as seen here. The layout and buildings of the royal palace in Myanmar were supposed to replicate Sakka's palace in heaven.

Late 1800s
Myanmar
Pigment on mulberry paper
Length 924 cm, width 53.5 cm
2010,3003.1

4. Leaf of a *pei-za* manuscript

The seventy-six leaves of this book have been incised with a Buddhist text in a combination of the Burmese and Pali languages. Texts that combine the two languages, using the Burmese to clarify the Pali for teaching purposes, are called *nissaya*. Wooden cover boards tied with a fibre string hold the leaves together, and the lacquered edges of the leaves protect them from damage and insects.

19th century
Myanmar
Palm leaf, wood, fibre
Length 52.7 cm, width 7 cm
Donated by the United Society
for the Propagation of the Gospel,
1989,1011.5

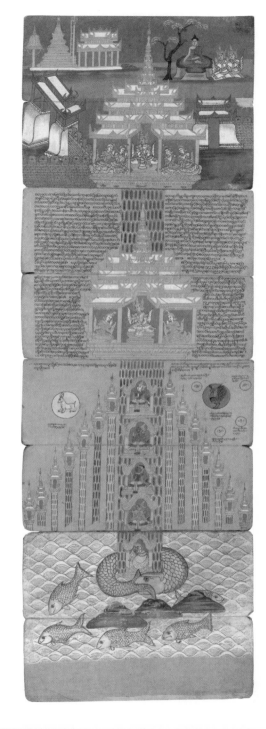

3 | 3 The Buddha and his relics in Lan Na and Lan Xang

Haripunchai was a kingdom in present-day northern Siam (Thailand) that lasted from approximately the 8th to the 13th centuries. It was succeeded by Lan Na, founded by King Mangrai (r. 1259–1311). From the mid-1550s to the end of the 18th century, Myanmar controlled the area, and it was absorbed by Siam (Thailand) in the 19th century.

Considered to have been founded by Fa Ngum (r. 1353–85), the kingdom of Lan Xang held sway over peoples occupying land to the east of Lan Na from around the 1350s to 1707. It split into several smaller kingdoms in the 18th century, and their territories eventually formed much of modern Laos. Substantial trade and the frequent wars that beset the region meant that the population often moved around or was forcibly relocated, which enhanced the transmission of artistic ideas throughout the area.

These kingdoms were Buddhist and produced Buddhist imagery in a wide variety of materials, including bronze, gold, silver, lead, wood and even resin and ash. Some of the Buddha images are famous across Buddhist communities and have extensive histories (3), while others were produced for use in domestic shrines.

One of the major characteristics of the region's Buddhist art is its diversity of form. Elements of Sukhothai sculpture including broad shoulders, elongated arms, or a walking stance are present. Also prevalent in Lan Na and Lan Xang were standing images, representing one of the four main postures – seated, standing, walking and reclining (1). Faces became more varied, often with pinched or angular features, raised eyebrows and pointed, flaring ears, and across the region from present-day eastern Myanmar to Laos, a puffy upper lip became common. High thrones and pierced or footed bases were widespread (2). Besides Buddha images, model shrines and stupas were made to house relics or to place on altars for worship (4).

1. Standing Buddha image
This Buddha figure holds its hands in an unusual gesture. More typically, the hands would lie flat over the abdomen, a reminder of the events occurring in the seven weeks after the Buddha's enlightenment. The Buddha spent one of the weeks in meditation looking at the tree under which he had attained enlightenment. The high arched eyebrows and puffy upper lip of the image indicate links with northern Thailand, Shan States and Myanmar.

18th century
Laos
Bronze
Height 65.8 cm
2003,0806.1

2. Seated Buddha image
The Buddha sitting on a waisted throne was a type popular from Myanmar to Laos during the 16th to 18th centuries. The high *ushnisha* (cranial bump representing wisdom) and large flame finial, as well as the curved earlobes, arched eyebrows and puffy upper lip, are of a type that emerged in the 15th century. Known from at least the early 16th century, the 'boat' shape of the upper section seems to have been a form made near Chiang Saen or Chiang Kham (near the present Thai border with Myanmar and Laos).

16th–17th century
Lan Na (northern Thailand)
Bronze
Height 41.5 cm
Donated by A. W. Franks, collected by Carl A. Bock, FBInd.11.a

3. Seated image of the Buddha Sikhi

The Buddha Sikhi appears in a northern Thai legend dating to the 1400s. The historic Buddha, Gotama, visited the area and gave a sermon while sitting on a black rock. The rock was carved into five statues, afterwards called Buddha Sikhi statues. This image may be named Buddha Sikhi because it is based upon the earlier models. It is inscribed with a dedication by three people expressing the wish that they will be reborn together in future lives until they attain Nirvana.

1540–41
Lan Na (northern Thailand)
Bronze
Height 55 cm
Donated by A. W. Franks, collected by Carl A. Bock, FBInd.5.a

4. Model shrine

Model shrines were another form of offering. Here, the Buddha sits on a textile cushion below roof tiers of lotus petals and buds supported by a double stylized lotus pedestal. Tiled roofs were a feature of Thai and Laotian religious buildings, as indicated by the scale pattern on the lowest roof here. The Buddha's features, with slight smile, curved and pointed ears and high finial, were common in provincial workshops of northern Thailand and Laos.

Late 19th–early 20th century
Laos or Lan Na (northern Thailand)
Wood, pigment, textile
Height 63.4 cm
1880.3452

3 | 4 Buddhism in Ayutthaya and under the Chakri dynasty

Founded not far from the Gulf of Thailand, Ayutthaya became a powerful Thai kingdom with a prominent role in international trade before being destroyed by Konbaung Myanmar's army in 1767. General Chakri, becoming King Rama I, re-founded the Thai kingdom (then known as Siam) in Bangkok in 1782, which has lasted to the present.

In the 15th century, Ayutthaya extended its sphere of influence, bringing the north-central kingdom of Sukhothai under its control, as well as attacking Lan Na in the north and occupying the Khmer kingdom in present-day Cambodia in the 1430s. Despite the almost continuous wars, Ayutthaya was cosmopolitan, welcoming new ideas, goods and peoples, particularly under King Narai (r. 1656–88), when there was tremendous commercial and diplomatic activity with Europe and the Middle East. Contributing to the exchanges, Buddhist monks travelled along religious networks across the region, and images of the Buddha's disciples started to be produced (**3**). As in other Southeast Asian Buddhist kingdoms, Indian Brahmins played major roles in court rituals, and Hindu deities were incorporated into royal and other contexts too (**4**).

Much Ayutthayan art perished in 1767, but surviving art forms demonstrate the kingdom's extensive cross-cultural interactions. The niello metal inlay technique was introduced by the Persians or Portuguese (**5**). The role of elephants in demonstrating royal power and spirituality developed from religious interactions with Sri Lanka (**2**). Crowns, headdresses, and the incorporation of mythical *naga* serpents into statuary and architectural designs reflect historic connections with Angkor (**1**). These historic connections are also visible in the rich art forms of the 19th and early 20th centuries.

1. Crowned Buddha head
Crowned Buddhas played an important role in Ayutthaya-period Buddhism, emerging in the early 16th century, though their meanings in different contexts are imperfectly understood. They may have represented the future Buddha Metteyya (Maitreya), or been associated with the episode in which Buddha humbled the haughty King Jambupati by a tremendous display of wealth, or linked with royal ancestors and the king. The wide decorated crown with layered *ushnisha* is found on 16th- and 17th-century Ayutthayan images, and harks back to Angkorian forms. Images became increasingly heavily decorated over time.

16th–17th century
Ayutthaya
Bronze
Height 29.9 cm
Donated by Mrs Shillito,
1949,0413.1

2. Stupa reliquary on elephant-back
This is a commemorative reliquary made to house the ashes of a senior monk or high-ranking person, as well as other precious items. The bell shape of the stupa supported by elephants, representing royal and spiritual power, resembles temple designs of Chedi Chang Rop at Sukhothai and Wat Maheyong at Ayutthaya, both dated to the 15th century. Reliquaries and stupas on elephant-back became popular after the Thai monk Si Sattha's journey to Sri Lanka in the 14th century.

15th century
Ayutthaya
Bronze, ivory
Height 34 cm
Donated by Reginald Le May,
1957,1014.2

3. Sculpture of the monk Kaccayana

Kaccayana was one of Gotama Buddha's main disciples, best known for explaining the Buddha's teachings to a lay audience. To prevent his attractive appearance distracting people from his presentation of the teachings, he used his spiritual powers to transform his body into that of an unattractive and fat man.

1700s or early 1800s
Ayutthaya or early Siam
(Thailand)
Bronze with lacquer and gilding
and a clay core
Height 28.4 cm, width 23.3 cm
Donated by William Raffles Flint,
collected by Stamford Raffles,
1859,1228.158

4. Ritual candleholder

Found in Thailand, Laos and Cambodia, ritual candleholders were used by all ranks of society in ceremonies, such as rites of passage, consecration, healing and agricultural rituals. They are usually in the shape of a leaf of the Pipal, the tree under which the Buddha sat when he became an awakened being, with the tip in the shape of a stupa (relic mound). This candleholder is adorned with an image of the Hindu god Brahma, incorporated into Buddhism as a protector, riding on his mount, the sacred *hamsa* goose. The candles would have been attached to the undecorated side.

Late 18th–early 19th century
Lan Na (northern Thailand)
Bronze
Height 28 cm
Donated by A. W. Franks,
1894,0926.16

5. Covered altar vessel

Used to make offerings to the Buddha, this gilded vessel was made using the niello technique, a complicated process in which a silver object is engraved with a design that is then filled with a black metallic alloy of sulphur and either silver, copper or lead. The whole piece is heated and the alloy melts and fills the incisions, providing a strong contrast with the surrounding areas.

Late 19th–early 20th century
Siam (Thailand)
Silver, gold, niello
Height 33 cm
Donated by A. Mitchell-Innes,
1934,0514.4.a–b

3 | 5 Thai religious furniture

The production of religious objects, such as Buddha images, manuscripts and offering vessels, necessitated places to put them. Elaborate manuscript chests and cabinets (**2, 3**), as well as stands and altars for Buddha images (**1**), were thus commissioned as a means to honour the Buddha and stave off the decline of the religion. Production of such objects declined in the first half of the 20th century as tables, rather than tiered stands, became popular for the display of Buddha images and printed Buddhist texts replaced palm-leaf and hand-illustrated ones. More recently, bookshelves and glass-fronted cabinets are used to display and store images, amulets, books and manuscripts.

Religious furniture was once lavishly decorated with lacquer, gilding, mirrored glass and paint. Tiered stands for Buddha images and cabinets for manuscripts could illustrate in paint or gold leaf representations of the Buddha, episodes from the Buddha's life and the *jatakas*, or scenes from the Ramayana, the epic narrative found in a variety of art forms in Thailand and other parts of Southeast Asia (**1, 3**). The narrative of the monk Phra Malai, who visited Hell and reminded people to make merit for unfortunate relatives, as well as images of the previous Buddhas, were also popular.

Practitioners placed vessels, stands, trays and boxes of silver, lacquer, mother-of-pearl and niello (a form of metal inlay) containing offerings to the Buddha on the altars and stands, while the chests and cabinets lined walls or were placed against pillars in monasteries and temples.

1. Tiered altar stand for Buddha images
Made of gilded and lacquered wood with coloured glass inlays, this altar stand has a series of platforms for Buddha images and offerings, as well as two drawers at the base. The painted background shows the Buddha seated in meditation on a throne in a landscape setting, being honoured by several deities. Such pieces of furniture were commissioned and donated to temples, but went out of fashion in the late 19th century.

Late 19th century
Siam (Thailand)
Wood, lacquer, glass, pigment, gold leaf
Height 153 cm, width 67 cm, depth 44 cm
Donated by the Doris Duke Charitable Foundation, 2004,0628.24

2. Manuscript chest
Gilded chests like this one would have been donated to a monastery to store religious manuscripts. Furniture with inlaid glass designs became fashionable in the late 19th century in Thailand. The diagonal trellis patterning was also found on imported Indian trade textiles made for the Thai market and on the Bencharong and Lai Nam Thong ceramics originally commissioned from kilns in China for consumption in Thailand, and therefore was associated with luxury goods. Its use on a donation would have added to the perceived value of the object, honouring the Buddha to the donor's greatest capacity.

Late 19th–early 20th century
Siam (Thailand)
Wood, glass, lacquer, gold leaf
Height 33 cm, width 82 cm, depth 27 cm
Donated by the Doris Duke Charitable Foundation, 2004,0628.34

3. Manuscript cabinet

Many manuscript cabinets were decorated with gold leaf on black lacquer and depicted narrative scenes from the Ramayana epic or Buddhist tales. The front panels here show the battle between Prince Rama and the demon Kumbakarna and their forces in the lowest segment, Kumbakarna fighting the monkeys Sugriva (left) and Hanuman (right) in the middle, and the deities of lightning (left) and thunder (right) at the top. The side panels portray further scenes and characters from the Ramayana, including the monkey Hanuman and the demon Indrajit. The back is undecorated.

Mid-20th century
Thailand
Wood, lacquer, gold leaf
Height 99 cm, width 67 cm,
depth 42 cm
Donated by the Doris Duke
Charitable Foundation,
2004,0628.36

3 | 6 Islamic kingdoms and coins

Islam in Southeast Asia flourished in part because it was linked with the international trade occurring along dynamic port city networks, but it was also adopted because it was compatible with pre-existing local beliefs and practices, such as the retreat from worldly life and meditation. Southeast Asian Islam was influenced early on by the Sufi tradition, a mystical form of the religion that emphasizes the inner search for God.

Centres of Islam initially spread from northern Sumatra across peninsular Malaysia, northern Borneo, northern Java, Sulawesi, parts of the Philippines and among the Cham of southern Vietnam. The conversion to Islam of the rulers of Melaka, one of the main entrepôts, in the 1430s enabled the religion to spread through the islands rapidly, and the city became a centre of Islamic learning. The Malay text *Sejarah Melayu* described it, claiming '... from below the wind to above the wind Melaka became famous as a very great city ... so that princes from all countries came to present themselves before (the sultan)' (Brown 1953, 59). In the western mainland part of Southeast Asia there were extensive connections between the Bengali sultanates and Rakhine Buddhist courts (**6**).

Initial evidence of Muslim traders in Southeast Asia comes from imported Islamic coins dated to the early 9th century, but it was not until the 14th century that Southeast Asian Islamic coinage was produced. Local sultans issued gold, silver, tin and lead coins. Most examples are inscribed in Arabic script, but later Southeast Asian Islamic coins use Arabic calligraphy to inscribe local languages, a format called Jawi. The coins also display floral and animal motifs and designs drawn from a variety of Muslim and trade contexts (**3, 4, 5**), and demonstrate connections with other Islamic centres, including Egypt and the Indian sultanates of Bengal and Gujarat (**2, 3**), as well as the Ottoman empire (**1**).

1. *Pitis* coin
Issued by Sultan Muzaffar Shah (r. 1445–59), this coin is inscribed in the Arabic language in the *tughra*-style script that developed in the Ottoman empire in the late 13th century, but which arrived in Melaka from Gujarat, India. *Pitis* were tin coins issued by several Southeast Asian kingdoms.

1446–56
Melaka, Malay peninsula
Tin
Diameter 1.8 cm
Donated by R. Bland, 1905,0101.69

2. *Kupang* coin
Sultan Abd al-Djalil (r. 1579), also known as Sri Alam and Ghiat ad-Din, of the Samudera Pasai Sultanate, a trading state on the north coast of Sumatra, authorized the issue of this *kupang* coin. Sometimes Egyptian Mamluk titles were added to Samudera Pasai coin inscriptions, as well as to coins issued by Aceh and Brunei. Small gold coinage was a principal issue minted by Muslim states in island Southeast Asia.

1579
Samudera Pasai Sultanate, northern Sumatra, Indonesia
Gold
Diameter 1.2 cm
Donated by Spink & Son Ltd, 1928,0608.47

3. *Pitis* coin

Gold, silver and tin coins were produced in Brunei from the late 16th century with the primary influences coming from Egypt and the Indian sultanates, particularly Bengal. On this example issued by Sultan Muhammad Hassan (r. 1582–98), the image is of a camel, probably originating with Chinese representations based on connections with Central Asia. The language and script on the reverse is Arabic.

Early to mid-1590s
Brunei
Tin
Diameter 3.7 cm
Donated by W. Williams, 1937,0704.3

4. *Mas* coin

This *mas* coin with Arabic language and script was issued by Sultan Malikussaid (r. 1639–53) of Gowa, whose father had converted to Islam in 1605. Gowa was a powerful trading kingdom in the 16th and 17th centuries, only defeated by combined Dutch and Bugis forces in 1669. According to the *Gowa Chronicle*, Sultan Malikussaid had diplomatic relations with the Spanish governor in Manila, the Portuguese viceroy in Goa and the Mir Jumla in Macchilipatnam, besides other rulers, demonstrating his political reach. *Mas* coins were the equivalent of four *kupang* coins.

1639–53
Gowa Sultanate, Makassar (Ujung Pandang), Sulawesi, Indonesia
Gold
Diameter 1.9 cm
Donated by King George IV, CH.420

5. *Pitis* coin

Issued by Muhammad Bahauddin (r. 1776–1803) of the Sultanate of Palembang, the coin's script and language are Arabic, but the shape, made with a central hole to allow coins to be stored on strings, is modelled on the Chinese *cash*. Chinese coins circulated extensively around island Southeast Asia from the 13th to 19th centuries.

1783–84
Palembang, southern Sumatra, Indonesia
Lead
Diameter 2.1 cm
1842,0409.13

6. *Tanka* coin

Owing to close connections with the Bengal Sultanate, Rakhine's Buddhist kings used Bengali coins in the 14th and 15th centuries. From the 16th century, they issued their own Bengal-style coins like this one inscribed variously in the Bengali, Persian and Rakhine languages. Here, all three languages have been used: Rakhine on one side and Persian and Bengali on the other. From 1638, inscriptions were only in the Rakhine language. The Rakhine kings also adopted Islamic-style names, as in the case of Dhammaraja Hussain (r. 1612–22), who issued this coin (*dhammaraja* is the title of a righteous Buddhist king).

1612–22
Rakhine, Myanmar
Silver
Diameter 2.95 cm
Donated by Arthur Phayre, 1882,0508.4

3 | 7 Ottoman and Middle Eastern connections

During the 1500s, the Islamic Sultanate of Aceh on the northern part of the island of Sumatra (Indonesia) forged diplomatic relations with the Ottoman empire to gather support against the encroaching Portuguese. Further diplomatic interaction occurred again in the 19th century when European expansion increased substantially. While political exchanges with the Ottomans and the Middle East may have been intermittent, trade and religion ensured the regions remained linked, as spices, goods (including Thai and Vietnamese ceramics) and people made their way westwards. Numerous Southeast Asians travelled (and still do) to Mecca on the religious pilgrimage of the hajj. Some stayed on to learn Arabic and study for long periods of time, becoming known as the Jawi community. Southeast Asian connections also stimulated the concept of a global Muslim solidarity, and Arab traders settled in Southeast Asia, establishing lineages that remain significant today.

In part because they controlled the holy cities of Mecca and Medina, the Ottomans captured the imagination of Muslim Southeast Asia, and local rulers sometimes claimed descent from Rum, the Southeast Asian name for the Ottoman empire, in their genealogies. Middle Eastern stories, designs, imagery and characters were incorporated into art forms, and the king of Rum became an important character in island Southeast Asian literature. The people who returned to Southeast Asia brought souvenirs, Qur'ans and prayerbooks, which served as models in the incorporation of Ottoman motifs into Southeast Asian art, including the *tughra* (royal monogram), some calligraphic forms, including animal shapes, and the Ottoman layout of Qur'an texts (**3**). Clothing too was affected (**1**). The two-bladed sword of Ali, the Prophet Muhammad's son-in-law, called *dhu al-faqar*, became popular on flags, coffin covers and banners across the region from Aceh on Sumatra to the southern Philippines (**2**).

1. Hat
Replicating the shape of the Middle Eastern fez, this woven hat is an early form of the black velvet hat (*peci*) that became part of male national dress from the late 1940s onwards in Indonesia. Basketry weaving was used to make a large range of items across Southeast Asia, and the skill of the producer can be seen here in the tight weaving and decorative embellishments.

Mid-19th century
Sumatra, Indonesia
Vegetable fibre
Height 7.5 cm, diameter 16.5 cm
As 1891,0815.103

**2. Calligraphic batik
(*tulisan Arab*)**
Since the colour red indicates courage, this cloth was probably a coffin cover for a warrior, although such batiks could also be made as military banners. This cloth is decorated with images of the double-bladed sword and powerful lions, associated with Ali (the Prophet Muhammad's son-in-law), magical numeric diagrams and the Islamic Creed written in Arabic, which were considered to be protective. Usually made in Cirebon on the north coast of Java, such cloths were exported to Sumatra, where they are primarily found, and elsewhere in the Malay world.

Late 19th–early 20th century
Cirebon, Java, Indonesia
Cotton
Length 219.5 cm, width 101.5 cm
2019,3034.1

3. Qur'an

Acehnese Qur'ans developed specific conventions for illuminating manuscripts that became influential across the island world. Coloured red, black and yellow, decorated pages were symmetrical with the text framed by rectangular, flanged borders filled with foliate arabesques. The regular layout of 1/30th of the text, called a *juz*, across twenty pages originated with the Ottomans, and it was a format that facilitated memorization and recitation. Each *juz* was subdivided with special marks, and in this Qur'an, these sections are indicated by ornamented features or roundels of Acehnese design in the margins and within the text.

1820s
Aceh, Sumatra, Indonesia
Paper, cloth, leather, gold leaf
Height 33 cm, width 20.5 cm
British Library, OR 16915

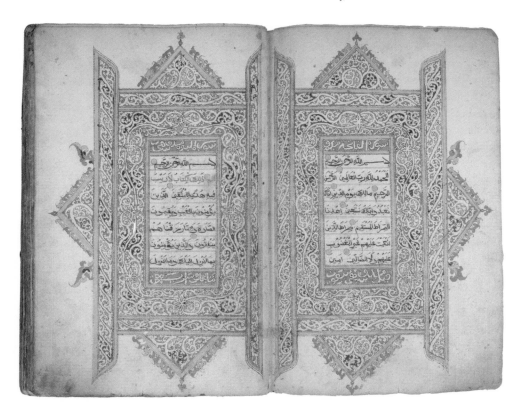

3 | 8 Christian ivory carvings

The Philippines and East Timor are the only Southeast Asian countries where Christianity is the main religion today. After the Portuguese conquest of Melaka in 1511, Christian missionaries started to arrive in the region as part of Portuguese and eventually Spanish policies, and Catholic missions were established on some eastern Indonesian islands. Later, Dutch Protestantism became dominant as the Netherlands gained control of swathes of island Southeast Asia, while French Catholics converted people in Vietnam and the Baptists were successful among minority groups in Myanmar in the 19th century. The various Christian denominations responded to local beliefs and imagery differently, with Anglican and Catholic churches adopting a more accepting attitude than the Baptist and Evangelical ones, which demonized other views.

In the 16th and 17th centuries, ivory sculptures with Christian subject matter were produced in Manila in the Philippines and possibly Ayutthaya (central Thailand). Carvers in other parts of Asia, including Goa (India), Sri Lanka and Macau in China, also made them. It is hard to identify where pieces were made and by whom because they are iconographically similar and they circulated around the Christian world. In Manila, many of the carvers were from China, particularly Fujian province in the south, but the city was also a major trans-shipment port, so ivories may have arrived there from various Asian cities to be sent across the Pacific Ocean to Mexico and other parts of the Americas, and via Mexico to Spain and Portugal.

Christian artistic production was linked to European ideas, practices, iconography and subject matter. Carved with a high degree of realism taken from European imagery circulating in Asia, the ivories (*santo*) included representations of the Virgin Mary and the baby Jesus, Christ on the Cross, and various saints (**1, 2, 3**). Christian imagery and emblems, such as motifs of angels and crosses, were incorporated into local objects too.

1. St Joseph
Christian ivories were sometimes painted with fine brushes, given inlaid glass eyes, real hair and cat-hair eyelashes, and dressed. In this example, St Joseph has painted black hair and wears a long mantle with traces of red pigment and gilding. Some of the detailing, such as the eyes and ears, betrays a Chinese influence, and the piece may have been made by Chinese carvers in Manila.

17th century
Probably the Philippines
Ivory, gold
Height 32 cm
Donated by A. W. Franks,
1882,1028.1

2. St Anthony

This figure of the Portuguese priest, St Anthony, shows him dressed in monk's robes and with tonsured hair that was once coloured. The now-missing Christ child would have stood upon the book in St Anthony's left hand.

17th century
Probably the Philippines
Ivory
Height 16.3 cm
Donated by Walter Hildburgh, 1927,0509.3

3. Head of St Francis Xavier

St Francis Xavier was a Catholic missionary who spent time in Southeast Asia, arriving in Melaka in 1545 and travelling on to the Maluku islands (Moluccas) the following year. He stayed in the area for eighteen months, learning about local communities and proselytizing on Ambon, Ternate and Morotai. For his service in Asia generally, he was beatified within seventy years of his death.

c. 1630
Philippines
Ivory
Height 10.8 cm
Donated by Molly Lowell and David Borthwick, 2017,8027.1

1. Jar

This jar was acquired in Brunei on the island of Borneo in the 1880s. It is a typical example of the rough Chinese blue-and-white ceramics that were exported to Southeast Asia and the Middle East in the 16th and 17th centuries. While jars of many types were imported from China, Southeast Asian kilns also produced them for local use and export around the region. Powerful serpent-beings associated with water are considered to be synonymous with the Chinese dragon by indigenous peoples. The importance of these creatures makes ceramics with dragon imagery of great relevance to communities on Borneo.

1573–1620
Probably Guangdong, China
Porcelain
Height 29 cm, diameter 13.5 cm
Donated by A. W. Franks, collected by A. H. Everett, Franks.3149

2. Swatow dish

Found in Indonesia, this dish is typical of Swatow wares made with coarse clay and decorated with hastily executed designs that were exported to Southeast Asia in the 16th and 17th centuries. This example is covered with a thick grey glaze and polychrome enamels depicting a single bird in a central roundel surrounded by six cartouches filled with floral motifs set against a repetitive geometric pattern. The bright colours and patterning that cover the surface appealed to Southeast Asian aesthetics, and were repeated in later forms, including ceramics, used among Peranakan and other local communities (see pp. 112–13).

1600–30
Pinghe county, Fujian province, China
Porcelain
Diameter 37 cm
1965,1014.1

The many roles of imported textiles and ceramics

Although Southeast Asia had its own extensive ceramic and textile traditions, over the millennia it has also imported Chinese silks and ceramics, Persian brocades, Turkish embroidery and European flannel and velvet. Known as a centre of cotton weaving and dyeing, India produced large quantities of textiles designed to suit specific markets that were exported all over Asia, as well as to Africa, the Middle East and Europe. In Southeast Asia, Indian textiles, including the *patola* and block-printed, mordant-dyed cottons, are still much prized for their designs and colour-fastness. Over time they have been kept as sacred heirlooms, utilized as currency in the spice trade and stores of wealth, and incorporated into rituals and rites of passage; they have also signified rank and status, embodied power and authority, and have been thought to have protective and healing properties (**3**).

Until the 17th and 18th centuries, when increasing European control of the textile trade reduced Indian imports, both high-quality cloths for Southeast Asian elites and coarser cloths for the general population were available. Southeast Asian weavers adopted some textile production techniques, particularly from India, including *ikat*, in which the pattern is dyed into the yarn prior to weaving, and supplementary weft, where additional yarns are added during weaving. Indian trade textile patterns and arrangements, such as the use of border designs separate from the centrefield and repetitive floral-geometric motifs,

were reinterpreted for local use (**4**). Patterns were also replicated in other media. Religious sculptures, puppets and other figures often appear wearing the luxury cloths, and religious wall paintings and relief sculptures could include Indian textile patterns and arrangements, making the buildings look as if they were hung with cloths.

Southeast Asians have long prized Chinese ceramics, and archaeological evidence suggests that communities in Vietnam and Thailand were using them as early as the 5th century BCE. Chinese potters produced specific objects for various Southeast Asian markets: ritual water vessels (*kendi*), covered boxes, jars and bottles, and later dishes are found across Southeast Asia in vast quantities (**1**). Some types were made specifically for the Southeast Asian market, such as Swatow wares (**2**). Chinese ceramics in Southeast Asia were employed in rituals, as a form of currency and as grave goods, kept as heirlooms to be passed down through generations like Indian textiles, and functioned as status symbols. Chinese techniques, materials, decorative methods and arrangements also provided models that were adapted at Southeast Asian kilns. Particular patterns, such as a stylized lotus petal around the lower edge of bowls and dishes or a central motif surrounded by floral and geometric designs, became prevalent, and as with textile patterns were repeated in other art forms.

3. Trade cloth

The Toraja region of Sulawesi
is where the largest number
of Indian trade cloths have
survived, some dating to the
13th century, and where
they were used as powerful
ritual textiles (*ma'a* or *mawa*)
particularly for ceremonies
associated with fertility and
agriculture. This example
displays a series of women
dancers and musicians holding
vinas, an Indian string instrument.
It would have been block-printed
with a resist of wax or mud and
dyed, and then decorated further
by hand painting with a red
mordant (substance that fixes
the dye to the material) dye.

16th century
Gujarat, India
Cotton
Length 502 cm, width 96 cm
Donated by R. A. Killik,
As1944,08.4

4. Batik cloth with *patola* patterns (detail)

Originating in Gujarat, India,
patola cloths were made by the
complex process of resist-dyeing
both the warp and weft yarns
prior to weaving, a technique
known as double *ikat*. The
weaving process was slow
to ensure the designs on the
yarns aligned accurately. Double
ikat cloths became the most
prized imported luxury textiles
in Southeast Asia, and because
of their cost, the patterns were
imitated through block-printing
and, less commonly, batik to
satisfy less wealthy patrons.
The narrow bands of floral and
geometric motifs at the ends
of this batik textile and the
centrefield of repeated eight-
pointed flowers were typical
patola patterns.

1880–1913
Java, Indonesia
Cotton
Length 183 cm, width 52 cm
Donated by Charles Beving,
As1934,0307.17

3 | 9 Vietnamese ceramics

The principal Vietnamese kiln sites, including the famous Chu Dau kilns, were in the Red River delta in Dai Viet (northern Vietnam). From there ceramics were exported to Southeast Asia, the Middle East and eastern Africa. Shapes and decoration were tailored to suit the receiving market. For instance, *kendi* ritual vessels and covered boxes were popular in Southeast Asia (**1**), while large plates and dishes were preferred by consumers in the Middle East (**2**). The export business became substantial in the 14th and 15th centuries, only diminishing in the 17th century, possibly because of competition from Chinese production centres.

Underglaze blue-and-white pieces are Vietnam's most well-known ceramic type, yet kilns produced highly varied wares (**3**). Shapes ranged from bowls to cylindrical, lidded jars, straight-sided cups, covered boxes, ewers, bottles, melon-shaped forms and *kendis*. Brushed underglaze iron-brown decoration, sometimes used to fill motifs carved into the body of a vessel, was popular, as were green-, cream- and brown-glazed vessels and filled, incised or moulded decoration. From the mid-15th century, polychrome decorative methods sometimes combined underglaze blue patterns with overglaze coloured enamels, a technique that required two firings, first to fix the blue underglaze painting and clear glaze, and then again at a lower temperature once the coloured enamels had been added (**2**). Biscuit details, where pieces of unglazed clay were incorporated into designs to create complex and busy surfaces, became common in the 16th and 17th centuries, mostly on ceramics used within Vietnam (**4**). Clays were of high quality, being fine-grained with few impurities, and produced pale grey or cream stonewares.

1. Covered box
Salvaged from a ship that sank near Hoi An in central Vietnam in the late 15th or early 16th century, this box is decorated with a Chinese-style landscape scene of trees and foliage on hills surrounded by a lotus motif and cartouches with sprigs of vegetation. Small, covered boxes were a popular export item, particularly within Southeast Asia, and exist in many different forms, ranging from blue-and-white to white-glazed and enamelled wares. Most displayed similar floral and vegetal motifs and landscape scenes.

Late 15th–early 16th century
Vietnam
Stoneware
Height 15 cm, diameter 15.2 cm
2000,1212.48

2. Dish

This dish has a decorative barbed rim and displays busy underglaze-blue and green-enamelled designs showing two birds perched among lotus blossoms, encircled by further stylized lotus motifs, an arrangement that elaborated upon Chinese design layouts.

Late 15th–early 16th century
Vietnam
Stoneware
Diameter 35 cm
2000,1212.49

3. Ewer

This underglaze iron-decorated ewer is in the form of a fish. Whimsically shaped water vessels were produced in both Vietnam and Thailand, though they were not the most common shapes.

1450–1550
Vietnam
Stoneware
Length 31.2 cm
2003,0728.2

4. Altar lamp stands

Made for use in a temple to venerate ancestors, this pair of lamp stands is decorated with underglaze blue floral and animal imagery, biscuit-fired dragons, clouds, Chinese characters applied to the sides, and iron-brown painted details around the baluster foot and neck. The inscription in Chinese characters on one reads 'May the emperor live ten thousand years', while the other gives a date that corresponds to 1589, during the reign of Emperor Mac Mau Hop (r. 1562–92) of Dai Viet's Mac dynasty.

1589
Vietnam
Stoneware
Height 48 cm
Donated by the British Museum
Friends, 1984,0604.1–2

3 | 10 Thai ceramics

During the 14th to 16th centuries, Thai kiln sites produced large quantities of utilitarian and domestic ceramics for local and international consumption, as indicated by excavations at kiln sites and on shipwrecks carrying Chinese, Vietnamese and Thai ceramics. The relationships between Thai and Chinese, particularly southern, kilns have yet to be established in detail, but some of the technology, such as the production of celadon glazes, originated in China (**2**).

The centrally located Sawankhalok and Sukhothai kilns and the northern Kalong kilns shared technology, such as up-draught and cross-draught kilns and stacking tools, as well as some decorative methods. They produced primarily stonewares with a variety of glazes, including greenish celadons and underglaze iron ceramics, some featuring original designs and others relating to Chinese blue-and-white patterns. The iron brown decorations were painted onto the body of the vessel before being covered by a clear glaze and fired between 1100 and 1300°C. Differences in the ceramics relate to the colour and composition of the clay, as well as the popularity of certain designs and glaze types. Sukhothai and Sawankhalok ceramics were produced in a variety of shapes from large dishes to bottles and jars (**4**), covered boxes (**3**), bowls (**2, 6**), covered jars, figures (**5**), roof tiles (**7**) and architectural pieces. Some of them were exported as far away as Indonesia, the Philippines and Japan, as well as the Middle East. Kalong wares were not exported and were primarily used in the northern region (**1**).

1. Plate

This plate displays the typical Kalong kiln patterning of boldly painted designs of flowers, birds, animals and abstract motifs in underglaze iron browns covered with a clear glaze. Other glazes included pale green, white and grey. The Kalong kilns used a strong, off-white clay to produce finely potted vessels.

14th–16th century
Kalong kilns, northern Thailand
Stoneware
Height 5.2 cm, diameter 24 cm
2005,0409.2

2. Celadon-glazed bowl

With scored sides, an everted rim and an elaborate incised floral medallion in the interior, this bowl displays typical decoration for celadon wares. It was produced with a fine reddish clay.

14th–16th century
Sawankhalok kilns, central Thailand
Stoneware
Diameter 21.5 cm
2001,0810.2

3. Octagonal box

Small, covered boxes were a major part of ceramic production in Southeast Asia. The decoration often connects across both box and lid, with a narrow ring left unglazed around the edge of the latter to prevent the glaze from fusing the two parts during firing. Underglaze iron-brown floral patterning was the most common form of decoration produced at the Sawankhalok kilns.

14th–16th century
Sawankhalok kilns, central Thailand
Stoneware
Height 7 cm, diameter 10.5 cm
Donated by Angus Forsyth, 1997,0326.88

4. Trumpet-mouthed jarlet with brown glaze, celadon jarlet and flattened iron-brown glazed jarlet

Glazed in a variety of colours, jarlets like these were another predominant form at the Sawankhalok kilns. They were probably used to hold precious oils and medicines. Some were exported to Japan for use in tea ceremonies.

14th–16th century
Sawankhalok kilns, central Thailand
Stoneware
Height 13.1 cm, height 7 cm, height 4.9 cm
1997,0326.65, 1997,0326.14, 1996,0613.8

5. Figurines

Figurines have been excavated in huge quantities in Thailand. Modelled by hand, they were decorated with the full range of glazes – celadon, white and brown, as well as underglaze iron-brown and white patterning. Not for export, the figures were used as offerings in spirit shrines, with birds being the most common shape. There were also animals, figures clasping a child or animal, and hunchbacked male figures in the form of waterdroppers. Some figurines were ritually broken.

14th–16th century
Sawankhalok and Sukhothai kilns, Thailand
Stoneware
Heights from 5–10.8 cm
1907,0320.6, 1907,0320.4, 1997,0326.83, 1997,0326.6, 1997,0326.12

6. Bowl

Sukhothai wares are characterized by a grey clay covered with a thick white slip on which underglaze iron decorations, often of floral and fish motifs, were painted. The whole was covered with a clear glaze. The famous design of a fish in the cavetto, as here, appeared first in the early 15th century.

14th–16th century
Sukhothai kilns, central Thailand
Stoneware
Diameter 24.3 cm, height 6 cm
1955,1022.1

7. Roof finial in the shape of a *naga* serpent

Thai temple buildings are often tiled, with sculptural pieces located at the end of roof ridges. The Sukhothai kilns produced these in brown with a cream-coloured glaze. In common with many cultures in Southeast Asia, Thai people viewed the serpent as a bridge between the human and spirit worlds.

14th–16th century
Sukhothai kilns, central Thailand
Stoneware
Height 45 cm
Donated by the Doris Duke
Charitable Foundation,
2004,0628,0.22

3 | 11 Bencharong and Lai Nam Thong wares

Decorated with Thai designs in overglaze enamels, Bencharong and Lai Nam Thong ceramics were made to order at the Jingdezhen kilns in China for the Thai market in the 18th and 19th centuries. Today, the wares are made in Thailand. Initially the preserve of royalty, by the late 19th century the ceramics came into general use for those who could afford them (**4**).

The name Bencharong literally means 'five colours', referring to the overglaze enamel decoration on porcelain. Lai Nam Thong indicates the additional use of gold in the multicoloured designs. Overglaze enamels require two firings in a kiln as the porcelain clay requires a higher production temperature (up to 1350°C) than can be tolerated by enamels (around 800°C). Lai Nam Thong is fired three times, the last to fix the gold to the piece.

The shapes of Bencharong and Lai Nam Thong wares were relatively standardized, comprising bowls with and without covers, jars, pots, stem dishes, spoons and spittoons (**1**, **2**), some of which are Chinese in form. In the second half of the 19th century, European shapes, such as candlesticks and teacups, were commissioned. In the 20th century, commemorative plates embellished with these techniques became popular. Motifs on these wares include imagery from Buddhist and Hindu mythology, such as the sacred animals and plants of Himavanta forest on the sides of Mount Meru, the universe's central axis (**3**). Floral and geometric patterns, many like those found on textiles and silver, as well as figures from Thai literature, are also common.

1. Bowl and spoon
Covered bowls such as this were made in the Bencharong and Lai Nam Thong styles from the early 19th century, becoming most popular during the reign of Rama III (r. 1824–51), who was a China enthusiast. They were used for royal table settings, along with spoons for serving or eating curries and other liquid foods.

Late 18th century
China
Porcelain, gold
Diameter 21 cm, height 20.9 cm
Donated by A. W. Franks,
Franks.575

19th century
Jingdezhen, Jiangxi, China
Porcelain
Length 16.5 cm
Donated by the Doris Duke
Charitable Foundation,
2004,0628.3

2. Lai Nam Thong container
Decorated with flower petals,
this is a container for cosmetics,
medicine, powder, oil or toiletries.
It is gilded around the rims and
on the knob.

18th century
China
Porcelain, gold
Diameter 6.6 cm, height 8.6 cm
Donated by A. W. Franks,
Franks.587.+

3. Covered bowl
Tall, covered bowls influenced
by the shape of funerary urns,
with a stupa shape as the knob
(a feature also seen in Thai
silver and other media), were
widely produced for serving
curry or soup or storing food.
This example is embellished with
floral motifs and male Buddhist
deities known as *thep phanom* in
cartouches, making the gesture

of homage (*anjali mudra*).
The cover is composed of
concentric rings of floral
and geometric patterns.

1750–1800
Jingdezhen, Jiangxi, China
Porcelain, gold
Diameter 12.4 cm, height 17.8 cm
Donated by A. W. Franks,
collected by Carl A. Bock,
Franks.1392.D

4. Stem dish
Stem dishes were used as
part of a dinner service and as
offering trays. Kilns in Thailand
began to produce Bencharong
wares in the 19th century. Less
well executed than the Chinese
versions, these locally made
examples were not controlled
by sumptuary laws and were
also sometimes exported. This
example was found on Borneo.

Early 19th century
Probably Thailand
Enamelled porcelain
Diameter 25.9 cm, height 10.7 cm
Donated by A. W. Franks,
collected by A. H. Everett,
Franks.3129

3 | 12 *Geringsing* cloths

Produced in Tenganan Pageringsingan village in east Bali by the Bali Aga people, *geringsing* cloths are made using the demanding double-*ikat* technique that originated in India – the pattern is tie-dyed separately into the warp and weft yarns before weaving, and the weaving itself is painstaking to ensure the pattern aligns accurately. The idea probably arrived in Southeast Asia with imported Indian *patola* luxury trade cloths, but this Balinese village is the only place in Southeast Asia where the technique was adopted.

The reddish-brown, cream and dark blue-black *geringsing* cloths have a loose weave (**1**), sometimes decorated with supplementary gold- or silver-wrapped or gold-coloured threads (**2**). Motifs are repetitive and include geometric and floral motifs, as well as figures that resemble sacred shadow puppets, and architectural forms. End panels display different designs from those of the central section. Because the cloths are believed to be sacred, particularly before the warp threads have been cut at the end of the weaving process, their manufacture is accompanied by rules and restraints.

The name *geringsing* means 'without sickness', and the textiles are associated with purity, believed to have a magical, protective power that shields the user from harm and impurity, and thought to protect the community. In particular, they play protective roles during transitions from one stage of life to the next, such as marriage and death. Boys and men use them as sashes and hip cloths, while girls and women wear them as breast or shoulder cloths, or as an outer garment. The cloths are also presented as offerings during rituals.

1. Cloth (*geringsing wayang kebo*)
The cloths with figural shapes that resemble sacred Balinese and Javanese shadow puppets and east Javanese temple reliefs of the 14th–15th centuries, called *geringsing wayang*, are the most sacred. Such pieces display three interconnected four-pointed stars filled with floral and geometric motifs. In the arches created by the stars' points are anthropomorphic figures. The end panels are composed of the repeated stylized floral-geometric motifs common on *patola* cloths.

Late 19th to mid-20th century
Tenganan Pageringsingan, Bali
Cotton, metal threads
Length 209 cm, width 52 cm
As 1980,08.1

2. Cloth (*geringsing wayang kebo*) (detail)

Some *geringsing* cloths have been embellished on the end panels, as here, with gold- or silver-wrapped supplementary threads added during the weaving process, but which are not part of the structure of the fabric. As is typical of end panels, the motifs are geometric and floral.

1920s
Tenganan Pageringsingan, Bali
Cotton, metal threads
Length 212 cm, width 49 cm
As1954,06.4

3 | 13 Batik from Java's north coast

Batik is a dye-resist method. Liquid wax is applied to the cloth, covering all areas not to be dyed in a particular colour. After dyeing the wax is removed, and the cloth re-waxed if other dye colours are planned. This process is repeated as necessary to produce the pattern. The wax was originally applied with a *canting* (a small cup with a handle and a spout), a traditional, time-consuming method practised by women. The process could take many months, depending on the complexity of the design and the number of colours. In the 19th century, the *cap* (a metal stamp for the application of the wax), primarily used by men employed in factories, was developed to speed up production.

While the intricate batik technique from Java appears to have emerged in the 17th century, the production of colourful batiks on the north coast by people of mixed heritage – Indo-Chinese, Indo-European and Indo-Arabian – started only in the early 19th century, with the patterning reflecting the multicultural trading settlements of the area (**1**, **2**). At this time, batik production changed gradually from family work to a commercial system organized by traders and entrepreneurs, who not only ordered designs in response to customer demand but also developed new patterns, colour schemes and layouts to entice clients.

In around 1860, mixed-heritage women in financial difficulties began establishing batik workshops on the north coast. Several became well known for producing cloths of the highest quality, such as Eliza van Zuylen, Catharina van Oosterom (**1**) and Tan Ien Nio.

Pasisir (north coast) batik's heyday from the late 19th–early 20th centuries ended after the two World Wars and the Depression.

1. Batik cloth (detail)
Decorated with angels, animals, crowned figures, buildings and floral motifs on the centrefield, and floral and figural images set in the usual triangles and diamond forms in the *kepala* (end panel), this richly coloured cloth is from an Indo-European workshop. The piece is inscribed with 'The World Exhibition', possibly indicating that it was included in the 1889 Paris Exposition, which had a Java section.

Late 19th century
Java, Indonesia; possibly from the workshop of Catharina van Oosterom
Cotton
Length 111 cm, width 109 cm
Donated by Charles Beving,
As 1934,0307.51

2. *Sarong bang biru hijau* (detail)
Probably made in a Peranakan (local Chinese) workshop, this sarong combines Chinese and Indo-European motifs and arrangements. The design of the end section (*kepala*), with diamond shapes and alternating long and short *tumpal* (triangle) motifs, was typical of north coast batiks, as is the Chinese combination of birds and flowers in the centrefield (*badan*) and the *banji* (swastika motif representing longevity and abundance) background. The three-dimensional appearance of the flowers was an Indo-European innovation. The pomegranates, indicating fertility, suggest the batik would be for a married woman. The elaborate colour scheme combines the traditional Pasisir red and blue with green.

c. 1880
Probably Semarang, Java, Indonesia
Cotton
Length 210 cm, width 105 cm
Donated by Charles Beving,
As 1934,0307.72

3 | 14 Glass beads found on Borneo

The numerous inland groups on the island of Borneo use beads to decorate clothing (**2**, **4**), to indicate rank and status, as money and wealth, in rituals, as heirlooms, for healing and as ornaments. Beads are also important to Borneo societies because they are often believed to be repositories of life forces and inhabited by spirits. While beads can be made from teeth, bone and shell, from at least 1,500 years ago trade beads of stone or glass had an impact upon bead fashions (**1**). Most of the beads from Borneo now in museum collections were not made on the island but were imported at different times from India, China, Southeast Asia, the Middle East and Europe, particularly Venice (**3**). Not only did ships stop at the cosmopolitan ports of Borneo, but also there is evidence that people from Borneo travelled abroad to purchase beads, and beads were exchanged along the many interior trade networks on Borneo itself.

Early glass was made in present-day India, but by the centuries around 500 CE, glass-making sites also existed in Southeast Asia. China became a major source of glass beads in the first centuries after 1000 CE; Venice emerged as a substantial producer in the 16th through to the 19th centuries; and Bohemia became an important manufacturer in the late 19th century.

There are still two main ways of making glass beads. The first involves pulling tubes of semi-molten glass off a larger lump and cutting them to size. In the second, heated glass is wound around a support, cut and heated again to smooth and shape the bead. Decorations, such as pieces of differently coloured glass, are added during reheating.

1. Islamic bead
Found on Borneo, this type of black and white bead was made in Islamic territories between approximately 700 and 1000 CE and was probably brought to Southeast Asia by Arab traders, who arrived in the region in the 8th century. When it was collected, in the late 19th or early 20th century, communities on Borneo would have considered it a bead of great power because of its age.

7th–10th century
Probably Egypt
Glass
Height 2 cm, diameter 2 cm
Donated by C. Collins,
As 1908,-.342

2. Cap
Borneo communities believed that the protective qualities of beads could transfer to the wearer, and so attached them to clothing. Warriors also wore them around the neck. This cap is made of fish scales and glass beads with a single large bead at the tip. Special beads were given names and were highly valued. While big beads were valued prior to the late 20th century, more recently, small tubular beads have gained in prominence.

19th century
Borneo
Fish scales, glass, fibre
Diameter 22 cm, height 18 cm
As 1908,0625.1

3. Polychrome beads

Most polychrome beads found on Borneo were made in Venice between the 17th and 19th centuries. First the basic bead was shaped, then thin rods of different coloured glass were heated and applied to it as dots, stripes and swirls. Their popularity and value have varied across the Borneo communities and over time. The black *lukut sekala* with a swirling motif has been particularly prized by many groups.

Lukut sekala bead
18th century
Venice, Italy
Glass
Diameter 0.9 cm, height 0.5 cm
Donated by Margaret Brooke, Ranee of Sarawak,
As1896,0317.51.a

Pyjama, millefiori, rosette and eye bead bracelet
18th–19th century
Probably Venice, Italy
Glass
Length 1.4 cm, diameter 1.1 cm (largest bead)
Donated by Diana Good,
As1936,1205.2

Polychrome beads on a necklace
19th century
Probably Venice, Italy
Glass
Height 1 cm, diameter 1.4 cm (bead)
As1900,–.756

4. Beaded tunic

This high-status tunic with a rare chequerboard pattern is made of vegetable fibre cloth covered with glass beads and has a fringe of metal cascabels and cowrie shells. Small opaque beads are still used to decorate clothing, hats and objects of use, such as baby carriers, because beads add to the value and power attributed to ceremonial items.

Late 19th century
Sarawak, Borneo
Glass, fibre, metal, cowrie shells
Length 48 cm, width 45 cm
As1908,0625.7

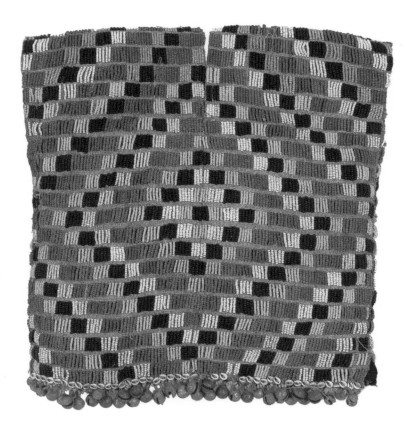

3 | 15 Peranakan and Chinese communities

Chinese and Indian intermarriage with Southeast Asians has created unique cultures known as Peranakan, meaning 'locally born'. Some trace their ancestry back to Melaka in the 15th century, but there are equally old communities in Myanmar, Thailand and across island Southeast Asia.

Also called Chetti Melaka, the Tamil Indian Peranakans are Hindu, combining Saivite practices with aspects of Chinese ancestral worship. Language, food, clothing and jewelry also amalgamated Malay, Chinese and south Indian traditions (**1**).

Similarly, Chinese Peranakans merged Chinese and Malay customs and food traditions. Myths, stories and auspicious animal and plant motifs came from Chinese contexts, including bats (wealth), bamboo (strength) and peaches (long life). Women were expected to excel in embroidery and beadwork, a major part of bridal trousseaus (**2**), with a popular aesthetic for bright colours and ornate details emerging in the 19th century.

Chinese communities played an important role in Southeast Asia as labourers, merchants, traders and moneylenders, as well as owning gambling houses. The tokens issued by such houses sometimes circulated as currency (**3**).

1. Necklace

Although produced in Southeast Asia, this necklace is in an Indian form known as an *addigai*. Demonstrating its Peranakan origins, it is not made of gold, as would have been the case in India, but of gilded silver, a technique used by the Chinese to prevent silver from tarnishing.

Early 20th century
Singapore
Gilded silver, beads, gems
Height 17 cm, width 13 cm
Peranakan Museum, 2016-00641

2. Table screen

Produced to show a Chinese Peranakan woman's patience and attention to detail, beadwork and embroidery objects ranged from shoes and slippers, belts, collars, purses, glasses cases and other items of dress or personal use to interior decor, such as hangings for a marriage bed, pillow cases, mirror covers, tablecloths and (shown here) table screens. Brightly coloured, in keeping with the preferred 19th- and early 20th-century aesthetic, the designs drew upon Chinese imagery, here mythical *qilins*, phoenixes and other birds, and a lion, deer and elephant surrounded by floral and vegetal motifs.

Early 20th century
Possibly Penang, Malaysia
Wood, glass, silk, metal
Height 71.7 cm, width 23.5 cm
(panel)
2021,3016.1

3. Tokens

Glazed ceramic, brass and glass pieces were used as gambling tokens, but they also circulated as currency in Bangkok prior to the 1870s. Tokens usually bore a Chinese inscription, and occasionally a Thai one, naming the issuing house along with good wishes and pictorial designs. Crabs have positive connotations for Chinese communities, and *fu* dogs function as protective figures.

Token with a crab and Chinese characters
19th century
Issued by Jin Yuan, Thailand
Porcelain
Diameter 2.2 cm
Donated by Richard Carnac-Temple, 1898,0901.20

Token with *fu* dog and Chinese and Thai inscriptions
19th century
Bangkok, Thailand
Porcelain
Diameter 2.2 cm
Donated by the Museum Galleries, 1977,0712.16

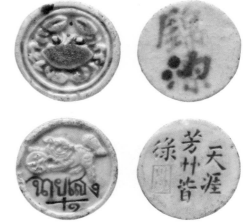

1. Horn and brass armour

Acquired during the British oceanographic expedition of 1872–76, this armour has horn plates, brass mesh and silver clasps. In some instances brass plates were used instead of horn ones. Known for their metalwork, Moro smiths living on the Mindanao, Sulu and Palawan islands started adapting European forms of armour and weaponry from the 1500s.

18th–early 19th century
Moro peoples, Mindanao, Philippines
Water buffalo horn, brass, silver
Length 74.5 cm, width 65.8 cm
Donated by A. W. Franks, collected by Lt. Hinds, As.9867

2. Helmet

Helmets such as this fell out of use as increasing British control limited warfare among the Chin in the late 19th and early 20th centuries. Although there are few written records of the Chin peoples, of which the Mara are a part, prior to the 19th century, British and later Chin records indicate that warfare and raiding were endemic during the cold season (November–February), when it was used to increase village land holdings and wealth, and to obtain slaves for this life and after death.

1900–1925
Mara people, northern Chin State, Myanmar or northeastern India
Bamboo basketry, hair
Height 25 cm, width 34 cm
Donated by James Chancellor de Vine, As 1927,0112.1

3. Sword

The British Museum's entry register from 1952 notes that this is an unusual hairy *kampilan* sword, with the shape of the hilt smaller and more rounded than customary. Tufts of animal or human hair added to the talismanic role of the weapon. Hilts were usually made of hardwood, as the quality of the weapon indicated the owner's social standing. Used both for warfare and war dances, *kampilan* are two-handed, single-edged swords found in the southern Philippines, as well as some eastern Indonesian islands with whom nobles in the province of Maguindanao had connections.

Late 1800s
Moro peoples, Mindanao, Philippines
Steel, wood, brass, hair, lime, fibre
Length 94.7 cm, width 27.3 cm
Donated by Webster Plass, As 1952,08.26

Southeast Asian warfare

Records in relief sculpture, inscriptions, literature and oral traditions show how warfare played an important role in many Southeast Asian societies, bolstering the claims of leaders and kings, proving men's prowess, and resulting in population movements around the region. People fought not only to prove their status, but also to acquire wealth and control the centres of production and various trade networks that had been a major feature of regional activity for thousands of years. Southeast Asia's traditionally low population density has also meant that capturing people was an important part of warfare, with the depopulation of areas a tactic used to prevent retaliation. People seized during ambushes, raids and wars comprised a large portion of communities, where they worked in a range of socio-economic positions. These included being incorporated into the royal court, placed in artisan communities, assigned land as farmers, conscripted as soldiers or being kept in permanent bondage. Such cross-cultural interactions resulted in shared imagery and practices.

Headhunting was another important form of warfare once practised in many parts of Southeast Asia, which colonial officials and missionaries attempted to end as the region came to be dominated by Western powers in the 19th and 20th centuries. Charles Hose, a colonial official working for Charles Brooke, the white rajah of Sarawak (r. 1868–1917), tried to institute rowing as an alternative competitive activity, but reports of headhunting on Borneo lasted into the 1960s. The purpose of headhunting ranged from revenge to challenging enemy groups, enhancing social status and prestige, and ensuring fertility for the community. While discussions of Southeast Asian warfare have focused on states, as with other parts of the world, the endemic nature of warfare among

4. Shield

Some shields were used in ceremonial war dances in preparation for headhunting and raiding expeditions. This example from the island of Solor in eastern Indonesia was for a person of high prestige. It is made of wood decoratively painted in red and black with inlaid cowrie shells and hair attached. There are both wood and cane handles at the back.

Early to mid-19th century
Solor, Indonesia
Wood, cane, hair, bast fibre, cowrie shell
Height 112 cm, width 15 cm
Donated by A. W. Franks, collected by Hakbyl, As.7289

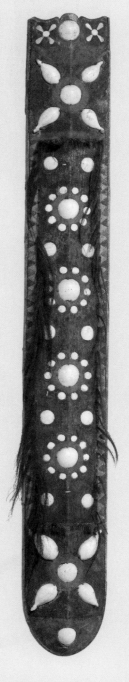

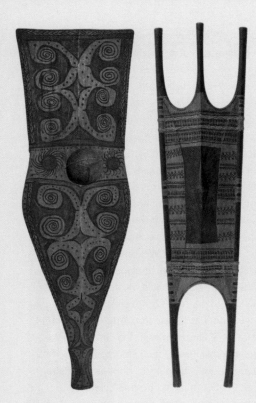

5. Shield (*koraibi*)

Mentawai shields were used for protection from arrows during headhunting raids. Made from the buttress roots of trees, they were first smoked to make them insect resistant, then shaped and painted in red and black with repetitive, symmetrical spiral designs. The maker abided by taboos during production, and an animal sacrifice was made upon completion to ensure the spirit's protection. The wooden grip at the back is protected by a hole covered with a half-coconut shell.

Early 1800s–1860s
Siberut, Mentawai islands, Indonesia
Wood, coconut wood, rattan
Height 110.9 cm, width 35.1 cm
Donated by the Amsterdam Zoological Society, As.7593

6. Shield

This shield was made by the Kalinga or Tinguian peoples of Luzon, for whom social position was acquired in part through warfare. The rattan lashings and the convex shape prevented the shield from splitting during combat in headhunting raids, and the five extensions were used to trip and trap victims. The geometric designs are related to those found on textiles and in tattoos.

Mid-1800s
Kalinga or Tinguian peoples, Luzon island, Philippines
Wood, rattan
Height 120 cm, width 30.3 cm
Donated by A. W. Franks, collected by Bryce M. Wright, As,+.3943

7. Gunpowder horn

This gunpowder container is made of bison horn with metal inlays and lacquer decoration. The plaited red and black wool cord was used to carry it. The Chin peoples once acted as mercenaries for surrounding rulers, and they were admired by the British for their martial abilities.

Early 20th century
Lai or Mara peoples, Zokhua village, Chin State, Myanmar
Bison horn, wood, wool, metal, resin, lacquer
Length 28 cm, width 9 cm
Donated by D. Hay-Neave, As1948,07.16

8. Flintlock pistol

After flintlocks became common during the 17th century, the VOC supplied them to numerous Southeast Asian rulers in the 18th century. Kings also acquired guns as gifts and captured them during raids, battles and attacks on ships. Mercenaries brought their own weapons, an added incentive for local rulers to employ Europeans in their armies. Some areas produced their own cannons and muskets, and by the 1700s the Bugis of Sulawesi and the Minangkabau of Sumatra had good reputations as gun producers.

18th–early 19th century
Acquired in Brunei
Wood, iron, brass
Length 41 cm
As.5707

large and small communities indicates that it played a cultural role, beyond the acquisition of people, resources and land, in the region.

Since Southeast Asia is so diverse, weaponry was also highly varied, ranging from swords and daggers to spears and lances, halberds, bows and arrows and blowpipes with poisoned darts. Helmets and shields were protective (**2**), although shields could also be used offensively (**6**). Little armour was worn (**1**), and then mostly by the elite, owing to the hot and humid climate. Many items were designed to present an aggressive and intimidating appearance to the enemy through patterns thought to be visually confusing, or the addition of enemy hair from previous conflicts (**3, 4, 5, 6**). Other forms of protection, such as amulets, magic diagrams, imagery and texts, and the forging of weapons with metals associated with invulnerability, were common, and remain so today. Some objects were also used in the rituals that accompanied preparations for warfare (**3, 4**).

While close combat was the norm, from the 16th century, firearms, cannons and gunpowder acquired from China, India and Europe increasingly became part of the arsenal. New accessories, such as gunpowder containers (**7**), were developed. Weapons were generally thought to be animated

by spirits. Like *keris* ritual daggers (see pp. 148–49), some firearms were decorated with *naga* serpents, whose power was associated with the capability of the weapon (**8**). Initially, cannons and guns were more often used to frighten the enemy with noise than to cause bodily harm. In the larger states, there was competition to acquire such objects, as before the 20th century local production was limited and sometimes not of high quality. Rulers welcomed European mercenaries, particularly Portuguese, for their military skills and possession of firearms.

Southeast Asians used weapons effectively, and Europeans took Southeast Asian warfare seriously before the 19th century. With the Industrial Revolution, European technology outstripped what the Southeast Asians could muster, although the latter's use of guerrilla-style resistance ensured that they were not easily defeated. After the complete annexation of Burma in 1886, the British fought against popular insurrections for more than a decade, and the war in Aceh, northern Sumatra, against the Dutch lasted from 1873 until 1904. States reformed their militaries along European lines in the late 19th century by hiring European engineers and other specialists. Smaller-scale battles between Southeast Asian groups continued to use traditional methodologies and weaponry into the 20th century.

3 | 16 The intensification of European colonial control

European presence in Southeast Asia before the end of the 18th century was primarily commercial and limited to the coast, but by the Second World War, the entire region, except for Thailand, was under colonial control. The acquisition of territories was achieved through warfare and military pressure (**4**), with the colonial heyday lasting from the 1880s to the 1930s.

While commerce provided a rationale for the control of Southeast Asia, colonial power was also an expression of diplomatic rivalry among the European countries, with each racing to ensure its own access to the rich resources of the region and using it as a gateway to Chinese markets. Materials and resources were exploited on a mass scale, often without regard to human life. Tin mines and rubber plantations became fixtures of the Malay landscape, as well as in Vietnam, which also produced coal and zinc; coffee and sugar were major exports from the Indonesian islands, and the teak forests of Myanmar provided another justification for annexation. Tea and rice were produced across the region. Grown in Malaya and Indonesia, gutta percha, tree sap tougher than rubber, was used for domestic and industrial purposes, such as the coating on telegraph lines, and later for tooth fillings. Silver and gold were also mined extensively (**2**).

Southeast Asia became an important market for various European goods, including textiles. It was observed in 1907 that local Myanmar blacksmiths struggled to compete with imported German knives, nails, axes and shovels (Bell 1907, 9–14).

1. Machine-minted coin
In the mid-19th century some Southeast Asian rulers began issuing coins for general circulation, using minting equipment purchased from Europe. Not all these coins were successfully adopted by local populations. Cambodians preferred to use Vietnamese and Thai coins rather than King Ang Duong's (r. 1840–60) first machine-minted copper and silver coins produced in the 1840s and 50s. The denomination illustrated here shows the sacred *hamsa* bird and a temple from Angkor, traditional imagery which in part has caused the king to be remembered as reviving Khmer culture. Cambodia became a French protectorate in 1863.

1847
Issued in Cambodia
Silver
Diameter 3.4 cm
Donated by Thomas Clarke-Thornhill, 1935,0401.12761

2. Silver ingot
Accessed by Myanmar and China, the silver mines at Bawdwin in Shan State, Myanmar, have been exploited from a very early date. In 1906, the Burma Mines Limited Company was established to recover the discarded metals in the slag heaps left from previous centuries of extraction. According to metallurgical analysis, this ingot from the Burma Mines is over 99 per cent pure silver.

Early 20th century
Myanmar
Silver
Height 1.4 cm, width 7.8 cm
Donated by Simmons and Simmons, 1989,0627.15

3. Machine-woven cloth

Made by Beving and Co. in Manchester, this cloth bears designs based on a Javanese batik textile owned by Charles Beving, who acquired African and Indonesian textiles for his firm to model. There were particular links between Ghana and Java as the Dutch shipped men from West Africa to work as colonial troops in Indonesia, and Javanese textile patterns, such as a patchwork design, may have originated in Africa.

c. 1880s–1910
Manchester, England
Cotton
Length 90 cm, width 60 cm
Donated by Charles Beving,
Af1934,0307.391

4. Box

Decorated in the *shwezawa* gold leaf technique on black lacquer, this box probably shows Myanmar people fleeing from British soldiers during the second Anglo-Burmese war of 1852. Britain annexed Myanmar in three phases over the course of the 19th century, culminating in the exile of King Thibaw (r. 1878–85) to British India.

Second half of the 19th century
Myanmar
Wood, lacquer, gold
Height 10.5 cm, width 28.2 cm,
length 43.4 cm
2002,0204.1

3 | 17 Models

Various colonial governments and individual officials studied the flora, fauna and cultures of Southeast Asia: naturalist Joseph Banks travelled with a draughtsman for the purpose of recording plants and animals (1768–71), and Stamford Raffles ordered ancient sites to be cleared and recorded during his time as Lieutenant Governor of Java (1811–16). Europeans also commissioned models, because they documented cultures during a time before easy photography and provided people back home with information about the foreign countries that they had colonized. Models and illustrations of foreign cultures in Asia, Africa and Oceania contributed to British projects to categorize and represent the cultural practices, forms of dress (1) and everyday activities that they encountered abroad. Southeast Asians have also made models for themselves for a variety of uses from toys to ritual paraphernalia.

The Southeast Asian collections at the British Museum include several hundred models, ranging from people and animals to boats (5), palanquins and other vehicles, musical instruments (2), weapons, utensils and tools, weaving equipment (6) and architecture (3, 4). These were usually made by local artists and craftsmen, whose skill in production is evident in both the original objects and their small-scale replicas. Models are still popular as souvenirs and intercultural gifts, and the British Museum houses some examples given to Queen Elizabeth II during state tours of Southeast Asia in the 1970s.

1. Model of a couple from Lombok
Models and drawings of couples were popular ways of representing the different peoples of Southeast Asia. Europeans were interested in cataloguing what was considered 'traditional' dress, although this drastically simplified the complex and fluid connections between peoples in the region.

Mid- to late 19th century
Lombok, Indonesia
Wood, resin, possibly gold
Height 30.7 cm (female); height 32 cm (male)
Donated by A. W. Franks, collected by C. M. Pleyte, As 1896,-.926–927

2. Model gamelan orchestra

These exceptionally fine replicas of Javanese gamelan instruments were illustrated in Sir Stamford Raffles' publication, *A History of Java*, in which he commented on the ubiquity of gamelan music on Java. Although Raffles also collected full-sized gamelan instruments, the volume's illustrator used the models to make his drawings, presumably because they were easier to transport and store.

c. 1812–15
Java, Indonesia
Wood, metal, cane, gold leaf
Heights from 7–36.5 cm,
widths from 9.5–34 cm
Donated by J. H. Drake,
collected by Stamford Raffles,
As 1939,04.2, As 1939,04.7–9,
As 1939,04.18, As 1939,04.18a,
As 1939,04.17, As 1939,04.17a,
As 1939,04.20, As 1939,04.31–32

3. Model of Minangkabau building

Providing shelter for extended families, Minangkabau houses, raised on piles and usually constructed of wood, have multiple roof layers and sweeping ridges that resemble buffalo horns, symbolism that is also present in other Southeast Asian cultures, such as the Toraja on the island of Sulawesi.

Early 20th century
Sumatra, Indonesia
Brass
Height 19.9 cm, width 27.8 cm
Donated by F. Killik,
As 1944,08.1.a–g

4. Model of a Balinese temple

Associated with the Hindu and Buddhist cosmic mountain Meru, diminishing, concentric roofs are a common superstructure found across many parts of Southeast Asia. The number of levels is always odd, between three and eleven, and reveals the status of the deity or person for whom it was built. More layers indicate higher status.

c. 1850s–early 1860s
Bali, Indonesia
Plant fibres
Height 37 cm, width 20.4 cm
As.5021

5. Model of a royal barge

During the annual Kathina festival at the end of the rainy season in October, when offerings were made to the Sangha (monkhood), royal barge processions were held on the Chao Phraya River in Bangkok. The British Museum's acquisition notes from 1937 indicate that such barge models were made for the festival.

Early 20th century
Thailand
Papier mâché, foil paper
Length 60 cm, width 8 cm
Donated by John Mallin,
As 1937,0414.1

6. Model loom

Textiles were of great significance to Southeast Asian societies, and Europeans collected numerous examples, as well as looms and models of the various loom types. This example from Myanmar is a frame loom, in which the strung warp threads are held taut by the loom itself. These were introduced to Southeast Asia during the late 19th century to stimulate the development of the textile industry, and successfully so; the region is now a major exporter of cloth and clothing.

1870s to mid-1880s
Myanmar
Wood, cotton
Height 18 cm, width 20.3 cm
As1919,0717.44

Timeline

10th century onwards	Ore smelting on Borneo
11th–21st centuries	Lacquer industry in Myanmar
13th–19th centuries	Circulation of Chinese copper *cash* in island Southeast Asia
16th century	Arrival of tobacco in Southeast Asia
c. 1500s to 1885	Production of bronze and brass market weights in Myanmar region
16th–17th centuries	Conversion to Islam of many trading areas in island Southeast Asia, including Brunei
Late 17th century	Rapid increase of Chinese trade and migration to Southeast Asia; Chinese men marry into local families and work as middlemen between Southeast Asians and Europeans, and as miners, labourers, craftsmen, traders, etc.
	The kingdom of Gianyar on Bali fails, and the island is divided into nine kingdoms, each with its own court
17th–18th centuries	Reports in VOC archives provide some descriptions of cultural practices
18th century	Increasing slave raiding in Southeast Asia
1755	Treaty of Giyanti divides authority in central Java between the courts of Yogyakarta and Surakarta
19th century	Christianity becomes significant in Vietnam
	Increasing artistic competition between the Yogyakarta and Surakarta courts
1811–16	British interregnum on Java; numerous cultural objects are collected and taken to Europe or sent to the East India Company headquarters in Calcutta (Kolkata)
Mid-19th century	Forced opening of Batak region of north-central Sumatra by Europeans
Mid- to late 19th century	New and synthetic fibres and dyes arrive in Southeast Asia
1867	Part of the Malay peninsula becomes a British colony
1881–1946	British North Borneo Company established to administer and exploit the resources of the region
1886	Colonial and Indian Exhibition in London
1893	International World's Fair in Chicago
Late 19th–20th centuries	Mass conversion of people to Christianity during the colonial period
	Expansion of Indian communities in lower Myanmar and west Malaysia
	Europeans form large collections of cultural objects from Southeast Asia
	Suppression of headhunting by Europeans
1900	Paris Exposition
1920s to 1930s	Javanese migrations to peninsular Malaya
Mid- to late 20th century	Plastic becomes a prevalent material
Late 20th century	Decline of the use of betel, although it still remains essential to rituals in many cultures
Late 20th to early 21st centuries	Thai Khon dance-drama, Indonesian shadow theatre, *keris*, gamelan, and batik are inscribed as UNESCO intangible world heritage
	Angkor, Sri Ksetra, Bagan, Ayutthaya, Sukhothai, Ban Chiang, My Son, Hué monuments, Borobudur and Prambanan become UNESCO world heritage sites

4 From the everyday to the sacred

c. 1600–2020

Southeast Asia displays a rich diversity of artistic forms, yet the extensive spheres of interaction around the region have also resulted in many commonalities. Archaeological finds have demonstrated that, from an early date, aesthetics were thought to imbue objects and imagery with meaning and value. There are substantial continuities between small-scale societies and the major religions of Hinduism, Buddhism, Islam and Christianity, visible through shared patterns and forms, related cosmologies and the ritual propitiation of ancestral and other spirits. Objects, including ephemera,

1. Offering
Discarded after use at the end of the ceremony or the day, intricately woven and plaited palm leaves or leaf cut-outs are common offerings or are used as containers for offerings on Bali. The size and extensiveness of ornamentation depends upon the importance of the ceremony. The majority of Balinese offerings to spirits and deities are ephemeral. Besides palm-leaf constructions, they can also take the form of performances, flowers, fruit, betel nuts, rice and rice cakes, or coloured and shaped rice dough.

1970s–1982
Bali, Indonesia
Coconut palm leaf
Diameter 13 cm
Donated by Anna Banks,
As1983,10.14

2. Covered box
Repeated geometric and symmetrical designs, as seen on this box, are common features of Torajan art. Each design is named, but the names can be applied to different motifs across Torajaland. Household items, plants, such as rice, and animals, particularly buffalo, are all sources of pattern names.

Early 20th century
Mamasa, Sulawesi, Indonesia
Wood, fibre
Diameter 48 cm, height 53 cm
As1976,02.1.a–b

3. Tattooing implement
Many people were once tattooed in Myanmar, with men often covered with tattoos from the waist to the knees, and displaying designs on the torso and arms (see p. 157). The tattoo instrument had a stylus with two or four slots to hold the ink and was topped with a weight in the form of a *nat* spirit or deity for protection.

Early 20th century
Myanmar
Brass
Length 28.5 cm
As2000,07.1.a–c

form part of rituals, exchanges and feasts, and confer prestige, indicate rank and mark out abilities. Some do not necessarily have spiritual connotations, but are cultural markers, identifying social connections, gender, age and marital status. Many function in a variety of ways.

Prescribed methods and rituals can accompany manufacture, from the weaving of an Iban textile on Borneo to the construction of a Buddhist temple in Myanmar, to ensure success and infuse power into the final product. In some societies, men and women have different, but complementary, spheres of labour. Both are considered equally necessary for the proper functioning of society, and the importance of this complementarity is seen across media. Artists can draw upon spirits and ancestors for inspiration, and trance can be part of production and performance. Except for modern and contemporary art for a Westernized market, most works are unsigned, owing to the fact that objects may be made by several people, or can be viewed as a channel for higher powers, or because the sponsor was considered of greater importance than the maker(s).

While there can be a hierarchy of materials – gold, for instance, was governed by sumptuary laws in many cultures – durability or ephemerality are not necessarily of significance. Sometimes, it is the essence that is important for spirits and deities, as in the case of Balinese woven-leaf offerings (1). The value comes from the appropriateness of the material to the purpose of the object. Significance also often exists in the pattern or design, which once could be controlled by sumptuary laws. Motifs, such as spirals and meanders, as well as geometric designs, based on animal and plant forms, survive from the earliest times and appear across media and art forms from baskets and puppets to stucco and wood carving (2).

Politics, too, played a role in the production of art and material culture. This was explored in greater detail in Chapter 3 through Theravada Buddhist kingship and European expansion, but it was also relevant in the island region. When the kingdom of Gianyar on Bali declined in the 1650s, nine kingdoms emerged on the island, each building its own palace (puri) and temples, necessitating the patronage of artists and

architects by the courts. On Java, the 1755 Treaty of Giyanti established two kingdoms in the centre of the island with their capitals at Surakarta (Solo) and Yogyakarta, sparking cultural competition in the production of art, including masks, puppets and textiles.

As international communities expanded rapidly from the 1400s, foreign artisans followed and settled in trading areas. The 18th century saw increasing numbers of Chinese migrants and South Asian Muslims involved in trade. The movement of peoples through slaving and warfare accelerated transcultural exchanges, and large percentages of city and state populations, including those of European-controlled ports, were relocated persons or their descendants. Europeans not only acquired political control of areas, but also formed local alliances that resulted in large mixed (mestizo) communities. In the 19th and 20th centuries, Chinese specialists were invited to train locals in Vietnam (4). The impact of these movements of people can be seen in the ways that objects combine ideas from a variety of sources into completely new methods of expression, such as on Malay silver or batik from Java's north coast.

Southeast Asia has a wealth of natural resources, but owing to the largely humid and warm climate, few plant- or animal-based objects, such as wood sculptures, basketry or textiles, survive that were made prior to the 19th century. This makes tracing changes or the emergence of new forms difficult. The arrival of tobacco in the 16th century, for example, must have

4. Louis Godefroy, *Sculpture d'une empereur d'Annam*
This etching shows the gateways and walls of a temple or tomb within a tree-filled landscape at Hué. The Nguyen dynasty (1802–1945) placed its capital in the centre of Vietnam at Hué, where the family had its roots. They constructed buildings modelled on Chinese designs. European forms such as lunettes – half-moon recesses – were also included among the architectural elements. Emperors were buried in large, landscaped areas with gates, buildings and pavilions for religious and recreational purposes, lakes and the tomb itself. The final tomb built in the 1920s was for Khai Dinh, father of the last emperor.

1919
Hué, Vietnam
Etching
Height 13.4 cm, width 31.4 cm
Donated by Louis Godefroy, 1930,0211.14

provoked the development of new objects, yet little evidence remains. Relief sculptures and wall paintings provide some information about everyday objects, and early cultural practices were occasionally described by traders and missionaries in the 17th and 18th centuries, as seen in the Dutch East India Company (VOC) archives. However, many societies were first recorded in detail only during the profound alterations to material culture between the 1880s and 1930s, the heyday of colonial control. The radical changes were visible in the rapid emergence of novel materials and techniques, different beliefs and ritual practices, and the absorption of new ideas and customs. By the early 20th century, many of the practices and art forms discussed in this chapter were waning. As royal courts were removed or left without power, patronage of the arts declined, and many artifacts were no longer made or else knowledge of how to produce them was held only by a small number of people. With colonial officials came Christian missionaries and efforts to convert the local peoples, and activities viewed as 'savage', such as headhunting, were banned. In some instances, the European impact was profound socially, culturally, religiously and politically; in others, the effect on cultural ideas and practices was less acute. As older ways of life were altered or abandoned in the face of modernization, the objects associated with them were sometimes destroyed, given away or sold. Some traditions, such as tattooing (3), have fallen out of favour, but other practices and attitudes have continued, such as the relevance of beads or hornbill sculptures to Borneo societies, and shamanism. Buddhist pilgrimage and the production of souvenirs remain common among practitioners on the mainland. Across the island region, *adat*, defined as customary practices or rules for living, continues to govern, in some instances, how clothes are worn, ritual interactions and behavioural norms. Traditional status symbols, such as *keris* ritual daggers, are valued but no longer worn regularly, while such protective *pusaka* (heirlooms) as luxury imported or locally made ritual textiles, sometimes given titles and individual names, are still treasured by families over generations. As customs and associated objects persist, they have been adapted for the changing Southeast Asian cultural worlds of the 20th and 21st centuries.

4 | 1 Objects of daily use

Southeast Asians produce objects using the abundant natural resources around them, including bone, horn, wood, bamboo, plant fibres, rattan and palms, metals and clay. These have all been shaped into practical forms for use in growing, preparing and consuming food (**5, 6, 7, 8, 9, 12**), caring for livestock, hunting and fishing, making clothes, trading goods (**11**) and storing necessities. Containers of all sizes are found across the region (**10**). Agriculture and the extraction of forest products spawned many utensils and implements (**3, 4**), and blowpipes, traps, bows and arrows and spears were used to hunt and fish (**1, 2**). Among some communities, easily obtainable materials were also made into ornaments or protective items (**13**). Combining aesthetics with functionality, such utilitarian pieces can be handsomely decorated, and some were once restricted to the nobility or for use in rituals associated with agriculture, food acquisition and fertility. The idea of art as separate from the everyday only emerged in the mid- to late 19th century through interaction with Europeans and in the 20th-century establishment of art schools. In some instances, artists have started to have their names associated with their work. In the British Museum's Southeast Asian collection, this is notable among objects purchased from the Kelabit peoples of Borneo. With the arrival of plastic and other modern materials and technologies in the 20th century, objects made of natural substances are becoming less common as a part of everyday life.

1. Blowpipe dart quiver
Blowpipes were once used by many societies in Southeast Asia, as they are an excellent tool for hunting game at relatively close range in forests, being silent and easily fired in rapid succession. Some peoples poisoned the tip of the darts for added efficacy. Darts were carried in quivers, and this example is made from a section of bamboo. It is accompanied by a woven cane cover, cord and metal toggle to fasten it to a loincloth.

Late 19th–early 20th century
Semai peoples, Malay peninsula
Bamboo, metal, fibre
Height 36 cm, diameter 8 cm
As 1997,Q.335.a

2. Fish trap
Made by the Temiar, an indigenous group living in the centre of the Malay peninsula, this woven trap has inwardly facing stakes of bamboo to prevent fish from escaping. Such traps were set in rivers and creeks.

Early to mid-20th century
Temiar peoples, Malay peninsula
Bamboo, cane
Length 64.9 cm, diameter 19.7 cm
As 1977,13.46

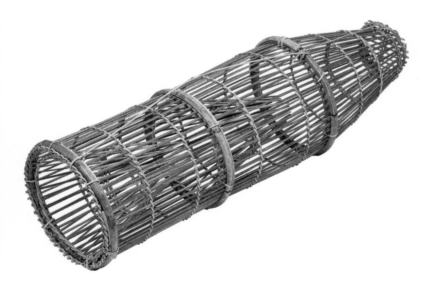

3. Sickle

Culturally and symbolically central for most of lowland Southeast Asia, the staple crop of rice has been cultivated in the region for about 5,000 years. It is grown in shifting cultivation or in permanent fields, using a range of methods from rain-fed dry cultivation to highly organized, communal wet-rice farming that requires transplanting the seedlings individually to irrigated *padi* fields. Cultivators use finger knives and, more recently, sickles to harvest rice. This sickle has a blade and two handles; the extra handle rests on the back of the neck when the sickle is carried.

1993
Cambodia
Wood, metal
Height 29.5 cm, width 38.5 cm
Donated by Sheldon Kent,
As1996,32.1

4. Merua' Ulun and Tepo Ben, Winnowing trays

Once harvested and threshed, rice has to be winnowed. Without mechanization, the rice is tossed into the air so that the chaff blows away, while the heavier grains fall back into the basket. Trays like these, which are also used for food preparation, are made of woven rattan and bamboo, and coated with tree sap to seal the interior surface. The hooks enable them to be hung up. Any painted decoration is found only on the exterior, to avoid contact with the food. The Kelabit have a custom where parents' and grandparents' names are changed after the birth of a child/grandchild. The names Merua' Ulun and Tepo Ben indicate that the makers are grandmothers.

1987/1986
Kelabit Highlands, Remudu,
Sarawak, Borneo
Rattan, bamboo, sap
Height 16.4 cm, width 47.2 cm;
height 16.7 cm, width 49.5 cm
As1988,22.89–90

5. Water jar

Earthenware vessels have served myriad purposes across Southeast Asia from at least 8,000 years ago to the present. As water jars, the porous nature of the clay allows evaporation, thus cooling the water inside. When placed on a fire, an earthenware pot does not crack and so can also be used for cooking, to make medicine or to prepare dyes for textiles. Although many such vessels look similar when finished, there are a variety of methods by which they are shaped, starting with either a single lump of clay or by adding clay during the construction process.

Late 19th century
Pulau Tiga, Perak, Malaysia
Earthenware
Diameter 26.5 cm, height 18 cm
Donated by the Perak
Ethnological Museum,
As1905,0316.23

6. Steamer

Acquired for the Colonial and Indian Exhibition of 1886 in London from the British Commissioners for the Straits Settlements (Penang, Dinding, Melaka and Singapore), to demonstrate the variety of cooking equipment in these communities, this food steamer is made of bark with a pandanus leaf cover held together with cane fibres.

Early 1880s
Straits Settlements, Malay peninsula
Bark, cane, pandanus leaf
Diameter 22.2 cm, height 35 cm
Donated by the Government of the Straits Settlements,
As1886,1213.75

7. Food cover

Covers are used across many parts of Southeast Asia to keep insects and other animals off food during preparation, as well as when setting out a meal. The ubiquity and flexibility of pandanus leaves, here supported by strips of rattan, make them ideal for lightweight covers.

Late 19th century
Baram River District, Sarawak, Borneo
Pandanus leaf, rattan
Diameter 50.6 cm, height 14 cm
As1900,-.687

8. Food box (*htamin kyaint*)

Probably used by office workers, this lunchbox is of a shape that arrived in Myanmar with the rapidly expanding Indian community of the colonial period in the late 19th century. Each section would hold a separate dish, and the lid could be turned over for use as a cup. The box was made in the town of Kyaukka, famous for its sturdy, plain-coloured lacquerware.

c. 1900–39
Kyaukka, Sagaing Region, Myanmar
Lacquer, wood
Diameter 14.1 cm, height 32.6 cm
Donated by Ralph and Ruth Isaacs, 1998,0723.221

9. Spoon

The Ifugao serve and eat from deep wooden bowls with spoons (*pakko* or *idu*) that are stored in a basket when not in use. Carved in a variety of woods, the decoration on the handles is mostly standing or seated figures. Spoons are carefully washed and maintained and are handed down as heirlooms.

Late 19th–early 20th century
Ifugao peoples, Philippines
Wood
Length 19 cm, width 6.3 cm
Donated by Miss Hirst,
As1927,0107.2

10. Container

On Timor, men produced decorated containers of bamboo, gourd, wood and bone for storing stimulants until the mid-20th century. Imagery was primarily floral and geometric, like that seen here.

c. 1880
Fatunaba, island of Timor
Bamboo
Height 18.3 cm, diameter 2.5 cm
Donated by A. W. Franks,
collected by Henry Forbes,
As,+.1896.a–b

11. Set of weights

For use on hand-held scales consisting of trays suspended from each end of a rod, sets of market weights provided the counterbalance to the goods in the opposite tray. Cast using the lost-wax method (see p. 28), the weights come in sets of up to ten, usually in the form of sacred birds (either the *hintha* or the *karaweik*) and, as shown here, the mythical *tonaya* (a composite creature combining the features of lions and bulls). Production ceased when Britain annexed Myanmar in 1886.

19th century
Myanmar
Copper alloy
Heights from 2.3–13.5 cm
Donated by Donald and Joan Gear, 1993,0731.13–14, 1993,0731.93, 1993,0731.88–89, 1993,0731.91

12. Coconut scraper

Until the invention of electric scrapers, examples like this one were essential for grating and removing the flesh of the coconut from its husk to make oil and milk, staples in many Southeast Asian diets. The oil is also used cosmetically, and coconut water is a refreshing drink that has become popular globally.

The tree's sap can be dried to make sugar, its fronds woven into functional basketry objects, the hard shells used for bowls and scoops, and the wood employed in construction. Because of its many uses, the coconut palm has been important in the region for millennia.

1940s–early 1950s
Made by Hanunóo peoples, Mindoro, Philippines
Wood, iron, aluminium
Length 60.8 cm, width 28.4 cm
As1958,06.97

13. Comb

Made from a section of bamboo, Semai combs were incised with patterns into which a dark-coloured material was then rubbed to make them stand out. The combs were apparently worn by women as protective talismans against disease.

19th century
Semai peoples, Malay peninsula
Bamboo
Length 25 cm, width 5.7 cm
Donated by A. W. Franks, collected by Rev. Dr. William S. Simpson, As1896,-.764

4 | 2 Lacquer

Lacquer in most of Southeast Asia is tapped from the *Gluta usitata* tree. The sap turns a glossy black upon exposure to oxygen, but it can be dyed. Lacquer is applied in layers over a base usually made of wood, bamboo or metal, although other materials are sometimes used, and each layer is left to dry before another is added. The technique has been used to create functional, waterproof objects, and lacquerware shapes include bowls, boxes, trays, offering vessels and water pots (**2**). Wooden monasteries, temples, palaces and other buildings were coated with lacquer for protection from the weather and insects, and gold leaf was adhered to images with lacquer.

Evidence for lacquer production varies across the region. In Myanmar it dates from the Bagan period (11th–13th centuries), and it continues to be a substantial industry today. There are similarities with the lacquerwares of Thailand, such as the *yun* decorative technique and a dense floral pattern called *Zinme*, the Myanmar name for the Lan Na city of Chiang Mai in northern Thailand (**3**). It appears that lacquer production spread from Lan Na to central Thailand, where it was used to decorate manuscript chests (see pp. 86–87), as well as smaller pieces, such as offering vessels and stands. Inlays of mother-of-pearl in floral and geometric patterns to create black and white designs may have developed in the 9th or 10th century and became highly sophisticated by the 18th century (**1**).

The Vietnamese lacquer tradition relates to the East Asian one, using the sap of the *Toxicodendron vernicifluum* tree, rather than *Gluta usitata*. Bowls, boxes, trays and other shapes are commonly made in lacquer (**5**), and since the colonial period, lacquer has been used to make paintings with great commercial success. The Palembang region of southeastern Sumatra has a long history of exporting a red resin called Dragon's Blood extracted from an indigenous palm tree for use in Chinese lacquer production. The lacquer products of Palembang are more recent and probably originated with Chinese artisans residing there since the early 19th century (**4**).

1. Footed stand inlaid with mother-of-pearl
This type of inlaid lacquer is particularly associated with the kingdom of Ayutthaya and later Siam (Thailand) with its capital city at Bangkok. Inlaid offering vessels are still made in sets to be used in Buddhist ceremonies to hold flowers, candles and incense, and sometimes inlaid stands were used to present small dishes of food to monks.

1980–90
Thailand
Lacquer, mother-of-pearl, wood
Diameter 21.6 cm, height 12.8 cm
1991,1023.96

2. Pair of *hsun-ok* offering vessels
Decorated in the *hmansi-shwecha* method, in which lacquer putty (*thayo*) is used for high-relief designs and as settings for glass pieces, these offering vessels were once used to donate food to the Sangha (monkhood). While most of the imagery comprises floral and abstract designs, there are also mythical creatures around the bodies of the vessels. The covers are topped with layers representing umbrellas, a mark of honour and status, and the sacred *hintha* bird.

Mid-19th century
Myanmar
Bamboo, lacquer, glass, wood, gold, metal
Diameter 60 cm, height 116 cm; diameter 56 cm, height 119 cm
1994,1116.1–2

3. Hsaya Kaing, Water vessel (*ye khwet gyi*)

The *yun* technique, in which the pattern for each colour is first incised into the lacquer and then filled with pigment, usually red, yellow and green, has been used to produce the imagery on this water vessel. Cartouches (a framing device) around the upper edge state that Master (*hsaya*) Kaing made this piece for Ma Hla Hpyu, and those among the narrative scenes name the characters and episodes of the Kusa Jataka, one of the stories of the Buddha's previous lives.

1900–25
Bagan, Myanmar
Bamboo, lacquer
Height 19.4 cm, width 23.9 cm
Donated by Ralph and Ruth Isaacs, 1998,0723.2

4. Box

Sumatran lacquer pieces are usually made of plaited bamboo, painted with Chinese-style patterns – here designs of stars and flowers – and covered with lacquer. Box sizes ranged from small, as here, to large enough to store clothing.

Early 20th century
Palembang, Sumatra, Indonesia
Lacquer, rattan, gold pigment
Height 14 cm, width 12.5 cm
Donated by Ralph and Ruth Isaacs, 1998,0723.180

5. Nested boxes

These three nested wooden boxes were covered with coats of black lacquer, each of which was dried and polished before the addition of the subsequent layer. The floral decoration was painted with coloured lacquer and covered with a clear lacquer coat. Boxes and other objects like this are made for a global market.

1995–6
Vietnam
Lacquer, wood
Height 5 cm, width 14.5 cm
(largest box)
Donated by Bich Tyler,
1996,0510.6

4 | 3 Betel equipment and tobacco

The chewing of betel quids was common among people of all ages and classes across Southeast Asia prior to the 21st century. It played a major role in personal aesthetics (black teeth were considered beautiful), social interactions and rituals from basic hospitality to cementing formal relationships, and as medicine, money and offerings to spirits and ancestors. At its most basic, betel was a combination of slices of areca nut, a betel leaf and lime paste, with other ingredients added to indicate status. As part of formal ceremonies, such as marriage negotiations and funerals, the arrangement and presentation of ingredients and equipment followed strict local custom.

In many parts of Southeast Asia, the trays, containers and cutting tools for storing, preparing and serving betel became art forms. Because the wealth and status of the owner was indicated by the level of decoration and the materials used, ranging from basketry (4), lacquer, wood and ceramics to iron (1), brass (2), silver (3) and gold, objects associated with betel linked with a person's social identity. Royal regalia confirming the legitimacy of the ruler also included betel sets.

While tobacco arrived in Southeast Asia in the 16th century, via Portuguese and Spanish traders, it was not until the late 20th century that it became dominant, replacing betel in popularity, but not symbolically or ritually. Prior to the rise of cigarettes, tobacco was incorporated into betel quids or smoked in pipes (6). As with betel, paraphernalia was developed for tobacco storage and use (5).

1. Betel cutter

Used to slice the hard areca nut, cutters were an essential part of betel paraphernalia. This betel cutter depicts a mythical winged lion (*singha*) embellished with Chinese swastika patterns that denote good fortune, zigzags, stars and geometric shapes.

Late 19th–early 20th century
Bali, Indonesia
Iron, silver
Height 10 cm, width 2 cm
Donated by Teresa Pattinson,
As 1932,0406.6

2. Betel box (*lotoan*)

Muslim communities of the southern Philippines are known for their production of a betel receptacle called the *lotoan*, a rectangular hinged box with silver inlays, usually with four compartments to hold the leaves, areca nuts, lime and tobacco. Indicating social status and wealth, the boxes were exchanged at ceremonies, such as weddings, and kept as heirlooms. They are decorated with floral and geometric patterns called *okir adatu* that are also reproduced in wood carving.

19th–early 20th century
Mindanao, Philippines
Brass, silver
Height 7 cm, width 13.5 cm
As1996,09.1

3. Betel leaf holder

This betel leaf holder is made of silver and decorated in the niello technique, in which sulphur is combined with another metal, usually silver, copper or lead, to fill designs that have been engraved on the metal surface. The exposed floral patterning has been gilded. This shape of holder is also found in Thailand, because of close cultural connections along the Thai-Malay peninsula.

Early 20th century
Malay peninsula
Silver, metal, gold
Height 13.9 cm, width 8.2 cm
As1931,0320.6

4. Betel box

Produced in the complex hexagonal plaiting called mad weave (*anyam gila*), this box was made by a Timorese woman for offering betel ingredients and food to ancestors. It is decorated with concentric stars picked out in coloured strips around the sides, and the cover is an elaborate roof-like structure with suspended woven stars around it. Stars were a frequent design element in Timorese art and were widespread in other Southeast Asian arts and in Indian trade textiles, such as the *patola*.

1840s–1850s
Island of Timor
Palm leaf, plant fibre
Height 20.8 cm, diameter 10.2 cm
As.5597.a–b

5. Tobacco container

Carved from a nut, this container was wrapped with a band of braided fibre so that it could be carried easily. On the Mentawai islands, two main concepts dominated artistry: an object should not merely be functional but also in harmony with its surroundings, a concept called *mateu*; and it should also be made as well as possible – *makire*.

Early to mid-20th century
Rogdog, Mentawai Islands, Indonesia
Nut, fibre
Diameter 6 cm, height 13 cm
As 1994,07.2.a-b

6. Smoking pipe

The silver mounts here, embellished with bands of geometric and floral patterning, indicate that this pipe was used for special occasions. While the silver and the wood elements were late 19th-century additions, the ceramic bowl is old. Numerous such bowls have been regularly found in the Shan States and used as pipes and also as touchstones, which are objects believed to identify precious metals.

19th century
Yaunghwe, Shan States, Myanmar
Pottery, wood, silver
Height 31 cm, width 24 cm
As 1904,0626.22

4 | 4 Malay silver

In the Malay states, many governed by sultans since the 15th century, courts retained silversmiths to create regalia items, including musical instruments, as well as jewelry and vessels for hospitality and ritual use. These included betel equipment, *kendi* ritual water vessels, weapon mounts, cosmetic containers, bowls, plates, spittoons, containers, trays, pillow ends and pubic covers worn by young children (**1**, **2**, **4**). High-ranking Malays wore elaborate belt buckles during court and state ceremonies (**3**). The production of Malay silverwork declined in the early 20th century.

Malay silver was made using chasing (in which the metal is shaped from the front), embossing (the shaping occurring from the reverse side), granulation (the addition of tiny balls of metal to the object's surface) and openwork (in which the background to the imagery is removed). The size of a piece and the intricacy of its decoration reflected the social and financial status of the owner. Silver pieces were often ornately decorated with auspicious emblems and floral, foliate and geometric motifs, including stylized lotus petals, cloud formations and bands of geometric shapes. Flat areas on boxes, buckles, pillow ends and plates contain a central motif surrounded by patterned borders of varying widths. Bowls often have bands of motifs around the rim with a larger section or sections of patterning around the middle. The geometric shapes and designs, as well as the non-figural decoration, indicate links with an Islamic aesthetic that was enhanced by connections between Southeast Asia and the Ottoman empire in the 19th century (see pp. 90–91).

1. Flask

Because mountains had spiritual significance among many cultures across Southeast Asia, mountain shapes were often incorporated into art forms, as the lid of this silver flask demonstrates. Stylized floral and geometric motifs encircle the upper and lower sections of the vessel, and the body is heavily striated. Small flasks were popular as containers for ointments and oils.

Late 19th century
Malaysia
Silver
Height 10.7 cm, width 5.7 cm
As1931,0320.1

2. Lime box

Slaked lime, an alkaline substance combining calcium oxide and water, is an essential part of a betel nut quid, and pots to hold it were an element of betel paraphernalia. This lime pot is simply decorated around the lid and the foot with stylized floral motifs found in Malaya and central Thailand. Such pots are usually identifiable by the white residue left by the lime on their interiors.

Late 19th–early 20th century
Malaysia
Silver
Diameter 5 cm, height 6.6 cm
As1931,0320.2

3. Belt buckle (*pinding*)

In the Malay states and on Sumatra, belt buckles, traditionally in an ogival shape, were a symbol of authority, with the material, size and ornament indicating rank and status. Royal regalia, the dress and accessories demonstrating the legitimacy of the ruler, also included buckles. Most likely made by Peranakan or Chinese silversmiths with silver imported from mainland Southeast Asia, this buckle was produced using the niello technique. Buckles could also be set with gems and inscribed.

19th century
Kuantan, Pahang, Malaysia
Silver
Height 10 cm, width 17.6 cm
Donated by Beatrice Satow,
As1963,01.12

4. Container and lid

Gourd-shaped containers such as this one are popular in Southeast Asia, and are seen in various media including Malay silver and lacquer from Myanmar. Inscribed on the base with 'Engku Basar owns this silver *lalu*', this container was probably once in the collection of a member of the nobility of Riau-Lingga, a Malayan sultanate (1824–1911) controlling an enclave on Sumatra and numerous islands in the South China Sea.

19th century
Malaysia or Riau-Lingga
Silver
Diameter 19.5 cm, height 20.6 cm
Donated by Brenda Seligman,
As1951,03.1.a–b

4 | 5 Jewelry

Glass and stone beads have been found placed as grave goods in Southeast Asia from ancient times up to the mid-20th century. Objects of adornment have continued to play a role in societies as a method of storing wealth and for personal embellishment (**2, 5**), but they also function as ritual items, forms of protection and indicators of rank and status within a community (**1**). Jewelry should be viewed along with other elements of self-adornment, such as tattooing, the filing of teeth, head-binding, clothing and ritual weapons, in understanding social communication via personal display. Adornment can reveal age, gender and marital status (**4**), and jewelry items are among those used as goods of exchange, during marriage ceremonies, for example. Some design elements, such as the spiral, extend across cultural areas (**3**).

Jewelry was often controlled by sumptuary laws. Myanmar's King Bagyidaw (r. 1819–46) issued a list of objects that his daughter was allowed to use upon her coming-of-age ear piercing ceremony, including golden footwear. Europeans were impressed with the wealth of the region, often describing it in detail. Francois van Boeckholtz wrote that Javanese princes 'wear one gold ring on the first finger and diamond rings on all the others'.

1. Bracelet (*geland sarung*)
The Karo Batak are Muslim, while the Toba Batak are Christian, yet both these Sumatran groups once adorned themselves with this type of bracelet. Now they are worn by Karo Batak men to indicate rank at ceremonies, such as those associated with their fathers' funerals and more recently, weddings, and as a protective amulet against bad dreams. The bracelets comprise three sliding metal tubes decorated with granulation (beads) and twisted wire strands in geometric patterns, which can also be seen on the jewelry of the Muslim nobles of Minangkabau and the Aceh and Deli sultanates on Sumatra.

Late 19th–early 20th century
Karo Batak peoples, Sumatra, Indonesia
Metal, gold, silver
Diameter (widest point) 17 cm
As 1988,28.1

2. Ring in the form of a *naga*
Myanmar has long been a major source of gems, particularly rubies and sapphires, which are still mined in mountainous regions occupied by minority groups. Rubies were associated with royalty, and their use was regulated by law.

Early 19th century
Myanmar
Gold, rubies, enamel
Diameter 3.1 cm
Bequeathed by A. W. Franks,
Af.2373

3. Ear ornaments (*padung-padung*)

Married Karo Batak women attach these earrings, which are formed of three tubes, to their headdress to help support the weight of the metal, which can be up to a kilogram. Older examples were solid and could not be removed from the ears. Now such earrings are mostly worn for festivals, if at all.
The spirals, an ancient motif in Southeast Asia, are usually arranged to face forward on one side of the head and backwards on the other.

19th century
Karo Batak peoples, Sumatra, Indonesia
Metal
Height 12 cm, width 8.3 cm
Donated by S. R. Robinson,
As 1895,0902.46–47

4. Necklace (*kalung*)

Among the matrilineal societies of the Muslim Minangkabau of central Sumatra, married women wear highly detailed and diverse necklaces. Wealth, of which jewelry is an important part, is passed from mothers to daughters. Alternating silver or gold beads with red stones, such as coral or carnelian, is a typical Minangkabau arrangement.
The red stones may have been imported from Yemen by traders and scholars called Hadhrami, after the Hadramaut region from which they came, who settled in island Southeast Asia where they were commercially successful.

1920s–1930s
Sumatra, Indonesia
Carnelian, silver
Length 65.1 cm
2016,3065.1

5. Necklace of coins

Indian silver *rupee* coins were used in necklaces and sewn on to clothing as a way of storing and displaying wealth among many mainland Southeast Asian communities, such as the Chin and Kachin, especially where the British were present. The coins here are quarter *rupees*, each of which weighs in at 2.92 grams of 91.7 per cent pure silver.

Early 20th century
Chin peoples, Myanmar
Metal, wool
Length 77.5 cm
Donated by D. Hay-Neave,
As 1948,07.21

4 | 6 *Keris* ritual daggers

Symbolizing refinement and spiritual and sexual power, and believed to possess magical abilities, *keris* daggers were once worn as weapons and adornment by men and women in many parts of island Southeast Asia (**3**). Their use could be controlled by sumptuary laws. For example, in Malay kingdoms, only *keris* gifted by the sultan could have a gold hilt. After colonial bans on carrying weapons and lessened relevance to contemporary society, *keris* have declined in importance, and the number of skilled smiths is now small. In some places, such as Java, *keris* are still part of formal dress and an integral element in cultural life, while in others, they are primarily symbolic.

Keris are formed of three parts – blade, hilt and sheath – though they are judged by the quality of the blade's shape and *pamor*, the metal alloy patterning composed of dozens or even hundreds of folds of iron and nickel compounds that create its famous damascened appearance (**1**). The narrow, asymmetrical, double-edged blades range from about 15 to 50 centimetres long. Older examples have straight blades, but the curved type eventually dominated, always with an odd number of waves. Complex rituals accompany the production of blades, although these differ across the various cultures that use *keris*.

Keris are believed to have spiritual qualities and essences that must be compatible with the owner or misfortunes will result. As amulets they are thought to protect against fire and enemies, and bring good fortune (**2, 4**). They are heirlooms (*pusaka*), royal regalia, part of ceremonial and court dress and ritual exchanges of gifts, and viewed as ancestral deities. Some were awarded names and titles by the nobility, and stories are told of warriors wielding legendary *keris*. Images of *keris* were used as seals on Malay manuscripts, and more recently, they have featured on flags, emblems, coins and logos in parts of the island region.

1. *Keris*
All the components of a *keris* had symbolic associations, particularly of masculinity and power, and a *keris* could stand for a man at his wedding if he could not attend, for example. While the blade is considered the source of power, it is the hilt that reveals the *keris'* origins. As many types of trees were viewed as having magical powers, specific woods were often used for hilts. The geometric formation of this wooden hilt is a style known as *cecak redut*, which was worn by Balinese soldiers into the 20th century.

19th century
Bali, Indonesia
Iron, gold, wood
Length 53.1 cm, width 10.5 cm
As 1926,0607.1.a–b

2. *Keris*
The mythical *naga* serpent is associated with the underworld and water, as well as marking transitional events and places across Southeast Asia. The *keris* blade was believed to represent a serpent, an idea enhanced by the depiction of the *naga* along its length on this example. The association between *nagas* and weapons can also be seen on cannons and guns (see p. 117). Supposedly a gift to the collector Carl Bock from the Sultan of Saribas, Borneo, this *keris* has a very simple sheath (not shown), which suggests that it was replaced or the source was reported inaccurately.

18th to mid-19th century
Made by Malays, Saribas, Borneo
Steel, gold, copper, diamonds or crystals, wood
Length 36.5 cm, width 6.5 cm
As,Bk.88.a

3. *Keris* and sheath

The large, heavy-looking blade is typical of Bugis *keris*, and the shape of the sheath is also standard with the flaring end and the boat-shaped flange around the opening. *Keris* often had angled hilts designed to ensure a good grip when thrusting. Here, the patterning is floral, rather than figural, in keeping with Muslim Bugis beliefs.

18th–19th centuries
Bugis peoples, Sulawesi, Indonesia
Steel, ivory, gold, silver, wood, diamonds
Length 39 cm, width 7 cm; sheath length 44 cm, width 17 cm
As 1972,Q.982.a–b

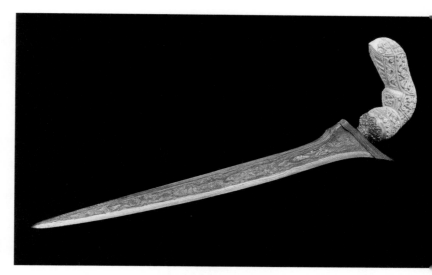

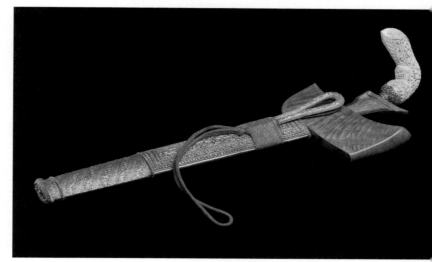

4. *Keris*

The relationships between the different parts of the *keris* were meaningful, with the sheath and blade representative of the unity of Allah and his creations on Java and Madura. Here, the hilt is in the form of a protective demon, but many were inspired by characters from the Mahabharata and Ramayana literary epics that had a major impact on Southeast Asian cultural life.

Late 18th–early 19th century
Madura, Indonesia
Iron, ivory, gold
Length 55.6 cm, width 9.6 cm
Bequeathed by John Henderson,
As 1878,1230.910.a–b

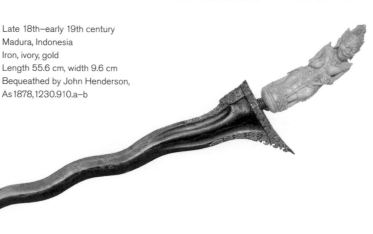

4 | 7 Balinese palaces and temple sculpture

Most people from Bali practice a unique form of Hinduism, combining the worship of Hindu deities with such elements as honouring ancestors and several calendrical systems. Spatial orientation towards the central mountain on Bali, Gunung Agung (a volcano that symbolically represents the axis of the universe) and the sea governs many aspects of life, including the layout of temples, palaces and houses, and the placement of offerings. The most sacred area is adjacent to the mountain, while gateways face the sea as they are transitional spaces, potentially admitting both the positive and the malign.

Palaces were major centres of art production. Doors to temples, shrines and palaces are carved with intricate details in high relief, painted and gilded by artists employed for the task by the ruler (**1**). Different decorative elements are arranged in specific positions on the brick, stone and wood elements of Balinese gateways. Corners usually display an animal or bird head, but most of the motifs are floral and vegetal patterns, many of which are based on lotus tendrils and some of which display Chinese or European origins, as well as exhibiting adaptations of patterns from luxury imported Indian textiles.

Sculptures are found within temples and residences as pillar supports, architectural ornaments or stands for *keris* ritual daggers. As temporary residences for deities, religious figures (*arca lingga*) are made by artists who have been consecrated by priests (**2, 3**). So that they are immediately identifiable, figures have standardized features that follow similar rules to those governing masks and shadow puppets. The artist is not paid, but is offered ritual gifts including Chinese *cash* coins and textiles.

1. Palace doors and detail
Although walls of temples and palaces are made of brick, the frame and door leaves are of wood. Doors are elaborately carved in high relief with details including floral motifs, lozenge forms and *kala* monster faces that mark transitions. The details have been emphasized with gold leaf, commensurate with the rank of the owner. The red pigment is cinnabar, which was imported from China. Because Balinese buildings are often formed of a series of separate compounds, such doors could also be internal features.

Early 19th century
Bali, Indonesia
Jackfruit tree wood, metal, gold
Height 253.7 cm, width 179.3 cm
1880.2486.1−15

3. Statue of Prince Rama on Garuda

The god Vishnu in his incarnation as Prince Rama rides his mount, the mythical and mighty bird Garuda, who clutches his enemy, the *naga* serpent, in his claws. Such statues were produced in soft wood with a straight grain to make intricate detail possible.

19th–early 20th century
Bali, Indonesia
Wood, pigment
Height 99.7 cm, width 50 cm
As 1970,20.1

2. Shiva

Shiva is the most important Hindu god on Bali, and in this representation, he is shown richly embellished. Each of the gods is associated with specific colours, numbers and directions. Shiva's are white, the number eight (representing the four cardinal and four inter-cardinal directions) and the centre, as indicated by the fact that he is believed to live on the mountain Gunung Agung, the world axis.

Early 19th century
Bali, Indonesia
Teak, gold, pigment
Height 107.5 cm, width 33 cm
Donated by Royal Botanic
Gardens, Kew, As.3438

4 | 8 Toraja architecture

Dong Son bronze drums, made in northern Vietnam from about 500–300 BCE, display images of buildings on piles with a saddle roof, an architectural format still prevalent in Southeast Asia. The house was not only a place of shelter, withstanding environmental forces, but could also be viewed as an origin house for a clan, enhancing clan rank and status within the community. This is the case among the Toraja societies of Sulawesi. Ornamented houses and granaries are reserved for the aristocracy among the hierarchical Toraja, with the carved imagery referring to specific forms of wealth (**2**).

The Toraja peoples pair the clan house (*tongkonan*) with a rice barn or several barns. While the house is considered to be private, the barn functions as storage and for public purposes, with the space underneath serving as a place to receive guests and socialize, as well as for more formal arrangements, such as settling disputes or arranging marriages (**3**). The space beneath the barn is also where such daily tasks as weaving and basket-making occur. The house faces north, which is the direction of the gods, while the barn faces south, oriented towards the ancestors. Barns are also ritual spaces, and among some Toraja communities, deceased family members are placed there temporarily during elaborate funerary ceremonies. Rituals also occur in the clan house, and room dividers separate the sections used in varying ceremonies associated with life or death (**1**).

Today, many Southeast Asian architectural traditions have fallen out of use owing to the rapid social and economic changes that began in the colonial period, and most people now opt for more modern housing. As a mark of wealth and status, some Torajans still maintain traditional clan houses and granaries, or construct new ones with such modern materials as corrugated iron. Fashion, too, plays a role, and in the 1990s, building extra-large houses became popular.

1. Sacred house divider (*ampang bilik*)

As the centre of a clan's ritual life, the Torajan house is designed to replicate the cosmos in miniature. Dividers separate the interior space into cosmologically significant units, each of which has designated functions in accord with *aluk to dolo*, the way of the ancestors. This example would have separated the southern part of a house from the northern one. Because the north is auspicious, the northern part of the house is reserved for guests, eating and rituals associated with life.

Early 20th century
Sa'dan Toraja people, Rantepao, Sulawesi, Indonesia
Wood
Height 159.5 cm, width 184 cm
As 1992,07.1

2. Door with buffalo carving

Among the Toraja, wealth is measured in numbers of buffalo, in addition to a family's titles and clan house. Buffalo are used for rituals, rather than for labour, and the horns of sacrificial buffalo are attached to clan houses to demonstrate wealth and rank, as well as strength. Houses, granaries and rock-cut tombs also have doors with buffalo carvings, and facades are carved and painted with buffalos.

Early to mid-20th century
Sa'dan Toraja people, Mamasa, Sulawesi, Indonesia
Wood
Height 106.7 cm, width 47.8 cm
As 1987,01.24

3. Rice barn (*alang*)

In 1987, the British Museum invited a group of Toraja men to build a barn for an exhibition in London. They constructed it over several months using traditional techniques with materials imported from Sulawesi. The elaborate imagery indicates that the barn would have been for a wealthy, high-ranking family. Governed by sumptuary regulations, these features would be closely connected with the kinship group's ancestral house (*tongkonan*), and designs are used interchangeably between the two. Inside, offerings of dried rice bundles for gods and ancestors, and rice for human consumption, are placed in specific cardinal directions depending on who they are for.

1987
Made by Toraja craftsmen at the Museum of Mankind, London, UK
Wood, bamboo
Height 800 cm, width 300 cm, length 1100 cm (dimensions approximate)
As 1987,01.94

1. Spirit shrine

Miniature temples have been made in Thailand since at least the 1500s. Early uses remain unknown, but more recently they function as shrines for spirits of place. Made of terracotta, wood, stone, lacquer or more modern materials, such as cement, the shrines are usually mounted on small platforms and placed in an auspicious spot within house and business compounds, as well as on top of skyscrapers. Incense, flowers, water, ribbons, coloured streamers and food and drink are offered to the spirits to keep them happy and avert ill-fortune.

2. *Bulul* figure

Made in pairs by the Ifugao peoples, *bulul* rice deities are carved according to complex production rituals, a process that can take more than six weeks. Once activated by being bathed in the blood of a sacrificed pig, they are believed to protect rice granaries and make rice grow. The figures are inherited by the eldest child of the family.

Early 20th century
Ifugao peoples, Luzon, Philippines
Wood, cowrie shell
Height 41 cm, width 16 cm
As 1974,20.1

Spirits and ancestors

All Southeast Asian societies once believed that spirits, supernatural beings or ancestors occupied the natural world around them (belief systems today called animism), and most still do. Spirits may be associated with natural features of the landscape. For instance, Thai *phii* and Myanmar *nat* spirits occupy specific locations like houses or fields, animals, and natural features, such a s stones, trees and bodies of water. For some groups in Borneo, the upperworld was symbolized by birds, and the underworld was watery, associated with crocodiles, fish and mythical serpents (*nagas* or dragons). The deceased are thought to remain a presence among the living or be reincarnated in their descendants, linking people with their progenitors.

Violent deaths or neglect can cause the dead to act harmfully, and spirits and other supernatural beings are dangerous if not treated appropriately. They are also thought to influence the success or failure of activities, present and future. Yet, spirits and ancestors can also bring blessings of protection, wealth and fertility to the living, and considerable effort is spent to propitiate or remember them (**1**), such as by living according to specific rules drawn from observing the surrounding environment, arranging the material world to please the spirits, or making offerings that range from incense, water and food to the sacrifice of animals or humans. Among some peoples, headhunting was once part of pleasing or honouring ancestors and spirits.

The role of a shaman, such as the Malay *bomoh* and the Myanmar *nat kadaw*, has been to act as an intermediary between the spirit and human worlds. Shamanism has long been the traditional means of healing, and shamans also produced ritual objects for these endeavours. While people now use modern medicine for many illnesses, traditional healing methods and shamanism continue to be widely practised, including in urban contexts, where they have been adapted to address new ways of life.

Across the region, art, expressed in sculpture and architectural forms or through offerings, feasts, sacrifices, music, oral histories, trance and performances, is thought to enable connections with the unseen world to ensure harmony, in accord with natural laws. Some spirits are an invisible essence, while named spirits are represented in art so that they are easily recognizable (**3**). In Myanmar, named *nat* spirits are associated with the kingdom, specific regions and royalty, and they each have their own iconography (**5**). Ancestor figures are kept by some groups, and this is sometimes associated with shamanism. Although there are a variety of ancestor figure types, the most prevalent is the seated or squatting form, often in male–female pairs (**2**). Usually the figures were carved nude, wearing jewelry, but they would have been wrapped in textiles or dressed with clothes and kept in a special location like the home or shrine. Guardian figures are often large and are placed to protect specific locations or areas of transition like entrances or crossroads (**4**).

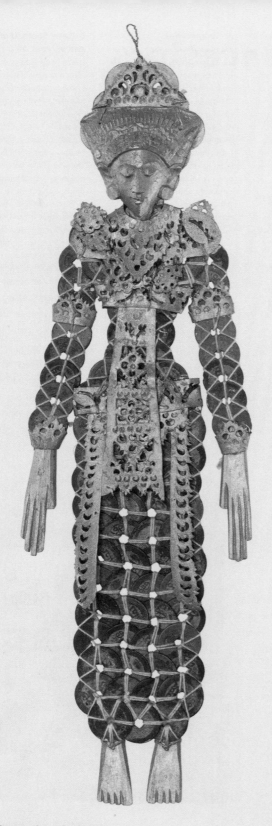

3. Dewi Sri

Dewi Sri, the goddess associated with rice and fertility, is still worshipped on predominantly Muslim Java and Hindu Bali. The figure of her here is formed of a pottery head, wooden hands and feet and paper decorations painted gold. The body is made of Chinese *cash* coins, which are often used for ritual purposes on Bali. The figure would have been hung in a temple pavilion.

1950s
Bali, Indonesia
Metal, pottery, paper, wood, fibre
Height 45 cm, width 10 cm
Donated by Eila Campbell,
As1994,20.3

4. *Hampatong*

Hampatong are images of ancestors and guardian figures used by many groups living on Borneo. They were placed in front of longhouses, chiefs' residences and headhunting and funerary shrines, as well as in places where there were believed to be malevolent spirits, such as cemeteries. The images vary stylistically among the different communities but are usually unpainted. The animal on this example's head would have been viewed as adding to its potency. Offerings were placed by *hampatong* to propitiate the spirits.

Late 19th century to mid-20th century
Kalimantan, Borneo
Wood
Height 198 cm, width 15 cm
As 1984,24.10

5. Kyaw Shein, *U Min Kyaw and servant Ah Ba Nyo*

U Min Kyaw Zaw is one of Myanmar's pantheon of thirty-seven *nat* spirits who are associated with kings and have died violent deaths. His attributes are alcohol, cock-fighting and horseback riding, as indicated by the imagery around him. There are links between *nat* beliefs and Buddhism: hence the Buddhist temple represented in the distance. U Min Kyaw Zaw's servant has been tattooed in traditional style across the thighs, arms and chest with repeated motifs, magic diagrams, protective Buddhist imagery and texts and potent animals.

Design 1979, painting early 1990s
Myanmar
Glass, pigment, metal foils, ink
Height 50 cm, width 39.6 cm
Donated by Ralph and Ruth Isaacs, 1996,0507,0.6

4 | 9 Funerary rituals

The size and diversity of Southeast Asia means that funeral practices are rich and varied, ranging from cremation by Buddhists and Hindus to burial by Christians, Muslims and a number of indigenous groups. Secondary treatment of the dead is also practised among some groups in the island region. This involves the retrieval of the bones after decomposition, their ritual treatment, and the re-interment of some or all of them in a different container, such as a ceramic jar or wooden box (2). Muslims require burial within twenty-four hours, while in communities that engage in secondary treatment of the dead the time between death and retrieval of the bones can be months or years. Among some island communities, funerals are major events that can take years to plan and occupy days or weeks of a community's time, as with the Toraja of Sulawesi. Rituals associated with death are accompanied by recitations, singing and dances, sometimes masked, as among the Batak of Sumatra (1). Funerals reaffirm the rank of the living and the dead, and provide opportunities for material and social exchanges.

Funerary traditions have a rich material culture. Besides sacrificial posts and ancestral sculptures, shrouds, coffins and other burial containers, specific clothing and cloths are produced for use by living participants, and temporary housing is constructed for guests. Objects are offered to, burned or buried with the dead to accompany them into the afterlife, as well as to maintain and enhance their rank. On Sumba, members of the nobility are buried with ceremonial mantles to indicate their high status in both worlds (3), and among the Toraja, high-ranking individuals are represented by effigies (4). Cemeteries are sometimes protected by carved images of ancestors (see p. 157). These traditions assist the dead to transition from worldly life to the afterworld and ensure that the dead view the living with favour.

1. Mask

Batak dancers once wore mourning masks to represent ancestors when they accompanied a high-status deceased person during secondary funeral rituals. Through this ritual, ancestors were assured that their descendants would continue to provide for them at ceremonial feasts, and they in turn were believed to ensure the future prosperity of the clan. Sometimes the masks were left by the grave, possibly a reference to the slaves that were once sacrificed to serve the dead in the ancestral world.

Early to mid-19th century
Sumatra, Indonesia
Wood, copper, hair
Height 30 cm, width 25 cm
Donated by S. R. Robinson,
As1895,0902.13

2. Jar

Made in Southeast Asia and China, these large jars were highly prized on Borneo as containers. They were also used as coffins, when the jar was cut in half for the insertion of the corpse, and in the secondary disposal of the dead, when the bones of the deceased were retrieved, cleaned, and some bones, particularly the skull, were placed inside. Because of the value of the jars, they also functioned as currency and were exchanged as marriage payments. They are still kept as heirlooms. Very old jars are thought by some people to be animated by powerful spirits.

18th–19th century
Possibly China
Glazed stoneware
Diameter 37 cm, height 79.3 cm
As1900,0616.1.a–j

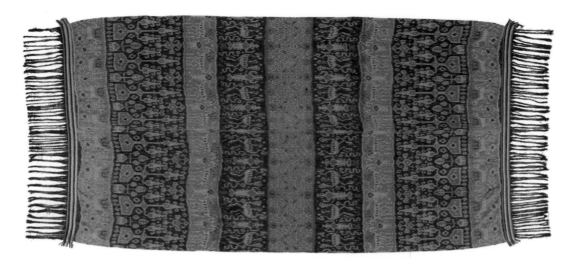

3. Waist and shoulder cloth (*hinggi*)

Full ceremonial dress for Sumbanese men included a *hinggi* cloth worn around the waist and over the shoulders as a mantle. Woven using the warp *ikat* method, in which the pattern is dyed into the warp yarns prior to weaving, these cloths were given by women's families as part of the gift exchange during marriage negotiations. Traditionally, men were buried in the cloths, and high-ranking individuals could be wrapped in dozens of examples.

19th century
Sumba, Indonesia
Cotton
Length 226 cm, width 119 cm
As 1949,09.1

4. Funerary figure (*tau-tau*)

Tau-tau figures are effigies of high-ranking people made from aged jackfruit wood. Called the 'soul that is seen', they are kept with the body during the extended funerary ceremony and accompany it when taken from the house to the rice granary and eventually to nearby limestone cliffs for interment. Caves and cliff grottoes have been sites for the disposal of the dead in Southeast Asia for tens of thousands of years.

Mid-20th century
Toraja people, Sulawesi, Indonesia
Jackfruit tree wood, textile, seed, bone, bamboo
Height 117.5 cm, width 35 cm
As 1987,01.88.a–l

4 | 10 Spirit papers

To honour and assist deceased ancestors, Southeast Asians of Chinese descent burn spirit papers during the annual Qingming tomb-sweeping festival, as well as on family anniversaries. Deceased family members are believed to use the offerings in the afterlife. This ritual fulfils filial duties in sustaining the family's ancestors, ensuring good fortune and prosperity for the living. The neglect of ancestors is believed to lead to their transformation into vengeful, dangerous and hungry ghosts.

Made of paper, the offerings include specially produced money (**4**), credit cards, passports, travel tickets and objects of daily use, such as clothing, televisions (**3**), cars and motorcycles (**1**), fans, pets (**2**), cooking equipment, jewelry, electronics, furniture and home decorations, fancy food and drinks and houses. Replicas of branded and high-end items are particularly popular. These goods are made in Southeast Asia in local workshops, but more recently it has been cheaper to import them from China.

1. Motorcycle
As Southeast Asian standards of living rose in the mid- and late 20th century, people replaced bicycle spirit papers with representations of motorcycles, which remain prevalent.

Mid-1980s
Penang, Malaysia
Paper, plastic
Height 107.1 cm, width 175 cm
As 1989,04.4

2. Dog

Dogs are popular pets in many parts of urban Southeast Asia. The burning of replicas such as this example would ensure that the deceased had an animal companion in the afterlife.

Mid-1980s
Bangkok, Thailand
Paper
Height 34 cm, length 62 cm
As1989,04.5

3. Television

Televisions were once an important symbol of status. This would be the fanciest model available at the time, and it is shown in full detail.

2000–2001
Singapore
Cardboard
Height 35.5 cm, width 39.5 cm
As2002,07.49.a

4. Banknote ('Hell money')

Printed to resemble legal tender, this banknote with a value of 1 billion yuan would become available to ancestors once it had been burned. The text states the value, the name Mingdu [Hell City] Bank, and that it is Hell money. The imagery represents auspicious Chinese symbols for good fortune, including bats, male children and a dragon. The boy in the rear holds a picture of the Chinese character 'fu' meaning good fortune, and the man appears in traditional-style Chinese official dress.

2000–2001
Singapore
Paper, plastic
Height 12.5 cm, width 23.8 cm
As2002,07.34

4 | 11 Spirits in Vietnam

Local traditions among many of the numerous cultural groups of Vietnam, including the Vietnamese Yao and Giê Trieng, include acknowledging and venerating nature, community or kinship deities and ancestor spirits (**1**). As a result of Chinese colonization and contact, Buddhism, particularly Mahayana conceptions and practices, Daoism and Confucianism also flourished. The Confucian god of agriculture was promoted at court from the 11th century, for instance. While China was the sole source for Daoist and Confucian ideas, Buddhism arrived via Chinese and Indian monks in the early 3rd century CE, becoming important among the general population in the 6th century with some concepts and practices remaining prevalent into the present (**2**). These three religions were called *tam gíao*, the three teachings, and they affected and intertwined with local beliefs (**3**). Daoist and local spirits overlapped and merged, for instance, and the monarchy also became linked with the ancestor spirits of great Vietnamese men. French Christian proselytizing began in the 17th century, but it was not until the late 19th that Christianity became a significant presence in Vietnam.

1. Guardian figure

Made of oblique twill weave (see p. 213) and painted by men, guardian figures replicating the shapes of humans or birds were placed in fields to deter both birds and malevolent spirits. The red, black and natural colouration of this example firmly links it with Southeast Asian aesthetics and colour symbolism dating back to early times.

Early 20th century
Probably Giê Trieng peoples, central Vietnam
Fibre, bamboo
Height 121 cm, width 110 cm
As 1956,06.1

2. Le Quoc Viet, *Ngày hoàng dao giò hoàng dao (Auspicious Day, Auspicious Hour)* woodblock

While there is a socialist-realist appearance to this woodblock, it also relates to the traditions of historical narrative and Buddhist paradise paintings that originated in China and the popular graphic art used to decorate Buddhist temples in Vietnam. The imagery indicates that if activities are undertaken at auspicious times, the spirit world will provide assistance to ensure the success of the endeavour. The artist Le Quoc Viet (b. 1972) grew up in a Buddhist environment, as a novice studying to be a monk between the ages of six and fifteen.

2001
Vietnam
Wood
Height 75 cm, width 145 cm
2003,0802.1

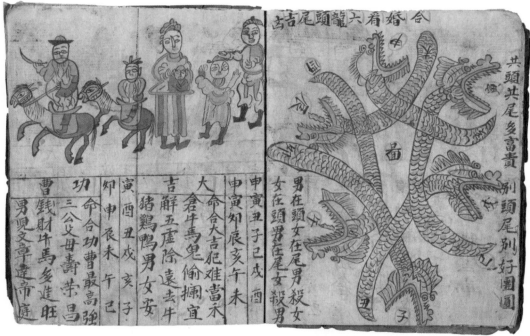

3. Shaman's book

Books were an essential part of a Yao shaman's repertoire and were usually produced by the shaman himself. Written with a brush and ink in Chinese characters and illustrated in two or three colours, they provide information on particular rituals, incantations and protective diagrams. Some relate to Daoism; others are medicinal books, astrology or divination manuals, ancestral records or even history texts. The diagram of the six serpents here represents the rotating *naga* formula used to determine auspicious times to undertake endeavours, such as house-building, in many parts of Southeast Asia, including Buddhist and Islamic cultures.

Mid-20th century
Yao peoples, northern Vietnam
Mulberry bark paper, fibre
Length 21.6 cm, width 18 cm
Funded by Pamela A. Cross,
2019,3032.1

4 | 12 Javanese amulets and their influence

Although used from the late 13th century until the present, bronze amulets were particularly popular on Java between the 15th and mid-18th centuries. They played a role in exorcisms, were placed in religious deposits at sacred sites and Javanese men wore them for protection, physical enhancement and as love charms (**3**). In areas with substantial contact with Java, including Bali and the east coast of present-day peninsular Malaysia, people also adopted these charms, primarily starting in the early 20th century.

Generally worn on a necklace or stitched to cloth, the amulets are usually shaped like Chinese coinage – round with a square hole in the centre – that functioned as currency in parts of island Southeast Asia into the 19th century. These Chinese coins were also used as ritual offerings, and in copying the shape, the amulets combined the idea of wealth with religious beliefs. Some of the later Islamic examples from the east coast of the Malay peninsula lack the central hole because they were based on British silver dollars.

The imagery on the amulets not only displays heroes from the Mahabharata epic in the style of shadow puppets (**1**), but also characters from *wayang gedog*, another theatrical form that narrates Prince Panji's adventures in search of his beloved Candra Kirana (**2**). The spiritual importance of epic literature and the ritually protective functions of the theatre on Java were transferred to the amulets through the imagery.

Islamic examples can display bearded figures holding a staff, who represent prophets and holy men, as well as Arabic inscriptions from the Qur'an invoking Allah's protection, magical formulae or declarations of the Islamic faith (**4**).

1. Amulet with characters from the Mahabharata
This amulet illustrates powerful characters from the Mahabharata (see pp. 190–91). On one side are the god Krishna and Arjuna, one of the Pandava brothers. On the other are Burisrava, a prince who joins the rival Koravas, and Karna, a complex character embodying various ethical and moral dilemmas, who fights on the Korava side despite his family relationship with the Pandavas. By showing characters associated with the Pandavas on one side and those fighting for the Koravas on the other, the forces are shown as stable, creating the balance sought by many Southeast Asian societies.

1500–1860
Java
Bronze
Diameter 5.95 cm
CH.661

2. Amulet with Panji imagery

Representing marriage and prosperity, the front of this charm shows Prince Panji and Princess Candra Kirana kneeling with a rice cone and water pot; on the reverse a woman kneels surrounded by domestic objects, including a spinning wheel and cooking pot. Other amulets with Panji imagery portray the prince's servants, Bancak and Doyok, or the prince on horseback making the ceremonial journey to claim his bride (see p. 190).

16th–18th century
Java, Indonesia
Bronze
Diameter 3.6 cm
Donated by Sophia Raffles, collected by Stamford Raffles, CH.646

3. Shadow puppet of the clown Bancak

Bancak is one of the clown servants from *wayang gedog* performances of the Panji narratives. In this representation, he wears one of the coin amulets on a cord around his neck.

Late 1700s–1816
Central Java, Indonesia
Hide, horn, gold
Length 49.5 cm, width 14.1 cm
Donated by William Raffles Flint, collected by Stamford Raffles, As1859,1228.579

4. One *dinar* protective coin

In southern Thai and Malaysian shadow puppet theatre (see pp. 202–03), performances begin with a ritual combat between two deities, which concludes upon the intervention of a holy man, like the one on this coin amulet, who restores harmony and balance to the universe. Here, he is in the form of a dervish carrying a begging bowl and water pot.

1950s
Malay peninsula
Silver
Diameter 3.6 cm
Donated by William Barrett, 2006,0929.7

4 | 13 The art of the Batak *datu*

Batak is a collective term for the six related peoples whose homeland is in the highlands of northern Sumatra and who share cultural, social, religious and artistic concepts. Once maintaining a deliberate self-isolation, the Batak region was forcibly opened up by Europeans in the mid-19th century, and by the early 20th century this led to the conversion of most Batak to Christianity and great changes to cultural and religious life, including the cessation of many traditions.

In addition to elaborately carved houses, ritual stone seats, tombs and objects of daily use, the Batak were once known for their literary skills, having developed a script based on old Javanese, as well as a ritual language called *poda* that is today almost obsolete. *Poda* was the preserve of male religious specialists called *datu*s, who were experts in the gods, spirits and black and white magic, as well as functioning as shamans and healers and determining the timing of ritual ceremonies. A magic staff (*tunggal panaluan*), a medicinal horn (*naga morsarang*), and a *pustaha* (book written in *poda*) were the three essential ritual objects made by *datu*s for their own use (**1, 2, 4**). They also developed ritual and seasonal calendars and inscribed amuletic imagery and charms on buffalo bone and bamboo to be worn around the body for protection (**3**). Although the objects were beautifully produced, it was their efficacy against negative forces that determined their importance.

1. Medicine container and stopper (*naga morsarang*)
As receptacles for magic substances, medicinal containers made from water buffalo horns with wooden stoppers were often carved in the shape of a protective creature that combined the characteristics of the mythical *singa* (a powerful animal) and *naga* (a mythical serpent) or buffalo.

Early 1800s to 1860s
Sumatra, Indonesia
Buffalo horn, bark, wood
Height 44 cm, length 51 cm
Donated by the Amsterdam
Zoological Society, As.7555.a–b

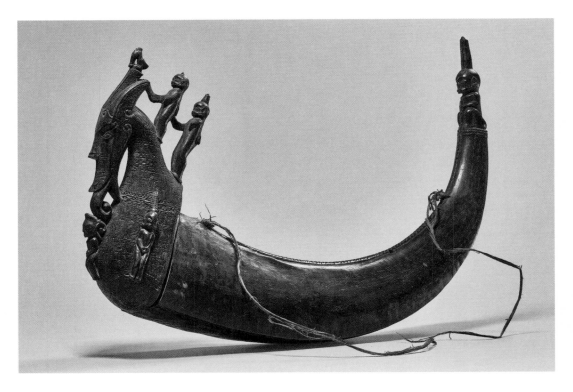

2. Book (*pustaha*)

Made of bark paper, folded
concertina-style between two
wooden boards, *pustaha* were
written by *datu*s as reference
works that recorded spells
and incantations, ranging from
love and divination formulae to
methods for removing enemies,
oracles, ritual procedures, and
recipes for potions. Only rarely
did they include records of
historical accounts or myths.
They were handed down
between *datu*s, each of
whom added to the contents
and to the listed genealogies.

19th century
Sibolga, Sumatra, Indonesia
Bark
Height 3.8 cm, width 9.6 cm
As 1913,1114.96

3. Oracle or amulet

*Datu*s often carved objects
for clients seeking protection,
cures for illnesses and advice
about engaging in activities such
as building a house, starting
a journey or marrying. This
example displays a combination
of texts written in *poda* and
ritually effective imagery of
stars and lizard-like forms
with human faces.

1850s–1930
Sumatra, Indonesia
Buffalo bone, fibre
Length (individual strips) 13.2
to 13.6 cm, width 1.8 to 1.9 cm
Donated by H. E. Miller,
As 1933,0307.39.a–e

4. Staff (*tunggal panaluan*)

Each *datu* carved his own magic
staff. The staff had several ritual
functions, including protection,
curing illness, making rain and
ensuring the fertility of the land,
people and livestock. The layers
of figures and animals carved
on the staffs refer to a Batak
origin myth, and in rituals, *datu*s
danced with their staffs and
rubbed them with the blood
of sacrificial animals.

Late 18th–mid-19th century
Sumatra, Indonesia
Wood, hair
Height 179.8 cm, width 4.7 cm
Donated by A. W. Franks,
As,+.3484

4 | 14 The island of Nias

Nias is the largest island off the western coast of Sumatra in the Indian Ocean, on what was once a major trade route. Remaining material culture, mostly from the 19th and early 20th centuries, shows that the island was culturally divided into three main areas – north, south and central – with highly stratified societies maintained through interclan warfare and headhunting and associated rituals.

Sculpted in stone and wood, ancestors played important and protective roles in Nias society. Ensuring fertility for people, land and animals, the largest wood sculptures (*adu siraha salawa*) represented the oldest known ancestor or an exceptional village leader and were given a place of honour within the clan house, which could hold hundreds or even thousands of such objects (**3**). The figures were carved nude but adorned with a high headdress and other jewelry to demonstrate their social rank. As is the case in many parts of Southeast Asia, status on Nias was partly confirmed by lavish feasts accompanied by the sacrifice of numerous animals. During feasts, people dressed as richly as possible in ceremonial headdresses, necklaces, anklets, bracelets and earrings, many of which were made of gold, as well as displaying their war dress (**1, 4**). Made of various metals, torques (*nifatali-tali*) were worn by men and women, but the *kalabubu* torque, made of gold, buffalo horn or graded discs of coconut shell, indicated a successful headhunter (**2**).

1. Sword (*telögu*) and sheath
The swords of Nias warriors who had successfully taken a head displayed hilts in the shape of a mythical composite beast called a *lasara*, which decorated all powerful objects. Each warrior also attached a personally assembled group of talismans, including small wooden ancestor figures, representations of hornbills and natural objects, to the sheath to protect himself during battles and raids.

Early to mid-19th century
Nias, Indonesia
Metal, wood, brass, cane, rattan
Length 68.7 cm, width 7.5 cm;
sheath length 53.9 cm, width 9.3 cm
Donated by the Amsterdam Zoological Society, As.7569.a–b

2. Torque (*kalabubu*)

Graduated buffalo horn discs that taper towards the ends over a brass core form this *kalabubu* torque. Such necklaces represented bravery and were restricted to noblemen who had participated in a successful headhunting raid.

Early to mid-19th century
Nias, Indonesia
Buffalo horn, metal, brass
Diameter 23.5 cm
Donated by the Amsterdam
Zoological Society, As.7571

3. Ancestral figure (*adu siraha salawa*)

This *adu siraha salawa* displays the features associated with ancestor figures of north Nias, including a seated posture, a cup held against the chest and the headdress and ornaments of a successful noble headhunter. After being activated by the final breath of the dying person, the figure was placed on the right wall of the main room of the house, where it was presented with sacrificial offerings.

Late 1700s–early 1820s
Northern Nias, Indonesia
Wood
Height 70.1 cm, width 11.9 cm
Donated by William Raffles Flint, collected by Stamford Raffles, As1859,1228.168

4. Shield

Besides being for protection in battle, shields were part of ceremonial attire. Made of a single piece of wood and shaped like a leaf with supportive ribs, Nias shields have a long extension capped with iron so that they can be rested on the ground. A central boss covers the area where the hand grasps the shield and provides additional protection when fighting.

Mid-19th century
Nias, Indonesia
Wood, iron
Height 121 cm, width 25 cm
Donated by the Amsterdam
Zoological Society, As.7568

4 | 15 Southeastern Maluku islands

The Maluku islands (Moluccas) in eastern Indonesia are known for their spices – cloves, nutmeg, mace – which once grew nowhere else. The peoples on these islands share cultural features, a result of the endemic warfare, raiding for slaves and water shortages that led to the regular movement of populations. The art from the numerous southeastern Maluku islands was once highly intricate, impressing 19th-century colonial visitors and becoming desirable to collectors in the early 20th century. Many of these objects were no longer produced after Christian missionaries converted the population, sometimes forcibly; and as society changed under colonization, such ritual objects became less relevant.

Related to beliefs about fertility, ancestors and social status, art forms ranged from sculpted figures and relief carving to textiles, drums (**2**) and jewelry (**3**), especially gold ornaments. Squatting figures carved in the round were once believed to serve as the homes of ancestral spirits who were installed in a sculpture through ritual ceremonies upon the death of a family member (**4**). Boats served as a metaphor for society, with the community viewed as the crew of a vessel. This related to mythical origin stories of a kind common to many parts of Southeast Asia, which tell of the arrival, often by boat, of exceptional male incomers who marry local females. Boats also played a physical role in Maluku. Used for journeys forming or renewing community alliances, trade and warfare, ceremonial outrigger boats were dug out of a single log and decorated with elaborate prow boards with spiral patterns and animal figures that represented guardian and ancestral spirits (**1**).

1. Ship prow board (*kora*)
In Maluku, as in many island areas, boats had ritual and social significance alongside their role as transport. Boats for important events were decorated with prow boards, which feature openwork spirals, often with an animal at the base, usually a rooster, snake, dog or fish, which was the emblem of the clan or village and a disguised ancestor. The dog seen here is symbolic of the bravery and aggressiveness necessary to become a successful headhunter.

c. 1850s–1870s
Ritabel, Tanimbar Islands, Maluku, Indonesia
Wood, hair, cowrie shell, cane
Height 111 cm, width 10.3 cm
Donated by A. W. Franks, collected by Henry Forbes, As,+.1876

2. Drum
In parts of southeastern Maluku, large standing drums were played at dances associated with festivities ensuring the fertility of the new year. In the 1880s Henry Forbes, a botanist who lived in the community for some months and collected this drum, described how men danced and sang accompanied by drums while guarding the village during periods of warfare.

Mid-19th century
Ritabel, Tanimbar Islands, Maluku, Indonesia
Wood, rattan, lizard skin
Diameter 15 cm, height 43.2 cm
Donated by the Royal Society, collected by Henry Forbes, As,HOF.36

3. Comb (*suar silai*)

At the beginning of the 20th century, this type of carved ivory and wood hair comb was reserved for use by senior men in the community. Earlier records indicate that once only warriors, chiefs and men who were successful in various competitions wore them as part of an ensemble to impress and intimidate enemies. The combs were inserted into the hair flat on the head with the handle, from which a plume of feathers extended, pointing backwards. Carved from a single piece of wood and inlaid with bone, the comb shares the designs and symbols associated with boat prows.

19th century
Ritabel, Tanimbar Islands, Maluku, Indonesia
Wood, bone
Height 13.3 cm, width 23.5 cm
Donated by the Royal Society, collected by Henry Forbes,
As,HOF.1

4. Ancestor figure

Ancestor figures from the southeastern Maluku islands are carved seated on a chair or stool, indicating their high status, with their arms resting upon their knees, and occasionally with a bowl in front, symbolic of the collection of offerings for spirits. Adorned with jewelry, figures typically have a long, tapering torso, a prominent nose, and features inlaid with shells. The carved figure would be ritually activated and placed on the top floor of the family home with other ancestral images when a family member died.

Late 19th–early 20th century
Leti, Maluku province, Indonesia
Wood
Height 50.5 cm, width 10 cm
Donated by the Wellcome Institute for the History of Medicine, As1954,07.182

1. Kettle

Kettles with Chinese elements, such as dragons, were found in many parts of the island world. They were manufactured in Brunei and were used at the court there and by Malays along the coast, while interior societies used them ceremonially, traded them like currency and kept them as a store of wealth.

Late 19th century
Sarawak, Borneo
Bronze
Height 29.6 cm, width 38.5 cm
As1908,0625.61.a–b

2. Shaman's box (*lupong manang*)

Iban shamans kept their equipment in boxes made of bark, plaited rattan and bamboo, and wood. These were powerful objects. There was a ritual when shamans made and incorporated them into their possessions, and they were handed down through generations as heirlooms. Sometimes they were decorated with figures used to treat illnesses, usually a male–female pair. Often the figures no longer match, as when one broke, it was simply replaced.

Mid- to late 19th century
Iban peoples, Borneo
Bark, wood, rattan
Height 30.2 cm, width 20 cm
As1906,0529.1.a–b

Borneo

Borneo is the world's third largest island and home to numerous cultural groups, including Malays, Chinese and people often collectively called Dayak, some of whom live on the coasts and others inland in the rainforest. For thousands of years, these communities have traded metalwork, pottery, luxury goods and forest products, such as aromatic woods, hornbill ivory, birds' nests, rubber, beeswax and camphor (1). Chinese goods reached inland communities in the 14th century, where the objects were treasured as heirlooms and used in already extant prestige traditions.

Archaeological evidence suggests that Borneo was first occupied about 40,000 years ago, but subsequently experienced multiple waves of arrivals from different parts of the island region. Within the past 2,000 years, some of the coastal areas saw the emergence of Hindu–Buddhist

polities, with most ideas arriving via Java and Srivijaya, rather than directly from India (see p. 61), and the Majapahit empire (c. 1293–1527) extended its control over parts of southern Borneo. The coastal polities started converting to Islam in the 15th, 16th and 17th centuries after Melaka became a major entrepôt and converted in the 1430s. Brunei became a prominent trading post in the 16th century and the ruler converted to Islam, but religious changes did not interrupt coastal–inland and far-reaching trading patterns. It has been assumed that the small-scale societies were ethnically different from the coastal peoples; in reality, as in much of Southeast Asia, ethnicity was flexible. Coastal Dayak peoples intermarried with traders from the Arab world and India; some eventually converted to Islam and came to be called Malays, who dominated the coastal

3. Bodice (*rawai*)
Iban women traditionally wore bodices (*rawai*) of small brass rings threaded on hoops of rattan. Worn over *ikat* skirt cloths, *rawai* covered either the hips, stomach and waist, or everything from the breasts to the upper thighs. Men wore smaller versions around their legs. The brass would have come from trade with coastal communities.

Late 19th century
Baram River District, Sarawak, Borneo
Cane, brass
Diameter 32 cm, height 19.2 cm
As1904,0416.6

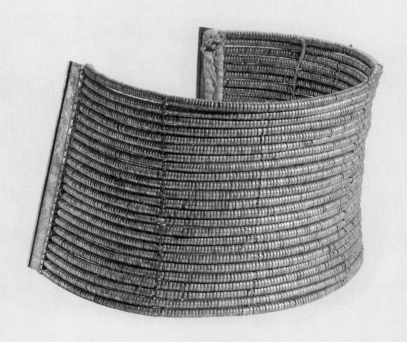

4. House board

Longhouses were once a widespread form of housing on Borneo, as well as in the Mentawai islands and highland Vietnam. Designed to accommodate multiple households, they usually consist of separate apartments, with each family responsible for maintaining their part of the building. Among hierarchical societies, such as the Kayan, the chief's section could be decorated with panels carved and painted with imagery indicative of their rank. This example displays the mythical *aso* dog-dragon motif in stylized form.

19th century
Baram River District, Sarawak, Borneo
Wood
Height 34.8 cm, width 276 cm
As 1905,-.797

5. Baby carrier

Baby carriers were decorated with designs that indicated the child's rank, as well as protective charms, such as bells, shell discs, tusks and teeth, and talismanic beads, to ward off malevolent spirits and ensure the good health of the child. Often made by the grandmother of a child, such carriers could take up to three months to complete.

Late 19th century
Kenyah peoples, Borneo
Wood, shell, glass, vegetal fibre
Height 31 cm, width 37 cm
As 1904,0416.104

kingdoms. The island today is divided among three countries – Brunei, Malaysia and Indonesia – because of colonial history. What became the Malaysian state of Sabah was largely controlled by the British North Borneo company, while present-day Sarawak state was ruled by the Brooke Rajahs from 1841 until 1946, when the territory was ceded to the British. Brunei opted not to join the Federation of Malaysia upon its independence in 1958; internal self-rule began in 1959, and it became fully independent in 1984. The Dutch part of the island was ceded to Indonesia only in 1950.

As the island was drawn into colonial capitalism in the 19th century, many Dayak groups were converted to Christianity, which Europeans saw as a means of 'civilizing' the locals and promoting European law and order, as well as undermining the Islamic states. The Europeans were in turn fascinated by, admiring of, and horrified by the small-scale cultures of Borneo. They aimed to eliminate headhunting and other practices that they considered 'savage', and this was relatively successful. Raiding and slave trading largely ended with colonial control.

In the process of interacting with Borneo's peoples, Europeans formed collections of objects that reflected fundamental ideas about the world held by these societies, as well as locally available materials and their trade networks (**3**). Some

groups have developed highly stratified societies, such as the Kayan and Melanau (**4, 5**), while others, such as the Iban, are strongly merit based, and this too is reflected in artistic production. While beautiful and requiring great skill to produce, Dayak objects serve functions both practical and spiritual. Many things are made to please and propitiate spirits, encourage their support and protect the wearer or user. Besides a principal deity or two deities, Dayak societies recognize natural and ancestral spirits. There is an upperworld and an underworld, in addition to the human one, and contact with the spiritual world comes through dreams, bird messengers (especially the hornbill), animals and shamanism (**2**). While headhunting was part of inter-group engagement, it was associated with the fertility and well-being of humans and animal and vegetal resources. Today, some rituals once linked with headhunting have been transferred to celebrate other difficult endeavours, such as long journeys or harvest festivals. Other practices fell out of use in the 20th century as they became less relevant to changing lifestyles. New materials, such as chemical dyes and synthetic fibres, have been embraced, but recently there has been renewed interest in earlier craft methods, as well as the ideas and beliefs associated with them, with the rise of a pan-Borneo Dayak identity.

4 | 16 Melanau sickness figures

The traditionally seafaring Melanau people live primarily in Sarawak state. While all are now Muslim or Christian, before the 20th century the Melanau engaged in healing practices based on animistic beliefs, and although these ideas remain in some cases, the related healing practices have largely ceased through lack of relevance to modern Melanau communities.

Some diseases were once thought to be caused by spirits who had wandered from their proper place, and part of the cure involved carving a sickness figure (*bilum* or *dakan*) to restore the balance of the unwell person's body and to assist the spirit to depart. Once the disease had been diagnosed by a spirit medium, the specialist carver rapidly created the figure from the soft pith of the sago palm, starting with the feet and finishing with the eyes or the ears. A repertoire of images, each associated with a particular disease, was used, and more than 140 such spirits were once known. Specific signs distinguished the spirit types, none of which could be omitted or changed.

After completion, the image was activated near the patient by chanting invocations and then kept close by for three days to force the spirit into it. After this, the figure was considered dangerous and was taken to a place associated with its spirit type – a river for water spirits (**3**), a relevant piece of ground for earth ones (**4**), and a tree for air spirits (**1, 2**) – to help the spirit begin its homeward journey.

In the late 20th century, carvers started making sickness figures for the tourist market.

1. *Naga terbang* figure
Some spirits had companions, human or animal, and in other instances, the spirits manifested themselves in the form of an animal, such as the *naga*, which is said to have arisen from the python or scaly anteater. There are several *naga* categories, and *naga terbang* (flying *naga*) have horns, legs with bird-claw feet, a spiked tail curved over the back and wings (here shown with a scaly pattern). They cause coughs and fever, and the figures would be hung from a roof or tree as they are associated with the air.

Late 19th century
Igan River region, Sarawak, Borneo
Sago palm pith
Height 65.5 cm, length 191.5 cm
As 1905,-785

2. Figure of a *langit bilum*

This may be a *dalong separa langit*, an air spirit that causes fever and sores. It is represented as a squatting figure with wings on the back, bird claws and a hairy body indicated by striated lines. The shaman would determine where to hang it once the spirit had entered.

Late 19th century
Igan River region, Sarawak, Borneo
Sago palm pith
Height 48.8 cm, width 11 cm
As 1905,-.651

3. *Durhig* water spirit

There are several sub-categories of *durhig* spirits, not all of which are associated with water, but most of which are female. Water spirits are represented seated, with flat eyes and spiky headdresses, and some have scaly appearances or tails. Most cause diseases of the digestive tract, and the figures would be deposited by water.

Late 19th century
Igan River region, Sarawak, Borneo
Sago palm pith
Height 44 cm, width 14 cm
As 1905,-.637

4. Tiong bin Nyalay, Carving of *geragasi tugan*

Earth spirit *bilum* have protruding eyes and hold a blowpipe, another weapon, or their tongue. They are disposed of on the forest floor. The fierce earth spirit *geragasi tugan*, seen here, has a hairy face and tusks and eats humans. Initially causing bloody vomit, it later drives the invalid mad. This example was one of many commissioned by Stephen Morris, an anthropologist, to record the tradition.

1971
Melanau peoples, Oya District, Sarawak, Borneo
Sago palm pith
Height 35 cm, width 13 cm
Donated by George Morris, collected by Stephen Morris, As 1994,05.55

4 | 17 Headhunting

Headhunting was significant among most interior groups on Borneo, except the nomadic Penan, but was practised only occasionally, often after the death of a prominent person. Among all groups, heads were revered and treated with care, because communal well-being was believed to depend on them. They restored cosmic order, maintained correct relationships with ancestors and spirits, and ensured the fertility of the group and its livestock and crops. Heads were a vital part of rituals associated with life and death, as they were necessary to end a period of mourning and were thought to accompany the deceased on its journey to the land of the dead. Headhunting was also political, as the various groups competed for resources and expanded territorially.

Shields, swords, caps and cloaks were made for use in warfare and headhunting and the rituals associated with them. Asymmetrical, repeating and intertwining mythical figures, deities and spirits, demonic faces, serpents and birds and curvilinear designs beautified the objects, but were also meant to be visually disconcerting to confuse and overwhelm the enemy. Shields, swords and sheaths were decorated with hair from previous victims to intimidate opponents (**2**, **4**). Designs associated with victory, fertility and status were carved or painted on sword sheaths, and powerful beads were attached for protection (see p. 110). Successful warriors and high-ranking men additionally wore special adornments and accoutrements (**1**, **3**).

1. War cap
Hornbill feathers were attached to caps for high-ranking men who had displayed bravery in warfare and headhunting raids. This elaborate example is embellished with dyed goat hair, metal plaques and braid over a cane frame. Such caps were used in ceremonies associated with war, headhunting and fertility.

Late 19th century
Kayan or Kenyah peoples
Cane, goat hair, metal, hornbill feathers
Length 71 cm, width 30 cm
As1900,-.680

2. Shield
On this shield, painted eyes and fangs are surrounded by human hair from previous raids to dismay the enemy. Under the hair are images of vine tendrils that contribute a sense of movement to the design, intended to disconcert opponents while protecting the bearer. Shields were also practical, being

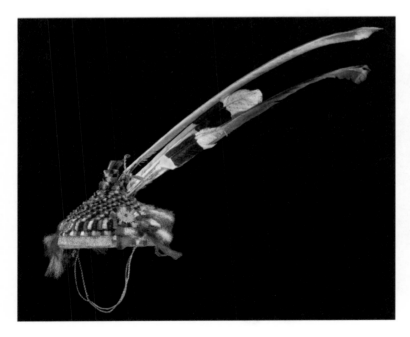

made of light, strong wood with horizontal woven rattan bands for reinforcement and a raised central line to deflect attacks. This shield is of Kenyah origin, but similar shields were adopted by other groups on Borneo.

Early 20th century
Kenyah peoples
Wood, iron, human hair
Height 117.2 cm, width 38 cm
As 1948,01.25

3. War cape
Among the stratified Kenyah societies, men of high rank and prowess had war capes made of hornbill feathers, shell, beads, hair and animal hide, including leopard, bear, goat and orang-utan. The shell disc would lie on the chest with the feathers cascading down the back.

Late 19th century
Kenyah peoples
Goat hide, hair, hornbill feathers, shell, glass beads
Length 173 cm, width 66.2 cm
As 1905,-.438

4. Sword and sheath
On Borneo there is evidence of ore smelting from about the 10th century, and Kenyah and Kayan men were known for their ability to forge high-quality iron swords, often embellished with fretwork and inlays along the upper edge. This hilt is heavily carved with the spirit of a trophy head and designs of leeches, associated with blood and water, connecting the fertility generated by headhunting with female agricultural activity. Elaborately decorated with beads marking status, the sheath is also covered in hair and the powerful *aso* dog-dragon design.

19th century
Kayan peoples
Iron, wood, human hair, glass, deer antler, vegetal fibre
Length 69.4 cm; sheath length 102.3 cm (including beads)
As 1905,-.717.a–b

4 | 18 *Pua* ceremonial cloths

Iban societies are meritocracies. Success in headhunting and battle once demonstrated the personal valour of Iban men, established their communal status and prestige and made them desirable marriage partners. While men strove to prove their prowess in these ways, Iban women demonstrated their abilities and acquired social rank by weaving warp *ikat* (see p. 213), ceremonial cloths called *pua*. Dyeing and weaving were known as 'women's warfare', and a woman's skills indicated her marriageability and were celebrated socially.

Pua patterns are abstractions from the natural world, ranging from rocks, clouds and water to floral and animal forms, heads and eyes, geometric shapes and objects of cultural relevance, such as boats (**1**). The oldest and most valued pattern was the small, tight coil, which was thought to encourage headhunting (**2, 3**). Originating in dreams believed to be sent by the gods, many designs were viewed as magically potent and required a spiritually strong woman to produce them. Ritually powerful *pua* were given praise-names and ranked by their effectiveness at inviting the protection of the deities. The potent cloths were used to form barriers against evil, invoke blessings from ancestors, demarcate sacred spaces, cover shrines and corpses, wrap newborns and receive severed heads. They were also worn at major events, kept as heirlooms and used as gifts or payment for ritual fees.

Before the late 19th century, women used such natural dyes as indigo, which produces a blue colour, and morinda, which creates the highly valued reddish-brown hue, as well as locally grown cotton yarns. These are still used by some weavers, but most examples are now made from commercial thread and synthetic dyes. Many Iban converted to Islam or Christianity in the 19th and 20th centuries, yet *pua* continue to be produced, including for the tourist market.

1. *Pua gajai*
The important bamboo plant is represented by the large triangular forms at each end of this *pua*, while the centre consists of repeating images of stylized birds. The latter pattern is found on textiles in several Iban areas, indicating that it originated before the communities migrated apart. The diverse Iban people now live in many areas on Borneo, including Sarawak (Malaysia), west Kalimantan (Indonesia) and Brunei.

Early to mid-19th century
Iban peoples, Saribas region, Borneo
Cotton
Length 202 cm, width 105 cm
As 1905,-.405

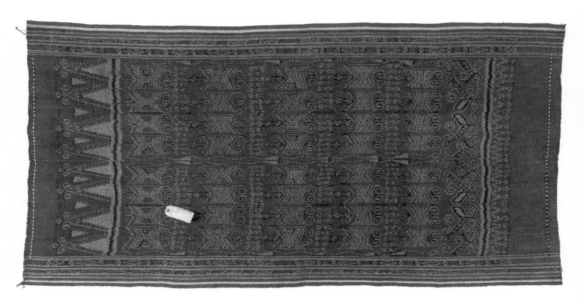

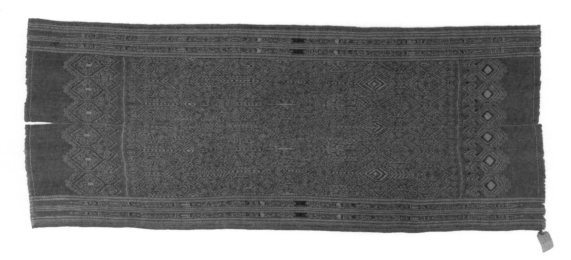

2. Pua bali bugau kantu
Framed by end panels and borders, this *pua*'s centrefield is composed of laterally symmetrical repeats with the imagery changing along the length of the cloth. A cloth's name is chosen by the weaver based on the main design, originating with the natural world and dreams sent by spirits. If a design proves potent, it is reinterpreted by other weavers. Demonstrating the difficulty of identification by anybody other than the weaver herself, the name of this *pua* pattern has been associated with successful warfare by some people and listed as without reliable identification by others.

Mid- to late 19th century
Iban peoples, Saribas region, Borneo
Cotton
Length 197 cm, width 82 cm
As 1905,-.410

3. Pua buah baya
On this cloth, the diamond-like pattern on the ends is called *selaku*, sometimes believed to be where Kumang, the guardian of weavers, resides. The central section, called *buah* (fruit), contains the main design of stylized crocodiles, who were thought to be protective spirits, with smaller coil and other motifs filling the empty spaces. This decoration could only have been woven by a high-ranking and spiritually powerful woman, because it depicts imagery associated with headhunting, such as fruit in the border representing untaken heads.

Mid-19th century
Iban peoples, Rejang River region, Borneo
Cotton
Length 254 cm, width 130 cm
Donated by Margaret Brooke, Ranee of Sarawak, As 1896,0317.6

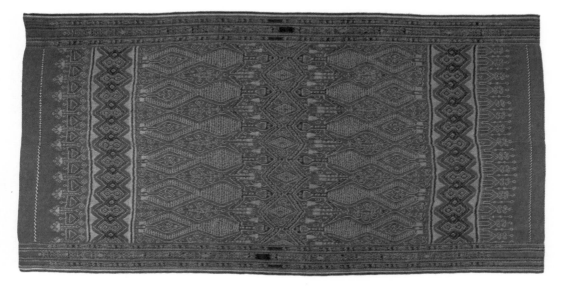

4 | 19 Iban hornbill sculptures

Birds play a central role in the animistic beliefs of many Borneo societies. The most significant birds are the rhinoceros hornbill and the brahminy kite, both widely associated with power and the ancestors. Among the Iban of Borneo, as with many island Southeast Asian groups, the underworld connects with serpents, femaleness and agriculture and the upperworld with birds and maleness. Associated with headhunting, the rhinoceros hornbill was thought to be a messenger to the god of war, Sengalang Burong, who was himself thought to be a brahminy kite.

The Iban made sculptures of hornbills, called *kenyalang*, which were displayed at feasts to honour Sengalang Burong and celebrate fruitful headhunting expeditions (**1, 2**). Only men who had taken heads could host such a feast, and the number of sculptures displayed indicated the number of successful headhunters in a family. In Iban society, within which status was achieved through personal ability and success, these events enhanced the rank of the host. At the end of the festival, which lasted several days, the *kenyalang* were consecrated and mounted on tall poles, and the spirit of the hornbill was thought to fly and weaken the enemy.

As it was believed to be a dangerous task, producing *kenyalang* required a number of rituals, including sacrifices to the tree being cut down and ceremonies to receive the tree in the village. While most *kenyalang* examples in museums and collections are made of painted softwood, there is evidence that older examples were once carved in hardwoods and left unpainted. Since the mid-20th century, the traditional format has changed to adapt to contemporary contexts in which many Iban are Muslim or Christian (**3**).

1. Kenyalang

Specialist carvers created hornbill sculptures with disproportionately large bills and tail feathers, reflecting the fact that the bird's casque was prized and its tail feathers decorated helmets, shields and sheaths for protection.

Early to mid-19th century
Saribas, Borneo
Wood
Height 59 cm, width 76.1 cm
Donated by George Darby
Haviland, As1894,0414.1

2. Kenyalang

Carvers first outlined the main features of the *kenyalang* in the forest, then brought it to the longhouse, where its arrival was accompanied by bards chanting literary texts and by offerings, and a month later added the details. Different communities produced *kenyalang* of varying appearances and sizes, following a standard formula but with individual detailing: in this case, elaborate floral tracery.

Late 19th century
Iban peoples, Borneo
Wood
Height 67.5 cm, length 107 cm
As 1905,-.819

3. Kenyalang

Despite the *kenyalang*'s intimate connection with headhunting and warfare, which are no longer practised, because they are important cultural markers they have been incorporated into other major communal events such as rice festivals. This example was used at a feast at the village of Skrang Skim on 28 June 1974 and again in 1975 at Lubok Antu. Although the spirit in the *kenyalang* departs once mounted on a pole, it can be summoned back with a special ceremony, enabling the reuse of the sculpture. Like *pua* cloths, the *kenyalang* are given praise-names, although this one's was not recorded.

1973
Sarawak, Borneo
Wood
Length 239.1 cm, height 116.1 cm
As 1977,06.1

Tattooing was once practised by many societies in Southeast Asia, including the peoples of Borneo. Since the afterworld was viewed as the mirror opposite of this life, the dark-coloured tattoos would be bright after death, guiding the deceased on the journey to the land of the dead. Among the Kelabit peoples, in the legend of the mythical ideal man, Tuked Rini, his wife says: 'I am a beautifully tattooed woman, tattooed with the soot from *damar* resin, With tattoo patterns laid out in the shadowy darkness ...' (Janowski 2014, 77).

Tattooing was carried out on both men and women and varied between the Borneo groups (**1, 2**). Europeans did not view tattooing positively but found the practice fascinating, collecting models and tattoo stamps in large quantities (**3**). Although the practice has become less popular as older cultural and religious practices have become less relevant in Christian, Muslim and globalized contexts, traditional tattooing has enjoyed a revival among some people on the island in recent years.

Among the Kayan peoples, tattoos (*tedek*) once indicated the achievements of a person (such as success in a headhunting expedition), ornamented the body to make a person attractive and marriageable, and functioned as protective motifs, as well as marking aristocratic status in highly stratified communities. Using a sharp needle and a special hammer, female tattoo artists forced the ink – made of soot, fat and sugarcane juice – under the skin. Different designs were associated with varying ranks. The mythical dog-like *aso* creature was used for chiefs, and a four-line pattern indicated a commoner's status. Other motifs drew on the natural world, including the full moon presented as concentric circles; various flora, such as ferns, tuba roots and aubergine flowers; and animals, such as the prawn and the dog, who had an honoured place in Kayan society. The representation of precious glass beads called *lukut* was another important motif.

1. Tattoo stamp
Tattoo designs were first drawn by hand or marked on the skin with stamps. This example shows common hook motifs that would be tattooed onto the thighs. Men were tattooed as boys and after major events with free-flowing designs on their thighs, hands, arms and shoulders, a process that could take several years owing to the ritual requirements and cost.

Late 19th century
Kayan peoples, Sarawak, Borneo
Wood
Height 16 cm, width 9.5 cm
Donated by Margaret
Brooke, Ranee of Sarawak,
As1896,0317.74

2. Tattooing stamp

Tattoo stamps took the form of inked wooden blocks, carved by men. Tattooing on both men and women was extensive, covering large parts of the body. Among the Kayan, designs covering women's forearms, backs of the hands, the thighs and the metatarsals consisted of abstract motifs associated with the natural world and fertility. Here, there are floral designs and eyes of the *aso* dog-dragon.

19th century
Kayan peoples, Baram River
District, Sarawak, Borneo
Wood
Height 35.2 cm, width 5.7 cm
As 1905,-.310

3. Model of a tattooed arm

This model arm displays designs appropriate for a Kayan woman. Before tattooing commenced there were ceremonies for the propitiation of spirits, and both the tattoo artist and the client were subject to various restrictions. Tattooing was not carried out during times of sickness, death or rice sowing, and particular foods were proscribed during the process.

Late 19th century
Kayan peoples, Baram River
District, Sarawak, Borneo
Wood
Height 35.5 cm, width 5.2 cm
As 1905,-.300

Timeline

Late 8th–early 9th centuries	Construction of Candi Borobudur and Candi Prambanan in central Java with extensive narrative reliefs
12th–16th centuries	Production of narrative reliefs in east Java showing shadow puppet-like imagery
12th–19th centuries	Production of wall paintings in Myanmar that link with literary and recitation arrangements
15th century	Possible development of Thai *nang yai* shadow theatre, which is related to the Cambodian form *sbek thom*
Early 16th century	Emergence of Thai *khon* dance-drama, possibly in connection with the *nang yai* shadow theatre
17th century	Kamasan becomes a centre for painting on Bali
	Thai banner painting is incorporated into a Buddha image, indicating the early importance of the art form by the reuse of such sacred objects in varying contexts
18th–19th centuries	Small metal figures of the Buddhas of the past and events from the historic Buddha's life are included in sealed relic chambers in Myanmar
19th–early 20th centuries	Probable emergence in the current format of the long story cloths used in northeast Thailand and Laos during the Bun Phra Wet festival
Early 20th century	Decline of court performances
	Production of Thai banner paintings wanes
1998	Shadow theatre banned in Malaysia as being un-Islamic
Late 20th to early 21st centuries	Thai *khon* dance-drama, Indonesian shadow theatre and gamelan are inscribed as UNESCO intangible world heritage

5 Narrative and performance

Narrative plays a major role in Southeast Asian art, with stories danced, sung, recited and dramatized across all echelons of society, as well as being carved, painted and reproduced in myriad ways. This is clear early on from epic literature, and also from wall paintings at Bagan in Myanmar (*c.* 11th–13th centuries) and relief sculpture at such sites as Borobudur and Prambanan in central Java (*c.* 770s–850s), temples in eastern Java (11th–15th centuries), the Bayon in Cambodia (late 12th century), and Wat Si Chum at Sukhothai (late 14th century). Storytelling was a major way of transmitting fundamental values, ethics and mores, and is still relevant in contemporary society.

1. Processional figure
Showing the strong connections between ritual and shadow theatre in Balinese religious practices, this dancing figure in the form of a shadow puppet of a soldier from the Panji story cycle was once used in Balinese religious processions, possibly those associated with cremations.

Late 1700s to mid-1800s
Bali, Indonesia
Rattan, bamboo, bark, wood
Length 87 cm, width 37.4 cm
As.7183

2. J. Wetherall, Drawing of Bima from Candi Sukuh
Characters from the Mahabharata and Ramayana became important in a variety of religious contexts. At the 15th-century Candi Sukuh temple on Mount Lawu in central Java, a stone relief sculpture shows the character Bima from the Mahabharata defeating an enemy while a clown servant watches. The replication of shadow puppet imagery and the character, who is believed to have great spiritual power, in sculpture demonstrates the ritual importance of both the story and the theatrical medium. Europeans did not understand the imagery of the temple, here drawing Bima's headdress like foliage curling around his head.

1811–15
Candi Sukuh, Java, Indonesia
Pencil on paper
Height 18.2 cm, width 26.3 cm
Donated by J. H. Drake,
collected by Stamford Raffles
1939,0311,0.7.98

Performance has been an important religious, social and artistic medium in Southeast Asia. There are many different forms, ranging from dance to dance-dramas and masked performances. Puppet theatre is another major type, particularly shadow theatre where puppets are used to cast shadows on a screen. Performances are associated with the spirit world and have been considered a way of communing with it. They help fulfil vows, function as offerings to spirits and ancestors at major life events, and are considered to depict ideal standards and principles (**2**). Given such connections, narrative imagery and performances often occur in religious settings.

Because of the theatre's popularity and its connections to ritual and the supernatural, other art forms, such as painting, sculpture, comic books and video games, also depict the characters and mimic the presentation of performances by using similar imagery (**1**). In many different ways, people have identified with particular characters, reified or rethought cultural norms and absorbed the powers generated through performance: some amulets, for example, depict shadow

3. Textile hanging with scenes from the Ramayana

The Ramayana was portrayed through theatrical performances, but also in stone, textile and ceramic. *Kalaga* or *shwe-gyido* are tapestries once used as room separators at court, in monasteries and in residences, as well as for wall decorations, horse and elephant trappings and coffin covers in Myanmar. The example here shows several scenes, including one found only in Southeast Asian versions of the epic – Hanuman the white monkey fighting the giant crab that was destroying the bridge to Lanka, the residence of the demon Ravana.

Late 19th–early 20th century
Myanmar
Cotton, flannel, sequins, metal-wrapped threads
Height 53.5 cm, length 290 cm
Donated by Henry Ginsburg,
2011,3013.1

puppet characters and forms (see pp. 165–66); in the 19th century, the Myanmar royal court modelled official dress on the costumes of the Thai theatre; and narrative reliefs replicate story cloths.

Performance and oral literature are less prominent today, but have remained relevant as a means of communication: shadow puppet theatre was used to promote birth control in Indonesia and Thailand in the mid-20th century, for example. Buddhist narratives, epic poems and other stories continue to play roles in rituals and as entertainment, although court performances, particularly in Thailand and Cambodia, have ceased. Some theatre forms retain symbolic and ritual importance, such as on Bali and Java and in southern Thailand.

In imagery and performance, Buddhist and Hindu narratives, Christian stories and Islamic legends mix with

numerous local folk tales and fables, as well as contemporary global stories such as *Star Wars*. Three epic stories can be found across many parts of Southeast Asia: the Mahabharata, the Ramayana and the Panji narratives. The last, which appears to have originated on Java and spread to other Indonesian islands and mainland Southeast Asia, concerns the adventures and trials of Panji, the legendary prince of Janggala, as well as the political activities and wars of his kingdom (1). They have come to have associations with Sufi Islam on Java, and a version of the Panji stories called Malat was prevalent on Bali until the 1930s. Both the lengthy Mahabharata and Ramayana epic poems originated in India and spread to Southeast Asia. The Mahabharata tells of the Pandava and Korava cousins who battle over the sovereignty of the kingdom of Kuruksetra, assisted by gods, deities, ogres and demons. It remains

**4. Stupa deposit representing
the Great Departure**
Images of the Buddhas of
the past and scenes from
Gotama Buddha's life were
sometimes depicted as a series
of metal figurines. These were
usually deposited in stupa
relic chambers by devotees
to enhance merit, add to the
building's sanctity and preserve
the religion from decline. Here,
to reject worldly life, Prince
Siddhartha (soon to become
the Buddha Gotama) departs
from his father's palace on his
horse Kanthaka. Chana, his
groom, clutches the horse's tail,
a typical depiction in Myanmar
art. The horse's hooves are held
aloft by deities to ensure that the
departure is silent and therefore
unhindered.

18th–19th century
Konbaung Myanmar
Bronze or brass
Height 23 cm
Donated by Florence MacDonald,
1981,1023.1

widespread on Java and Bali, particularly in shadow puppet
theatre, but is less popular elsewhere in Southeast Asia. The
Ramayana centres on the demon Ravana's abduction of Prince
Rama's wife, Sita. In the prince's quest to regain his wife, he is
aided by Hanuman, the white monkey. In Malaysia, emphasis
was placed on Ravana's role with the renaming of the story as
Great Forest King. In mainland Southeast Asia, the Ramayana
was once performed frequently and represented in sculpture
and painting in Myanmar, Thailand, Cambodia and Laos.

Adapted in Hindu, Buddhist and Islamic contexts to suit
local cultural and spiritual values, the three story cycles

have been told and retold in countless iterations as artists, puppeteers and others have embellished skeleton plot elements, characters and relationships to create relevant narratives for contemporary environments. For example, on Java, Arjuna, one of the Pandava brothers, has become the main character of the Mahabharata and the quintessential hero – handsome, strong and virtuous. New adventures using traditional characters from the epics are called branch and twig stories in Malaysia and Indonesia, and in all contexts additional characters, such as the clowns in shadow theatre, have been developed (**3**).

The tales of the previous lives of Gotama Buddha (the historic Buddha), of his final life in which he became a Buddha, and of the lives of the Buddhas of the past are also prevalent on the mainland (**4**). These and other Buddhist stories demonstrate the exceptionalism of enlightened beings, tell of the virtues necessary to become a Buddha, are a source of merit, and enable people to feel a part of the Buddha's community.

In some instances, such as the Panji tales or the Javanese Damarwulan cycle of stories that tells of a legendary hero engaged in the battles between the kingdoms of Majapahit and Blambangan, association with changing royal courts resulted in a decline over the 20th century, and performances and representations are now rare. In other instances, sponsorship has shifted, as in the case of *nang yai* shadow theatre in Thailand where remaining troupes are now based at Buddhist monasteries, rather than the royal court. Today, the epics, folk tales and Buddhist narratives are also told in modern forms, such as graphic novels, magazine entries, cartoons, films and serial television programmes. Buddhist stories are also painted in modern contexts, as can be seen at Wat Buddhapadipa in Wimbledon in the United Kingdom. In 1998, Thai King Bhumibol Adulyadej (r. 1950–2016) published his own cartoon version of the Mahajanaka Jataka. However, new stories based on novels and films with new heroes and villains are emerging too. UNESCO has acknowledged the importance of narrative and performance in Southeast Asia by inscribing some of these art forms on the list of intangible world heritage.

5|1 Kamasan painting from Bali

The village of Kamasan in southeastern Bali is famous for its paintings, dating back to the 17th century, and its specialists in drawing and painting (*sangging*) once were in service to the kings and nobles of the many kingdoms on Bali.

Ceilings, canopies, flags, banners and coffin covers are among the objects that were painted. There are several main formats: square, rectangular (**2**), or long, narrow strips called *ider-ider* that were hung in the eaves or ceilings of religious and palace pavilions (**1, 3**). Paintings were also used as offerings.

Before the arrival of modern paints, all artists used natural mineral and vegetal dyes and soot; some continue to do so. Painting is a communal activity, with the design sketched out by the master artist and filled in by apprentices and colour specialists, many of whom are women. The form of imagery relates strongly to the Balinese shadow puppet theatre tradition and relief sculptures from east Java, with which Bali once had close connections. As with puppets, the inner nature of each painted character is made clear by his or her appearance. Narrow eyes and slim bodies indicate refined characters, and large or hairy bodies with big or round eyes specify a coarse person. The social status of the characters is revealed by the style and elaborateness of headdresses and clothing.

There are numerous stories portrayed in Balinese paintings, including the Mahabharata and Ramayana epics, but the most common are the Panji narratives (of which the Malat is one of the main Balinese examples), in which the prince travels extensively in search of his missing beloved.

1. Detail of a temple hanging (*ider-ider*)

Painted in the two-dimensional Kamasan style using scarlet, ochre, blue and black natural pigments, this hanging portrays the Macangkrama episode of the Malat (Panji) story cycle, in which Prince Panji and his lost betrothed encounter each other while wandering in the mountains. As an indication of their high status, the main characters are shown sitting on an elephant-headed rock. The stylized rock here is pink and white and identifiable by its tusks and wiggly trunk to the right of the embracing couple. Some silk hanging ties remain.

c. 1850
Kamasan, Bali, Indonesia
Cotton, silk
Length 509 cm, height 27 cm
1996,1211,0.1

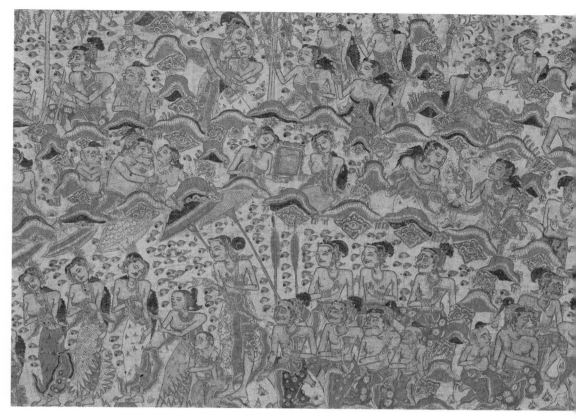

2. Detail of a hanging (*langse*)

Taken from the Malat (Panji) story cycles, this painting on cotton depicts the episode when the courts of Malayu and Panji independently retreated to the mountains, and the prince and his beloved met accidentally. Used in temples, palaces and houses as wall hangings or curtains, this type of broad, rectangular hanging would once have had another piece of cloth attached to the lower edge and, at the top, Chinese *cash* coins with central holes to hang it.

Late 19th century
Kamasan, Bali, Indonesia
Cotton
Length 230 cm, height 94 cm
1957,0511,0.1

3. Detail of a temple hanging (*ider-ider*)

Produced by a master artist, this *ider-ider* illustrates male and female figures from the Malat (Panji) story cycle. Such imagery is typically used to represent the beginning of the narrative.

Early 20th century
Kamasan, Bali, Indonesia
Cotton
Length 336 cm, height 26.5 cm
1957,0511,0.2

5 | 2 Javanese theatre

The various forms of theatre on Java still play a part in social, religious and artistic life, with performances accompanying rituals, vows, celebrations and major life events, though they are less prevalent than they once were. Performances traditionally created connections with the unseen world to summon helpful spirits, purify people and places, ensure good harvests and bless rites of passage, such as marriages or circumcisions. The environment of a performance is still believed to be auspicious (**3**). The stories narrated in the theatre include the epic tales, the Mahabharata and the Ramayana. The Damarwulan and Panji story cycles were once commonly performed as well, but are now very rare.

Javanese theatre includes unmasked (*wayang wong*) and masked (*wayang topeng*) dance-dramas (**9**, **10**), as well as several forms of puppet theatre: *wayang kulit*, shadow puppets (**4**, **5**); *wayang klitik*, two-dimensional wooden puppets (**6**, **7**); and *wayang krucil gilig*, three-dimensional wooden puppets (**8**). The main character types – refined, semi-refined, strong, emotionally uncontrolled, clowns and demons – each characterized by specific features, are shared across the theatrical forms.

The theatre is accompanied by gamelan music, which is also played during formal events, rites of passage, ceremonial processions and rituals. A gamelan orchestra is an ensemble of mostly percussive instruments, consisting of xylophones, metallophones and gongs struck with mallets, drums sounded by hand, string instruments played with a bow or plucked, and singers. It usually comprises fifteen to twenty instruments, but can range from four to over 100 in royal courts (**1**, **2**).

1. Gendèr
The gendèr is a gamelan instrument on which the melodic pattern is played with two beaters. Exuberant designs with bright colours and animal shapes are associated with the Javanese north coast, whereas central Javanese gamelan instruments have a more restrained appearance. Here, the sacred Garuda spreads his wings against the bamboo resonating chambers, while his foes, the mythical *nagas* associated with water and the underworld, slither down each side.

Late 1700s–1816
Java, Indonesia
Wood, bronze, gold, lacquer, bamboo
Height 74 cm, width 134 cm
Donated by William Raffles Flint, collected by Stamford Raffles, As 1859,1228.207

2. Kenong
Gamelan music is highly complex, consisting of interlocking patterns intertwining with the central melody. Kenongs mark segments of time between the beats of the gong. Gamelan orchestras are made and tuned together, and instruments are not interchangeable with other orchestras.

Late 1700s–1816
Java, Indonesia
Wood, fibre, gold, bronze
Height of support 49.4 cm; height of gong 30 cm
Donated by William Raffles Flint, collected by Stamford Raffles, As 1859,1228.196.a–b

3. Lamp

In shadow theatre, a puppeteer (*dalang*) manipulates puppets between a white screen and a light source to cast shadows. Oil lamps, in this instance in the shape of the sacred Garuda bird, were once used, but they have now been replaced by electric lights. Performances usually last all night.

Late 1800s–early 1900s
Java, Indonesia
Brass
Height 59 cm, width 61 cm
As 1955,03.1

4. Shadow puppet of the demon Kumbakarna

Kumbakarna is the younger brother of the demon Ravana, who kidnaps Prince Rama's wife in the Ramayana. Ogres and demons are depicted as large with round eyes to reveal their coarse natures. The angle of the head also indicates temperament, with a downward tilt denoting humility and a forward-facing look showing a bold nature.

Late 1700s–early 1800s
Cirebon, west Java, Indonesia
Hide, horn, gold
Height 101 cm
Donated by William Raffles Flint, collected by Stamford Raffles, As 1859,1228.781

5. Shadow puppet of Arjuna

Arjuna was the third of the five noble Pandava brothers in the Mahabharata epic and is a character whose exploits are particularly emphasized on Java. A puppeteer would have several Arjuna puppets at different life stages and in different moods. The black face here indicates an active moment. The slim body and limbs and delicate features signify the refinement and ability to control emotions that marks an exceptional individual. Some of the puppets, particularly the heroes, gods and clowns, are considered to be sacred and are used in divination or to make holy water.

Late 1700s–1816
Central Java, Indonesia
Hide, horn, gold
Height 72 cm
Donated by William Raffles Flint, collected by Stamford Raffles, As1859,1228.501

6. *Wayang klitik* puppet of Brawijaya

Wayang klitik puppets are made of carved and painted wood. Unlike in shadow puppet theatre, these performances do not use a screen and usually occur during the day. This is a royal male character, Brawijaya of the Majapahit kingdom, from the Damarwulan stories. He wears an elaborate headdress, *keris* ritual dagger, trousers and skirt cloth with luxury Indian trade textile patterns. While the downturned face indicates humility, the pink colouration and rounded eye reveal a forceful nature.

Late 1700s–1816
Java, Indonesia
Wood, hide, gold, fibre, horn
Length 43.7 cm, width 18 cm
Donated by William Raffles Flint, collected by Stamford Raffles, As1859,1228.471

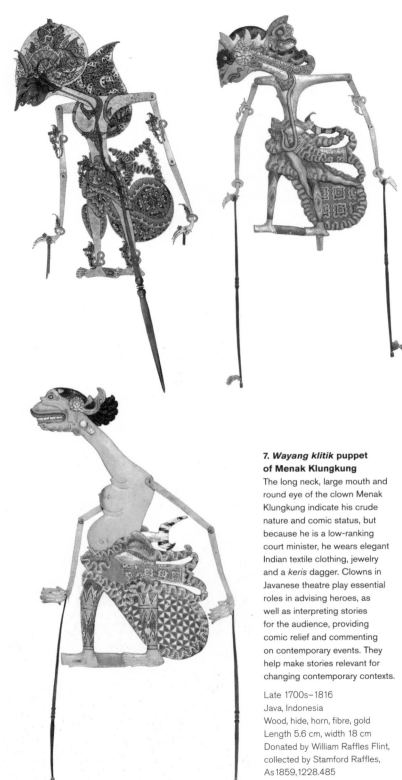

7. *Wayang klitik* puppet of Menak Klungkung

The long neck, large mouth and round eye of the clown Menak Klungkung indicate his crude nature and comic status, but because he is a low-ranking court minister, he wears elegant Indian textile clothing, jewelry and a *keris* dagger. Clowns in Javanese theatre play essential roles in advising heroes, as well as interpreting stories for the audience, providing comic relief and commenting on contemporary events. They help make stories relevant for changing contemporary contexts.

Late 1700s–1816
Java, Indonesia
Wood, hide, horn, fibre, gold
Length 5.6 cm, width 18 cm
Donated by William Raffles Flint, collected by Stamford Raffles, As1859,1228.485

8. *Wayang krucil gilig* puppet of Dewi Puyengan

This high-ranking female character, Dewi Puyengan, from the Damarwulan narratives is a type of three-dimensional puppet the use of which died out in the late 18th or early 19th century. The few remaining examples are found only in museums. Such puppets were used in performances of Panji stories. The support rod that would have extended from the base has been sawn off, possibly to facilitate transportation to Britain with Stamford Raffles' other collections or for easier display once in Europe.

18th century
Possibly Surakarta (Solo), central Java, Indonesia
Wood, gold, fibre
Height 28 cm, width 7.5 cm
Donated by William Raffles Flint, collected by Stamford Raffles, As 1859,1228.436a–c

9. Mask of the white monkey, Hanuman

Incorrectly labelled by Stamford Raffles or his assistants as the warrior character Rangga Megantara, this mask represents Hanuman the white monkey, a major character in the Ramayana who aided Prince Rama in recovering his wife. The Ramayana and the Panji stories were once performed by masked *wayang topeng* troupes, but this form of theatre is now mostly staged for tourists. Masks are carved from soft local woods and painted, with court versions also decorated with gold leaf. Bite cords or pieces of wood inside the mask are gripped between the performer's teeth to hold the mask to the face.

1800–1816
Central Java, Indonesia
Wood, gold, fibre
Height 20.3 cm, width 15.9 cm
Donated by William Raffles Flint, collected by Stamford Raffles, As 1859,1228.349

10. Mask of Prince Panji

A Javanese label inside this mask states that the character is Panji Pinanji, while a separate English label adds that he is the son of the king of Janggala. Masks of Prince Panji are either white or pale green, indicating a refined character able to control his emotions, and usually have a mark on the forehead to represent Panji's inner (spiritual) eye. The triangular shape of the mask indicates a central Javanese provenance.

1800–1816
Central Java, Indonesia
Wood, gold, fibre
Height 19.3 cm, width 16.3 cm
Donated by William Raffles Flint, collected by Stamford Raffles, As 1859,1228.282

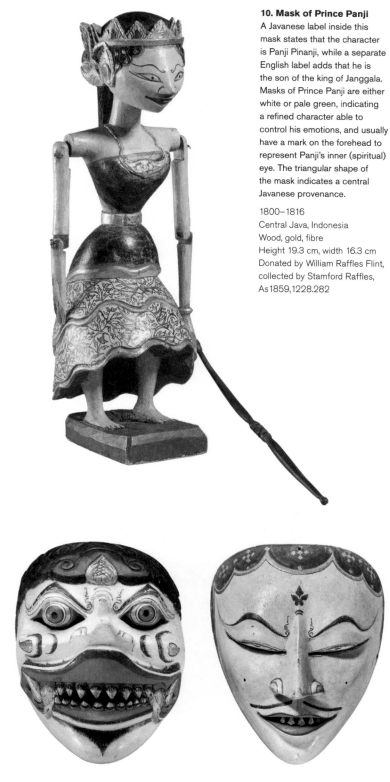

5 | 3 Thai theatre

There are many Thai theatrical traditions, most of which are accompanied by an orchestra that can include plucked zithers and lutes, stringed instruments played with a bow, two main types of woodwind instruments, and numerous percussive cymbals, clappers and drums (**1**). There are three different types of instrumental ensembles, each performing at different types of event.

Used for the performance of the Ramayana (*Ramakien* in Thai), masked *khon* dance-drama was developed for the Ayutthayan royal court in the 16th or 17th centuries with its own musical form, songs and highly stylized movements. The masks are made with lacquered papier mâché and decorated with paint, gold leaf and glass pieces (**3**). *Khon* is now primarily performed for local and foreign tourist audiences and sponsored during national events. Other forms of performance include the Manora dances of the Thai-Malay peninsula, Likhe improvisational theatre and Lakhon dance-dramas that mostly present Buddhist *jataka* stories.

Thailand has two main shadow theatre traditions, the *nang yai*, which was once associated with the royal court, and the *nang talung* shadow theatre found in the southern part of the country. Both are traditionally performed at night against a screen lit from behind. *Nang yai* uses large puppets, each of which was manipulated by a single performer, in telling the Ramayana accompanied by music and song (**2**). Despite King Vajiravudh's (r. 1910–25) support, arts patronage declined in the 20th century, and training shifted from troupes to official schools, the first of which was established in 1934.

1. Drum (*thon chatri*)

The *thon chatri* was used for wedding ceremonies, auspicious social events and the theatre. This example may have been a royal gift to John Bowring, a British diplomat and colonial official, who was in Thailand negotiating a treaty with King Mongkut (Rama IV) in 1855, because the gilding suggests that it was made by a royal craft maker. Bowring donated it to the British Museum in 1857.

Early 1850s
Thailand
Earthenware, snake skin, bamboo, glass, gold, metal
Diameter 24 cm, height 37.5 cm
Donated by John Bowring,
As1857,0101.11

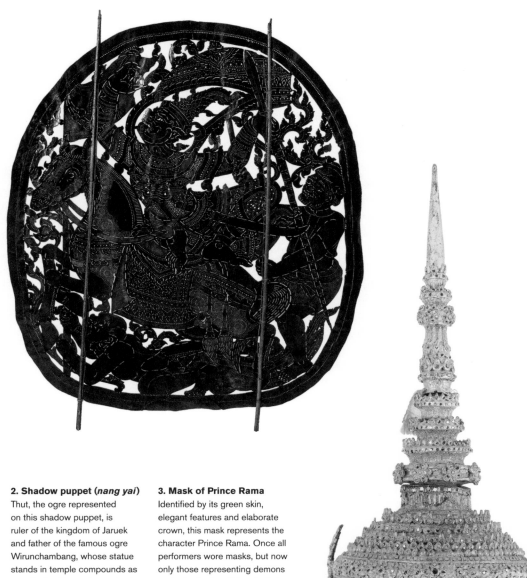

2. Shadow puppet (*nang yai*)

Thut, the ogre represented
on this shadow puppet, is
ruler of the kingdom of Jaruek
and father of the famous ogre
Wirunchambang, whose statue
stands in temple compounds as
a protective figure. Appearing in
performances of the Ramayana
in Thailand, Thut wears a crown,
carries a spear and rides a magic
horse. *Nang yai* puppets are
carved in detail and painted,
though older examples were
only coloured black with soot
or brown with tamarind, as here.

Late 19th–early 20th century
Thailand
Hide, wood
Height 177.5 cm, width 142 cm
As1929,0815.3

3. Mask of Prince Rama

Identified by its green skin,
elegant features and elaborate
crown, this mask represents the
character Prince Rama. Once all
performers wore masks, but now
only those representing demons
and animals do, while celestial
figures and royal characters
wear crowns.

1900–1920s
Thailand
Papier mâché, gold, wood, glass,
silk, resin, metal, lacquer
Height 35 cm, width 24 cm
As1929,0108.1.a–b

5 | 4 Southern Thai and Malaysian shadow puppets

Because of historic and cultural ties, there are strong connections between the shadow theatres of Malaysia and southern Thailand. The puppets are iconographically similar (1), and shows often begin with a ritual sequence involving a fight between two deities, which is resolved by a holy man who restores balance and harmony to the universe, although in Thailand there is an additional ritual scene with the god Shiva on his mount Nandi (3). The performance of episodes from the extended Ramayana narrative follows, although now stories can also be drawn from novels, films and television programmes with new heroes and villains, such as bureaucrats, business and military leaders (4), and such global icons as Darth Vader. In southern Thailand, *nang talung* shadow theatre continues to flourish as ritual and entertainment. It is performed at festivals and fairs, and families and communities sponsor shadow puppet performances to accompany life events, such as marriages, to celebrate a successful harvest, and to heal the sick or ward off ill fortune. In Malaysia, conservative Islamic politicians have banned or restricted performances since the 1990s, accusing shadow theatre of encouraging the worship of gods other than Allah.

As in the Javanese shadow theatre, Malay and Thai puppets are manipulated by a single puppeteer against a screen, accompanied by an orchestra of drums and other percussive and wind instruments. The mostly male, but occasionally female, puppeteers chant poetry, voice the characters, tell the story and conduct the orchestra during all-night performances. In modern innovations, electric lamps have replaced oil ones, and amplification and electric instruments are also now common. The carved, brightly coloured puppets are made of animal hide, sometimes by the puppeteers themselves. More recently, some puppeteers have experimented with using plastic instead of hide (5). Although the puppets reflect political, social, religious and aesthetic changes in new character types and new forms of dress, there is substantial continuity as the nobles still wear traditional court clothing and the semi-divine clowns are still coloured black (1, 2).

1. Tok Awang Lah, Puppet of Prince Rama
The representations of noble characters are similar in the southern Thai and Malaysian shadow theatres. This puppet of Prince Rama from the Malay tradition shares visual elements – the curved fingers, face in profile, high crown, stance with the bow held behind and a *naga* serpent ground – with painted representations and puppets of nobles and deities from Thailand.

Early to mid-20th century
Kelantan, Malaysia
Animal hide, wood, bamboo
Height 94.2 cm, width 31.3 cm
As 1970,02.109

2. Tok Awang Lah, Puppet of Pak Dogol

Clowns are an important part of shadow theatre across the region. Like clowns in other Southeast Asian traditions, Pak Dogol has a distorted body, and as with clowns from southern Thailand and Malaysia, he is painted black with a collar of sacred thread indicating his divinity. The puppet itself is believed to be sacred and is stored with offerings separately from other puppets. Before performing, puppeteers used to recite prayers to Pak Dogol.

Early to mid-20th century
Kelantan, Malaysia
Animal hide, wood, bamboo and cotton
Height 58.2 cm, width 24 cm
As1970,02.129

3. Shiva on his mount Nandi

The puppet of the god Shiva is an important part of the ritual scenes performed by puppeteers at the start of a show in southern Thailand. Elements of Hindu rituals have formed part of Thai traditions for many centuries. In Thailand, the benign and merciful Shiva is honoured during the new year Triyampavai ceremony, which includes swinging on a giant swing, a period of inauguration and renewal. Shiva in the shadow theatre ritual marks the beginning of the performance, makes it sacred and ensures the prosperity of the endeavour.

Mid-1970s
Southern Thailand
Animal hide, bamboo
Height 77 cm, width 40 cm
As1977,19.72

4. Military general

In southern Thailand, puppets can be based on actual people. The individuality of the red glasses in this example suggests that this was once a locally known person, but the glasses have now become a common element and are seen on many military puppets.

Mid-1970s
Southern Thailand
Animal hide, bamboo
Height 77 cm, width 40 cm
As1977,19.32

5. Midin, puppet of a young Peranakan woman

During the 1960s, some puppeteers tried making puppets out of plastic sheeting. The puppets are usually small, and the details are produced through painted colouration. An unsuccessful innovation, few plastic puppets are now in use. This puppet portrays a young woman dressed in Chinese-Malay style with a local batik sarong and fitted shirt.

Late 1960s
Kelantan, Malaysia
Plastic, bamboo
Height 43.2 cm
As1970,02.43

5 | 5 Thai religious paintings

In Thailand, Buddhist paintings were produced on cloth and wood, as well as on temple and monastery walls. The paintings are religious objects depicting the historic Buddha, Gotama, and stories from his life or previous lives (*jataka*), as well as the Buddha flanked by his two main disciples, Sariputta and Moggallana, with select narrative episodes below (**1**). Other topics include the five Buddhas of this era, sometimes in conjunction with the story of their birth (**3**), or all twenty-four Buddhas of the past who made prophecies to Gotama in his previous existences about his future Buddhahood. Such paintings were displayed inside and outside temples to serve as reminders of the Buddha and his teachings, and the cloth examples were paraded during festivals and ceremonies. People commissioned paintings to honour the Buddha, gain merit and protect the religion, hoping to ensure better rebirths for themselves and individuals with whom they shared the accrued merit.

Used as screens, the painted wood panels are relatively small (**2**), but the cloth paintings can be over 1 metre wide and up to 4 metres high. When not in use, paintings made on paper and textiles were stored rolled. Owing to their ephemeral materials, most surviving examples are in poor condition and only date to the late 19th and early 20th centuries, after which painting was replaced by prints. A few rare examples have been found in well-protected locations that can be dated back to the 16th century, revealing that the production of paintings was a long-standing part of Thai religious practices. Rarely, paintings were signed by the artist or inscribed with the name of the donor (**2**).

1. Painting (*phra bot*) of the Buddha and his two main disciples

Set against a typically Thai backdrop of floral motifs, the Buddha in this painting stands on an elaborate plinth with his right hand in the gesture of reassurance. He is flanked by his two main disciples, Moggallana and Sariputta, in attitudes of adoration. Above the figures, two flying *vidyadharas* (hermits with supernatural powers) honour the Buddha with gestures and flowers. Below, in a common banner painting format, there is a separate scene, in this case of offerings. The animals may be associated with the zodiac signs of the donors. The inscription panel is blank.

Mid- to late 19th century
Siam (Thailand)
Textile, paper, pigment
Height 289 cm, width 89 cm
1959,1010,0.9

2. Painting of the Buddha's departure from Tavatimsa Heaven

Although this painting is on wood, its inscription states: 'Monk Krum's cloth painting was made for the Buddhist dispensation'. The term 'dispensation' refers to the time during which the Buddha's teachings exist. Because the Buddha taught that everything is impermanent, people commission Buddhist objects to ensure the survival of the religion for as long as possible before it declines and disappears. The Buddha was believed to have travelled to Tavatimsa Heaven, the home of the deity Indra, to preach to his mother who had been reborn there.

Mid- to late 19th century
Siam (central Thailand)
Wood, gold leaf, pigment
Height 54.3 cm, width 38.5 cm
Donated by the Doris Duke
Charitable Foundation,
2004,0628.39

3. Painting (*phra bot*) of the five Buddhas of this era

The current cycle of time is believed to have five Buddhas, four of whom have already attained Nirvana with the fifth (Metteyya/Maitreya) to come. This banner painting shows the five Buddhas seated on thrones, each accompanied by an animal. The Buddha at the apex is Gotama, the historic Buddha. Lotus leaves and blooms spring from the lake in the lower panel, which tells a Thai version of the Buddhas' births. Their mother was a white crow who fell from a tree dead from grief when a storm blew her nest with five eggs into the water. The eggs were individually rescued, and the babies raised by the animals shown with them.

Late 19th century
Siam (central Thailand)
Textile, paper, pigment
Length 303 cm, width 92 cm
1959,1010,0.8

5 | 6 Buddhist processional cloths

In northeastern Thailand and lowland Laos, people wishing to generate merit commission the production of lengthy cotton cloth scrolls depicting the Vessantara Jataka, one of the stories of the Buddha's previous lives, which tells of how Prince Vessantara (the Buddha in a previous rebirth) perfected the virtue of generosity by giving away his possessions and eventually his family (1). Painted in regional workshops, these cloths vary between 15 and 75 metres in length. They are used in the important annual Bun Phra Wet festival held after the harvest in March or April. During the festival, monks chant the entire story, and at the end, lay participants take the cloth out of the village, unroll it fully, honour the Buddha and form a procession carrying the cloth, unrolled, back into the village accompanied by music and dancing. In the village it is circumambulated clockwise around the local temple three times before being hung in the temple's meeting hall. A communal merit-making effort, this procession inclusively re-enacts the ending of the *jataka* story when the prince is triumphantly welcomed home after being banished for giving away the kingdom's precious rain-making elephant, and it enables the participants, usually nearly the entire village, to take an active role in the story.

1. Section of a Vessantara cloth from the Bun Phra Wet festival
Although the complete story is composed of thirteen chapters and 1,000 verses, pictorial representations of the Vessantara Jataka often concentrate upon specific groups of scenes from the chapters that provide evidence of Vessantara's ability to suppress desire and attachment and the perfection of his generosity. This section of the cloth focuses on Vessantara's donation of his children to Jujaka the Brahmin, although the narrative is not in chronological order. It starts on the left with the death of Jujaka followed by the preparation of the feast at which he overate, causing him to die. Next he is sleeping in a tree. The children are tied up at the base of the tree being comforted by deities disguised as their parents. Jujaka presenting the children at the palace follows, and after that is the court procession to bring Vessantara back into the kingdom (the end

of the story). Above these scenes is a row of vases filled with lotus flowers, symbols of the Buddha's purity. The cloth ends with Vessantara giving away the children to Jujaka, telling his wife Maddi about the donation and reviving her after she faints at the news, and giving away the children again after they escape and hide in a lotus pond. Above these scenes, Maddi is seen collecting food in the forest and being blocked from returning to the monastery by three deities disguised as ferocious animals to ensure that Vessantara's gift of the children proceeds unhindered. Unusually, this cloth has a border all the way around it, suggesting that it is complete, even though it only depicts a part of the narrative.

Mid- to late 20th century
Northeastern Thailand or Laos
Pigment on cotton
Height 89 cm, length
approximately 500 cm
2003,1027,0.1

Timeline

c. 5,000–2,000 BCE	Linguistic evidence indicates the early and wide distribution of the basketry term *anyam*
c. 3,000 BCE	Evidence of cord-marked ceramic vessels
c. 1000 BCE	Early use of backstrap looms
1–800 CE	Importation of Indian trade cloths begins, as demonstrated by the use of textile patterns on stone sculpture and reliefs
17th century	Development of 'traditional' dress in many parts of Southeast Asia, which is later modified in the late 19th and early 20th centuries under colonial influence
	Gradual emergence of a VOC monopoly on the textile trade and decline in Indian textile imports
18th century	Development of new local textile centres, such as Java, southern Sulawesi and Panay in the Philippines
19th century	Importation of cheap mass-produced textiles from Europe gradually replaces local industries and homespun cloth
1860s–70s	Introduction of chemical dyes for use on textiles and basketry fibres
Late 19th century	Introduction of synthetic fibres
1980s	Southeast Asia becomes a major exporter of textiles
Late 20th century	Increasing use of plastic instead of natural materials, replacing traditional basketry; development of basketry made with discarded plastic
2009 and 2021	Indonesian batik and Malay *songket* are inscribed by UNESCO as intangible world heritage

6 Textiles and basketry

Textiles and basketry are major and complementary art forms in Southeast Asia. Local conditions have given rise to a diversity of forms and functions, and religious, trade and cultural connections have promoted similarities in structures and patterns. Yet, production of basketry and textiles is not static, and as new ideas, materials and fashions appear, they can be incorporated in innovative ways. Likewise, communities move, and meanings and fashions shift over time (3).

Basketry is usually produced by women for use within the household, for ritual purposes and commercially as a source of income, but it is not governed by the same ritual restrictions as textiles, and men can also be involved. While most basketry pieces are woven without patterning, those with ceremonial functions often display elaborate colouring, designs and attachments. As with many art forms in Southeast Asia, it is the technical quality of the product that is valued as pleasing.

Textiles in Southeast Asia are associated with women and made almost exclusively by them. In some cultures it is taboo for men to touch looms once in use, and women follow physical

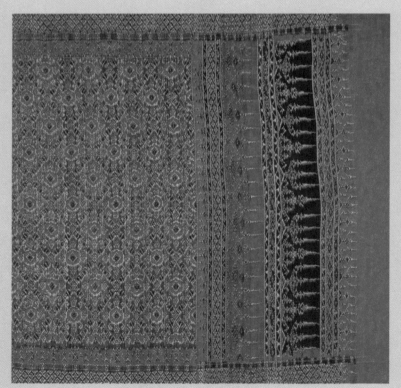

1. Skirt cloth (*sampot chawng kbun*) (detail)

This twill-woven, weft *ikat* cloth was tied around the waist and looped between the legs to form a trouser-like garment worn by men and women. Dyed in Cambodian traditional colours of yellow, green, red and blue, it is set with a diamond lattice pattern with eight-petalled 'flowers' in the centrefield in a *patola* (Indian trade cloth) layout. The border motifs are protective diagrams called *yantras*, found in a variety of cultural contexts and media across Southeast Asia. Together, the designs resemble the Indian textiles specially produced for the Thai market because of the political and social connections between Thailand and Cambodia.

Early to mid-20th century
Cambodia
Silk
Length 308.5 cm, width 95.5 cm
Donated by Douglas Barratt,
As 1962,02.1

2. Coat

This cotton coat belongs to the group of peoples called the Red Yao who live in southern Yunnan, China, and in northern Vietnam, but the patterning is typical of textiles made around Sa Pa in the Lao Cai region of northern Vietnam. The coat displays appliqué strips around the cuffs and edges, as well as embroidery on the back panels and around the collar. Further embellishments include glass beads, wool pom-poms and yarn bundles.

Mid-20th century
Sa Pa, Vietnam
Cotton, wool, glass
Length 100 cm, width 120 cm
As 1995,27.1

and spiritual restrictions at different stages of the dyeing and weaving processes to ensure their own and their community's safety. Textiles supply income, function as repositories of wealth, are sources of prestige to individuals and families and create alliances. Women were once responsible for producing a family's clothing, as well as ritual items, religious hangings, theatrical costumes and royal necessities. The cloths of great spiritual and ritual importance are often associated with the myths and legends that narrate the beginnings of a textile technique or the textile-related origins of a culture. Textiles are of great social significance, as the designs, forms, complexity, the way they were worn and the value of the raw materials could contribute to identifying the user's social status and origins, clan affiliation, marital availability, age and gender. As highly potent objects, textiles can be worn as talismans for protection, and they once played an important role in economic exchanges when they were commonly used as currency. High-status cloths and imported textiles were kept as heirlooms. As religious objects, textiles were used in such rites of passage as childbirth, marriage and death, as well as at rituals and feasts to demonstrate an owner's social status within the community. In some communities, textiles were presented by women's families during gift exchanges in return for metal and wood objects associated with men, or were given as ceremonial exchanges among the women of a family or clan. Textiles were also offerings

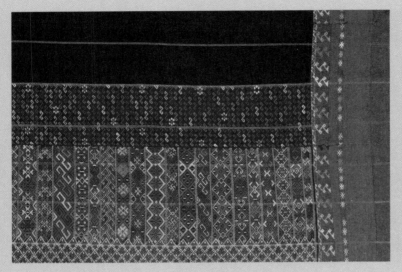

3. Skirt cloth (detail)
Produced in the Kachin State or
northern Shan State of Myanmar,
where there are substantial
Kachin communities, this skirt
cloth is heavily patterned with
twill weave and multi-hued,
continuous and discontinuous
supplementary weft designs
against black and red grounds.
The vertical patterned stripes at
the lower edge are now more
closely associated with the
Lachik, a Kachin subgroup, but
in the past they seem to have
been more prevalent among the
Jinghpaw subgroups. The skirt
would have been worn with the
black panel at the top.

Early 20th century
Myanmar
Cotton
Length 188 cm, width 71 cm
Donated by Anne Smith,
As1992,01.5

to ancestral spirits who would protect the deceased on their
travels to the afterworld. The immense significance of textiles
is further indicated by the fact that patterns were replicated in
other media, including being carved in stone on Hindu temples
such as Candi Prambanan (9th century CE) in central Java and
painted on the walls of 18th- and 19th-century Buddhist temples
in Thailand and Myanmar.

Materials for producing textiles vary from bark and plant
fibres, including cotton, to silk (probably initially arriving from
China) and, more recently, synthetic fibres. Most of the textiles
discussed here were woven on frameless backstrap looms;
the tension of the fabric is controlled by the weaver leaning
against the strap that passes around her. Frame looms, a later
development in which the cloth is held at the correct tension by
beams, are mostly used for silk, fabrics patterned with metallic
threads (*songket*) and tapestry weave. The predominant dye
colours were blue-black from indigo and reds and browns from
a variety of sources, including the *Morinda citrifolia* tree and the
yellow flame tree (*soga*). When chemical dyes arrived in Southeast
Asia in the late 19th century, they were enthusiastically adopted,
eventually almost entirely replacing the vegetal dyes.

The great technical complexity of many textiles requires
substantial command of yarn production, dyeing techniques and
the weaving process, and the maker's abilities are judged by these
criteria. In weaving, the warp yarns are tied to the loom, and the

wefts are woven in with a shuttle. When a cloth is called warp-faced, it means that there is a greater density of warp threads concealing the weft ones; for weft-faced textiles, the reverse is true. The most basic form of weaving is plain or tabby weave, in which the warp and weft yarns interlace each other in a basic one-over-one-under arrangement. Float weaves are where warp or weft yarns travel over and under two or more of the opposite element (warps or wefts). An example is twill weave, where the weft yarns float over two or more warp ones in a staggered manner creating a diagonally aligned pattern (**3**). Twining involves twisting two or more weft (or warp) yarns around each other while wrapping successive warp (or weft) threads. These methods of weaving cloth in Southeast Asia can be the primary patterning of a textile or provide a ground for other weaving or decorative techniques. Widespread in the region is the use of supplementary patterning, involving the addition of further warp or weft threads during the weaving process (**3**). These can be continuous, running the full width or length of the cloth, or discontinuous, when the threads are worked back and forth within a design element. When the discontinuous supplementary threads are weft yarns, then the technique can also be called tapestry weave. Brocading cloth is a means of adding supplementary threads, often of silver or gold, to a woven cloth, and embroidery refers to various types of stitches – such as couching, chain, running and satin – usually produced with a needle to decorate the fabric. The process of stitching additional pieces of cloth to a ground fabric is called appliqué (**2**). Beads, shells, seeds, gold and silver threads, pom-poms and pieces of mica or glass are also often incorporated into designs (**2**). Not all textiles have a woven pattern. In batik production, hot wax or rice paste is applied to the surface of a textile to prevent dye penetration. After dyeing, the resist is removed. *Ikat* is another resist-dye method, in which the warp or weft threads (or both) are tie-dyed with the pattern prior to weaving (**1**).

The 19th century saw the importation of cheap, mass-produced, printed textiles primarily from Europe, and these gradually replaced local industries and homespun clothes. Over the course of the 20th century, Southeast Asia itself became a centre for mass textile production and an exporter of clothing.

6 | 1 Bark, barkcloth and vegetal fibres

Matting, interlacing (plaiting) and twining of plant fibres have existed in Southeast Asia since the most ancient times, as demonstrated by the imprints found on early pottery. Mallets for pounding bark discovered at Neolithic sites in Southeast Asia indicate that people developed barkcloth early on. Leaves, vegetal fibres and bark can still form part of the clothing repertoire (3). On Borneo, barkcloth was once used as the basis for jackets associated with warfare and headhunting (1, 2). It is still worn as protection against malign spirits during rites associated with death. Barkcloth textiles are also part of funerary rituals among the Ifugao of the northern Philippines. Although once widespread across Southeast Asia, barkcloth and coarse vegetal fibre items are now used as clothing only by a few isolated groups, as they have been replaced in many communities by woven cloth.

Barkcloth ranges from rough untreated pieces of bark stitched together to soft, fuzzy cloths produced by soaking and pounding the fibres with beaters. The resulting fabrics can be painted, as well as ornamented with shells, seeds, beads and mica (1). Thin pieces of barkcloth were once also used as paper for manuscripts and paintings at courts, including those on Java and Bali. In some places, rough examples were used as armour, while finer cloth was employed for everyday and festive dress. In southern Sumatra, barkcloth remains in use as a garment liner.

1. Jacket (*baju buri'*)
Made of pounded barkcloth with cowrie shells stitched to the fabric, jackets such as this one were once used while headhunting. The hooks and spirals are part of a Southeast Asian aesthetic that emerged during the deep past, and the crocodile is here seen making ripples as it swims upriver. Iban peoples associate the crocodile with water and the underworld and believe it is a spirit that assists men when headhunting.

Late 19th–early 20th century
Iban peoples, Borneo
Bark, cowrie shell
Height 55 cm, width 65 cm
As 1923,1018.1

2. Iban war coat

The bark fibres of this Iban war coat are loosely woven with thin strips of rattan and covered with pangolin scales to protect against projectile weapons. Warfare was endemic among many communities on Borneo into the 20th century.

Late 19th century
Iban peoples, Borneo
Bark, pangolin scales, rattan
Height 66.5 cm, width 42.5 cm
As 1905,-437

3. Rain cape

Made of grass fibres twined compactly to form a short upper jacket but left loose beneath it, capes such as this one were worn as raincoats by men and women over backpack-baskets among many groups in Southeast Asia.

Early 20th century
Probably Chin peoples, Chin State, Myanmar
Grass fibre
Height 86.4 cm, width 56.7 cm
As 1935,1008.1

6 | 2 Ifugao textiles

Ifugao is the collective name for speakers of four related languages who live in the central Cordillera region on Luzon island in the Philippines. Here, as in almost all Southeast Asian cultures, textiles are a woman's art and have occupied important roles in daily life, economic exchanges, marriage settlements, funerary practices and other ritual contexts.

Women wore a wrap-around cloth held in place by sashes (**2**), and occasionally jackets, while men donned loincloths and jackets. Blankets were used as needed, and everybody carried woven bags and pouches (**1**). Few wear the full complement of these clothes daily now, but many items remain in use for important occasions. With the extensive circulation of textiles in the Cordillera, weavers have adapted designs, patterns and colours as they encountered new ideas, and today many textiles are also made for tourists.

Among the Ifugao, the warp *ikat* technique is primarily reserved for funerary textiles. There are several types of blanket that function as shrouds, such as the *gamong* (**3**). Bodies are wrapped and buried in as many textiles as the family can afford, and widows also cover themselves with such cloths. The Ifugao once practised secondary interment of the dead, and when bones were exhumed, they were wrapped in new funerary cloths and kept in the home until sufficient resources to host an expensive reburial ceremony had been gathered. During burial ceremonies, the textiles are sometimes ritually damaged so that they will not be stolen in the land of the dead.

1. Bag (*pinu'hha*) and detail
Small bags used by Ifugao men to hold amulets, carved wooden spoons, betel quids and other necessities were triangular and closed with brass rings. The circular brass handle was used to attach the bag to the loincloth. The patterning here is formed with supplementary yarns added to the warp and weft yarns.

Late 1800s–1910
Luzon, Philippines
Cotton, brass
Length 71 cm, width 25.5 cm
As1914,0414.99

2. Woman's sash (*mayad*)

Women sometimes adapted dark-coloured men's loincloths to make sashes for themselves. The use of indigo-dyed dark fabric in this case suggests this alteration, with red and yellow yarns tied to the fringe to make it appropriate for a woman to wear. The body of the fabric has a central red stripe and two flanking strips of red and blue supplementary warp threads, with the end panels made of red and yellow supplementary weft yarns.

Late 1800s–1910
Luzon, Philippines
Cotton
Length 196 cm, width 18.5 cm
As 1914,0414.88

3. Blanket (*gamong*)

Gamong blankets are woven on backstrap looms in four pieces, two of each type, which are then joined together. The central panels here are executed as blue and white stripes overlain with blue supplementary weft patterning at the ends, and the sections to each side have blue and red stripes that alternate with supplementary warp blue and white stripes. Separate, narrow bands of weaving have been added to the ends of the blanket.

20th century
Philippines
Cotton
Length 235 cm, width 159 cm
As 1995,11.2

Originating among approximately eighteen ethnolinguistic groups, Timorese textiles are highly diverse and difficult to categorize, since historical and political events, population movements and the geography of the island have all affected access to materials and production and the cultural importance of textiles over the centuries. Timorese textiles are highly individual, while retaining design arrangements, colouration, techniques and motifs relating to family and regional identities, as well as social status. Often there are only two main colours on a textile, but there are numerous techniques used to weave the warp-faced cloths on backstrap looms, including plain weave, warp *ikat*, warp-faced float weaves, supplementary weft wrapping, tapestry weave, discontinuous supplementary weft patterning and twining.

As with many groups in island Southeast Asia, Timorese weaving features in creation myths, textile production is associated with women, and textiles form part of the gift exchanges accompanying marriage agreements. Today, there are three main forms of textile: tubular women's cloths worn wrapped high above the breasts (**4**), a man's rectangular cloth with fringes (**1**, **2**) and a long, single-panel fringed cloth worn over the shoulder that became popular in the 20th century (**3**). Head and waist cloths, as well as bags for holding betel paraphernalia, are now rarely produced, if at all. Most handwoven textiles are now used only for festive wear.

1. Man's cloth (*selimut*)

Made of two pieces of indigo-dyed, warp *ikat*-patterned fabric woven on a backstrap loom, this skirt cloth would have been worn tied around the waist by a man. The design format, with eight red and yellow warp stripes enclosing *ikat* patterns in the centrefield flanked by wider bands of stripes to each side, is found in many parts of the island. In some areas, the large, white *ikat* patterning is identified as a betel box and the indigo centrefield associated with men's cloths.

Early 20th century
East Timor
Cotton
Length 233 cm (excluding fringes), width 125.5 cm
As 1927,0215.1

2. Man's cloth (*selimut*)

The complexity of the weaving, using supplementary weft and warp float yarns, and the patterned white centre stripe suggests that this cloth was made for a high-status man. Today, a man would wear two of these for formal occasions, one around the waist and the other draped over the shoulder. Whether this was the case in earlier times is not known.

Early to mid-20th century
Possibly Atoin Meto peoples, Timor
Cotton
Length 190 cm, width 115 cm
As 1981,11.3

3. Shoulder cloth

Narrower pieces of fabric used as shoulder cloths are a development from the second half of the 20th century, when shoulder sashes emerged as part of Indonesian 'national' dress after independence from the Netherlands in the

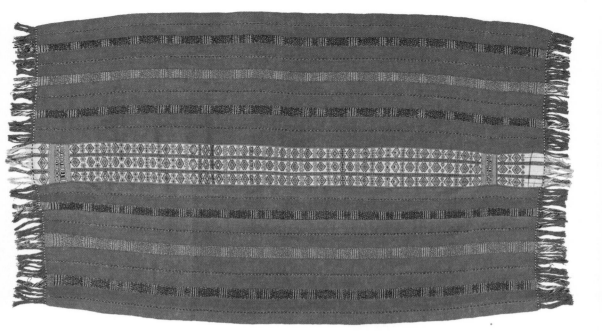

late 1940s. The techniques on this piece include warp *ikat*, weft twining and supplementary weft.

Mid-20th century
Timor
Cotton
Length 256 cm, width 71 cm
As1982,12.4

4. Skirt-cloth

Made of four pieces of fabric, this woman's skirt-cloth displays dark bands on a brown ground with two outer panels of red, yellow and pink stripes and cream warp *ikat* patterning against an indigo blue background. The upper and lower panels are plain indigo blue.

Early to mid-20th century
Ayotupas, Timor, Indonesia
Cotton
Length 122 cm, width 52 cm
As1992,05.87

6 | 4 Batak cloths

Among the six related Batak societies of Sumatra, women once wove and presented textiles as part of life cycle ceremonies and ritual gift exchanges to cement family relationships, but while cloths are still used as gifts, production is substantially reduced as it is not financially viable. To make the elaborate textiles, women used backstrap looms with continuous warp cotton threads coloured with natural plant dyes. When the warp threads were cut after completion, they were twisted, braided, knotted or crocheted into a fringe. Symmetry following established rules is an important feature of Batak textile design, which can comprise groups of three. This is most often seen as two side panels and a central section. Sometimes the centre panel is also composed of three sections (**2**). Borders are a standard element and vary in their elaboration. Textiles with end panels that have been elaborately woven with supplementary weft patterning are the most valued by the Batak groups (**1, 2**).

There are a number of different types of *ulos* cloths in Batak societies, all with different uses. The *ulos ragidup* is the most important cloth among the Toba Batak and is worn only by older, high-ranking individuals (**2**). The name means 'pattern of life', referring to marriage exchanges. While it is sometimes given as a form of protection to a high-ranking woman during her seventh month of pregnancy, she cannot wear it until she has become a grandparent. The dominant patterning of the centre field includes an odd number of stripes and supplementary weft designs, often in red, blue-black and white, the three main Batak textile colours.

1. Cloth (*ulos na marsimata*)
Ulos na marsimata are cloths with beads. This *ulos* is made of two equal-sized pieces of dark indigo blue cloth sewn together lengthwise. There are identical bands of diamonds, zigzags, cross shapes, triangles and chevrons at each end and stripes along the edges produced using tapestry weave, discontinuous supplementary warp, twill weave and discontinuous and continuous supplementary weft techniques. The fringe is twined, threaded with glass beads or covered with strips of metal. Red flannel pieces have been added at each end.

c. 1800–24
Sipirok Batak of South Tapanuli or Angkola Batak, Sumatra, Indonesia
Cotton (possibly), glass, wool, metal, fibre
Length 196 cm, width 95 cm
Donated by J. H. Drake, collected by Stamford Raffles, As1939,04.121

2. Cloth (*ulos ragidup*) and detail
Ulos ragidup are woven as three separate panels that are sewn together lengthwise, with the central section here displaying narrow indigo blue and white stripes and intricate patterns in supplementary weft with fringes at each end. The designs at each end differ, and one is considered female and the other male. The stripes to the sides of the centre fabric piece are made with supplementary warp yarns.

Early to mid-19th century
Toba Batak, Sumatra, Indonesia
Cotton
Length 185 cm, width 137 cm
Donated by the Amsterdam Zoological Society, As.7563

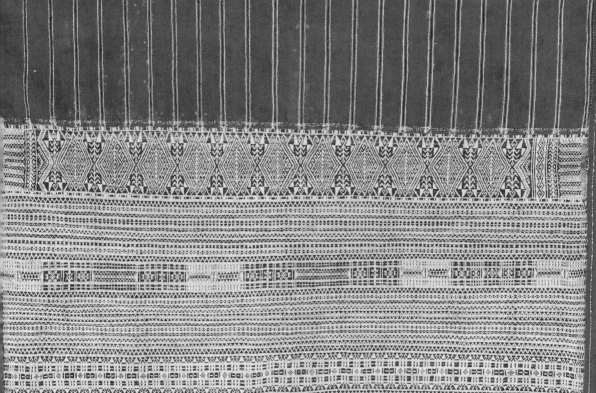

6 | 5 Textiles from Lampung

Lampung province occupies the southern tip of the Indonesian island of Sumatra along the Sunda Strait. Part of a major trade route since ancient times, the area is famous for its tube-skirts called *tapis*, jackets and *tampan* and *palepai* cloths, which are ritual and ceremonial items used by Lampung peoples, of whom the Kauer are one group, during festivals and such rites of passage as birth, circumcision and death. Young women used to create them as part of their wedding preparations, and they were also offered as prestige gifts.

Tapis skirts and jackets are time-consuming to make, sometimes taking up to a year, and incorporate expensive materials, demonstrating to the community a family's wealth and social standing (**1**, **2**). The colouration of skirts and jackets combines yellow, dark red and green, browns, indigo blue and creams in stripes. The all-important surface designs consist of gold- and silver-wrapped threads, beads and embroidery, mirrors, mica or muscovite, and pieces of felt and wool, which are attached to the surface of the cloth, sometimes with elaborate stitching.

The colours and organization of the designs reflect the different social groups that occupy Lampung, each of which has particular clothing conventions, although some patterns indicate the extensive interactions that have occurred between them. Images of ships sometimes occur on *tapis*, demonstrating their ongoing practical and symbolic roles from early times into the present in many parts of island Southeast Asia (**1**). In Lampung, in addition to having symbolic associations with marriage, boats also provide the conceptual structure for ceremonial processions in which *tapis* skirts and jackets are worn.

1. Jacket

Only Kauer women wore jackets such as this one, along with their *tapis* skirts. This example is made with appliquéd shells and printed fabric, couched pieces of mica, stripes, running and satin stitch embroidery and supplementary weft weaving. It is lined with plain cotton.

1870s–1883
Kauer peoples, Lampung, Sumatra, Indonesia
Cotton, nassa (mud snail) shell, mica, muscovite
Length 30.5 cm, width 128 cm
Donated by A. W. Franks, collected by Henry Forbes, As,+.1917

2. Tube-skirt (*tapis*)

This ceremonial skirt is made of five pieces of cloth hand-stitched together with embroidery, couched pieces of mica, muscovite and silvered metal threads, and metallic supplementary warp stripes. The imagery is of human figures in pavilions built for a festive occasion with banners between them in the lower band. In the upper register, a single figure is enthroned on a boat with two prone figures below him, possibly sailors or enslaved people. The surrounding flourishes emulate the sea. The colouration indicates that this *tapis* was made by a Kauer woman in the Semangka area along the southwestern coast of the Lampung region.

1800–1880
Kauer peoples, Semangka Bay, Sumatra, Indonesia
Cotton, metal, silk, mica, muscovite
Length 118 cm, width 64 cm
Donated by A. W. Franks, collected by Henry Forbes, As,+.1914

Belonging to the brocade family of textiles, *songket* is found in many parts of island Southeast Asia, including Sumatra (**1**), Bali, Lombok, Kalimantan and Sumbawa in Indonesia, the Malay states, particularly Kelantan and Terengganu on the east coast of the peninsula, and Brunei. It is made on a backstrap or frame loom using a supplementary weft technique in which extra gold and silver threads or metal-wrapped yarns are inserted between the structural silk or cotton warp and weft yarns, giving the appearance of a design floating on the surface of the cloth (**3**). More recently, polyester fabric and coloured metallic threads have become popular. Geometric and floral motifs compose the main designs, and *songket* is occasionally added over *ikat* patterning or in the borders surrounding an *ikat*-patterned main field (**2**). *Songket* designs can cover the entire cloth, the areas that are visible when worn, or just the borders and end panels.

Songket and its patterns were associated with *adat*, customary law, and were made for *adat* ceremonies. The end of sumptuary laws and the decline of royal sponsorship moved the main centres of *songket* production out of the courts. Today, *songket* is a source of income for women weaving from their home or in handicraft centres, as well as being mass-produced on mechanized looms by major textile manufacturers. Since the mid-20th century, the use of *songket* has spread widely in the island world to represent 'tradition' as part of general displays of wealth, status and ethnic identity on ceremonial occasions ranging from weddings and circumcisions to festivals and state functions.

1. Man's sash (*cawek*) or shoulder cloth (*slendang*) (detail)

The silver *songket* on this red silk textile comprises bands of varying widths and multiple patterns, which in some instances cover the base fabric entirely. A red ground is typical colouration for textiles from Sumatra, with brighter hues for younger people and darker ones for elders. The sash has long fringes with pom-poms, which are typical for a man's ceremonial waist sash, but usually the patterns at either end of a sash are separated by a long plain section, which is not the case here. It is possible that the two end pieces were repurposed into a shoulder cloth by sewing them together.

1860s–1870s
Padang highlands, Sumatra, Indonesia
Silk, rattan, silver
Length 176 cm, width 22.5 cm
As,Bk.30

2. Cloth (*slendang*)

The combination of silk *ikat* fabric with *songket* was produced for the royal courts in Trengganu and Kelantan on the east coast of peninsular Malaysia, as well as on Sumatra. Here, the end panels and borders, composed primarily of floral and floral-geometric patterns, almost completely cover the silk fabric, leaving the *ikat* pattern visible only in the centrefield, a standard format that may have developed from design arrangements on imported Indian cloths.

Late 19th–early 20th century
Kelantan or Trengganu, Malaysia
Silk, gold
Length 220 cm, width 85.5 cm
As1955,06.2

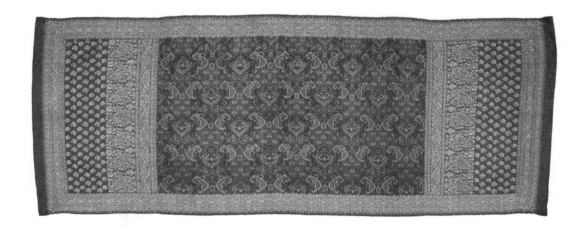

3. Skirt cloth (detail)

This skirt cloth displays patterns and arrangements related to Indian cloths that became prominent in many parts of island Southeast Asia, including the triangular *tumpal* motif, the eight-petalled floral design, stylized birds and leaves, and narrow strips of geometric elements framing larger bands of floral-geometric designs, such as stars. Many *songket* textiles from around the region share designs, indicating the extensive political and family alliances among Southeast Asian elites and the fact that in some centres textiles and pattern samplers circulated readily.

Early to mid-20th century
Possibly Sumatra, Indonesia
Silk, gold
Length 184 cm, width 87 cm
As 1992,05.15

6 | 7 Chin textiles

Comprising more than seventy different groups, the Chin peoples live in Chin and Rakhine States in Myanmar, as well as India and Bangladesh. Given this wide geographic distribution, their textiles are likewise highly variable.

Among the Chin, blankets were once the main form of clothing for men, along with loin cloths and headwrappers, while women wore tunics and skirts. Bags were carried by both sexes. Patterning indicated whether the wearer was male or female and his or her rank in society. It also indicated the event at which a cloth was being used, with some textiles reserved for festivals and exchanges, including marriages and ritual feasting (1). Production could also be associated with rank, and particular patterns were restricted to weavers of high-rank and specific clans. Because of the complexity of producing Chin textiles, they were prized heirlooms kept within families.

The earliest textiles were made of local cotton and flax and coloured with vegetable dyes. Later examples also incorporate Chinese silk, commercial cotton from India and synthetic materials and dyes. Chin textiles tend to be warp-faced, meaning there are more warp yarns (which are tied to the loom) than weft ones (which are woven into the fixed warps). Along with warp stripes, geometric shapes, produced with supplementary weft yarns and twill weaving, dominate the textiles (2, 3). As indicated by old records and travellers' accounts, patterning was gradually expanded to cover more and more of the textile over the course of the 19th century (4). All Chin textiles are woven on a backstrap loom.

1. Ceremonial blanket (*cong-nak puan*)

Cong-nak puan are worn by men and women at feasts of merit and other ceremonies. Made of two backstrap-woven loom widths, this blanket is decorated with warp stripes, diamond twill weave and discontinuous supplementary weft patterning. Such designs could take a year to complete.

Early 20th century
Mara or Lai Chin peoples, northern Chin State, Myanmar
Cotton, silk
Length 209 cm, width 140 cm
Donated by D. Hay-Neave,
As 1948,07.99

2. Man's ceremonial mantle (*tawnok*) (detail)

Displaying the prevalent arrangement of warp and weft stripes typical of Chin textiles, this man's ceremonial blanket has numerous green, black and red warp stripes and two horizontal bands of yellow diamond twill weave that divide the textile approximately into thirds. The discontinuous supplementary weft *vai puan* stripes in red, white and black are the most technically difficult element and can also be seen on other textiles besides the *tawnok*. While used at feasts of merit, *tawnok* could also function as shrouds.

Early 20th century
Siyin Chin peoples, Tiddim area, Chin State, Myanmar
Cotton, silk
Length 193 cm, width 131 cm
Donated by D. Hay-Neave,
As 1948,07.107

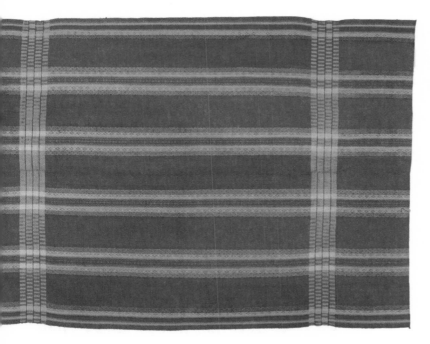

3. Ceremonial blanket (*vai puan*) (detail)

Only women from high-status clans were allowed to weave *vai puan*, ceremonial blankets identified and judged by the technically difficult, discontinuous supplementary weft-patterned red, black and white stripes in the centres of six decorative bands.

Early 20th century
Mara or Lai Chin peoples,
Haka area, northern Chin state,
Myanmar
Cotton, silk
Length 190 cm, width 148 cm
Donated by D. Hay-Neave,
As1948,07.102

4. Ceremonial blanket (*can-lo puan*) (detail)

Worn by high-ranking men, *can-lo puan* display the discontinuous supplementary weft, diamond-shaped *tial* pattern that the Mara peoples say represents animals' and birds' eyes. Made from two backstrap loom widths, these cloths are recognizable by their six white stripes. Traditionally, they were woven by the wives of high-status men of the Zahau, Zotung and Mara Chin groups.

Early 20th century
Mara Chin peoples, Haka area,
northern Chin State, Myanmar
Cotton, silk
Length 209 cm, width 131 cm
As1928,0605.81

6 | 8 Karen textiles

The Karen peoples, some of whom are now Christian, comprise a number of related groups that live in Thailand and Myanmar. They once produced clothes, blankets and bags on backstrap looms using locally cultivated cotton and natural dyes. Men and women wore decorated, dark-coloured tube-skirts, tunic-style shirts and head cloths, while children dressed in relatively plain, light-coloured, long shirts composed of two widths of cloth sewn together lengthwise leaving holes for the head and arms.

Karen textiles are mostly made of warp-faced plain weave with warp *ikat* patterning on the most elaborate items (**1**). Additional decoration was added with continuous and discontinuous supplementary weft threads of varying colours to produce small, repetitive geometric and figural patterns. The lavish use of Job's Tears (*Coix lachrymi*) seeds is another common decorative technique among the Pwo and Sgaw Karen (**2**), while the Pwo and the Paku also embroidered textiles.

Depending on the conservatism of the group, many Karen people now wear traditional clothing only on special occasions, if at all, and home-woven items have increasingly become heirloom objects. Recently, a new trend has seen ethnic identity being reasserted by wearing home-woven Karen clothing.

1. Skirt cloth (*ni*)
Decorated with warp striping, warp *ikat* and complex supplementary weft designs, the skirt consists of two joined cotton panels. The central section is dominated by 'python skin' patterning, a series of repetitive geometric shapes created with the warp *ikat* technique on women's skirt cloths by the Sgaw Karen. The origin of this pattern is related in a Karen legend.

c. 1860
Sgaw Karen peoples, Myanmar
Cotton
Length 114 cm, width 71 cm
Donated by A. W. Franks, collected by Morden Carthew, As.6881

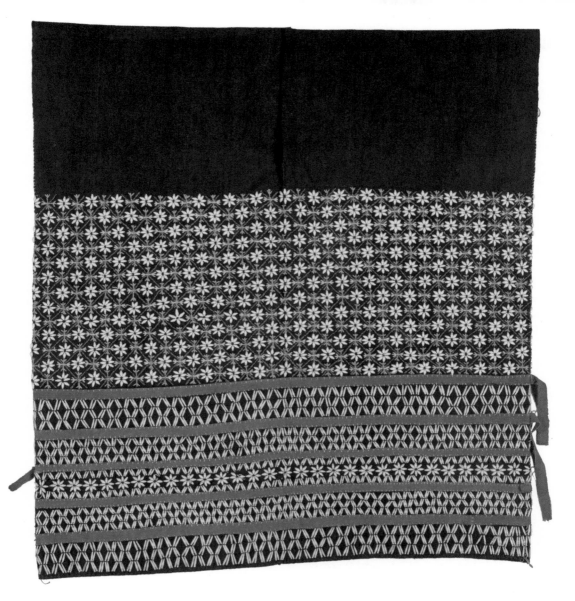

2. Shirt (*hse*)

Acquired in Tenasserim, now lower Myanmar, and presented to the biology section of the British Museum in 1844 for its seeds, this tunic comprises two pieces of indigo-dyed cotton cloth stitched together. It is a beautiful example of a Pwo Karen woman's shirt, decorated with Job's Tears seeds in floral and geometric patterns, embroidery in red, yellow and white, and appliquéd strips of red fabric. Some Karen women in Thailand still produce this type of shirt.

1800–1840
Pwo Karen peoples, Tanintharyi (Tenasserim) region, Myanmar
Cotton, Job's Tears seeds (Coix lachrymi)
Length 77 cm, width 69 cm
As 1979,Q.101

6 | 9 Shan States and Lan Na

The Shan and northern Thai of Lan Na are related people. They are part of the Tai groups occupying eastern Myanmar and northern Thailand, Laos, and Vietnam that share textile designs and weaving techniques. Using frame looms, women once made wide cotton trousers, headcloths and loose shirts for men and striped skirt cloths and sometimes Chinese-style jackets for themselves (**1, 2**). Bags were used by men and women (**3**).

The region was a major trade hub between China and mainland Southeast Asia, with patterns, clothing and materials, such as coloured yarns, sequins, beads, velvets and silks, traded at the regular regional markets visited by many different ethnic groups. Textiles sometimes functioned as a form of political interaction. Princess Dararatsami (1873–1933) from Chiang Mai continued to wear northern dress after she became the fifth consort of Thailand's King Chulalongkorn (r. 1868–1910) and lived in Bangkok. There are photographic records of 19th-century Tai princes showing their wives in traditional dress to demonstrate the extent of their political alliances.

1. Skirt (*phasin*)
Produced for a wealthy woman, this skirt is made of four pieces of cotton cloth. The ground is a plain weave decorated with supplementary weft diamond and zig-zag designs typical of Tai textiles in yellow silk yarn. The elaborate lower border displays a diamond-patterned band framed by floral-geometric patterning in discontinuous supplementary weft silk threads coloured yellow, green, blue and white. The lower edge of the end panel displays the typical fringe-like motif found in central and northern Thailand in a variety of media.

Late 19th century
Northern Thailand
Cotton, silk
Length 93.5 cm, width 69 cm
Donated by H. B. Garrett,
As 1910,-.54

2. Skirt (*phasin*) (detail)
A high-status skirt cloth, this piece is embellished with supplementary weft silk and gold-wrapped threads in diamond and eight-point star motifs on a diamond twill black ground. Some of the appliquéd chequerboard patterning is made of gold-covered leather pieces.

1850–1860s
Shan State, Myanmar
Cotton, silk, gold, leather
Length 93 cm, width 77 cm
Donated by Edward Sladen,
As.7158

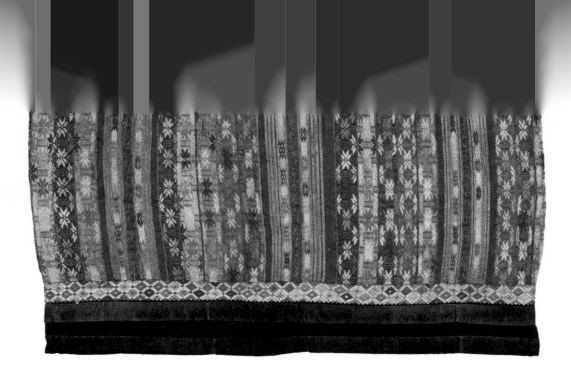

3. Shoulder bag and detail

This beautifully produced bag, a type commonly used among many ethnic groups in Myanmar, is patterned with bands of continuous and discontinuous supplementary weft geometric designs in green, orange, pink, black and white yarns, as well as embroidered with red yarns. Job's Tears seeds have been applied as stripes and stars.

Late 19th or turn of the 20th century
Tawngpeng, Shan State, Myanmar
Cotton, silk, Job's Tears seeds
(*Coix lachrymi*)
Height 86 cm, width 20 cm
As 1904,0626.6

Living in the highlands of southern China, northeastern Myanmar and northern Thailand, Akha groups grow their own materials for weaving, including cotton and indigo to dye the yarns a deep blue-black colour. Men's dress is relatively plain, consisting of turbans, dark short jackets and trousers for everyday wear and similar clothing embellished with appliqué, embroidery and silver ornaments for festive occasions. Women wear a short plain skirt pleated at the back, leggings, highly decorated coats that reach to mid-hip over a halter-top, a sash and elaborate headdresses (1). Both men and women carry bags. Clothing identifies a person's age group, economic position and marital status, and unmarried people tend to wear brightly coloured textiles with extensive patterning. Young children wear caps but not sashes. Additions, such as Job's Tears seeds, to clothing are made during the teenage years as a person approaches a marriageable age.

Akha textiles are distinctive for their embroidery and appliqué patterns, some of which are now made from commercial fabrics purchased at markets that take place at intervals in the hill villages. The embroidery consists of rows of running and cross-stitch lines, as well as patches of satin stitch. Triangles, diamond shapes and narrow strips in a variety of colourful cloth pieces are couched in place to make dense patterns (2).

1. Headdress

Hats are embellished according to marital and economic status with whatever appeals to the wearer, including beads, feathers, fur and silver coins. Made of a framework of leaves with a bamboo rim and decorated with red and white seeds, bamboo and basketry strips, nut shells and beetle wings, this headdress would have been worn by an unmarried woman. Once, Akha women wore these hats constantly, but since the 1990s, they are more commonly donned on special occasions.

Late 19th century
U Lo-Akha peoples, northern Thailand
Leaves, bamboo, seeds, nut shells, beetle wings
Height 29 cm, width 23 cm
As 1903,-.23

2. Woman's jacket

The designs on the sleeves and back panel of this jacket are composed of appliquéd strips, as well as repeating diamonds and triangles of coloured fabric and multicoloured embroidery, including couching and cross, running and chain stitching. Job's Tears seeds, tassels and metallic beads add to the lively appearance. The base fabric comprises four pieces of indigo-dyed cotton. The jacket was made for festive occasions.

Early to mid-20th century
Loimi-Akha peoples, northern Thailand
Cotton, metal, seeds
Length 69 cm, width 136 cm
As1981,21.75

6 | 11 Textiles of the Hmong

Large groups of Hmong emigrated from China to the highlands of Vietnam, Laos and Thailand in the 19th century. More recently, owing to the war in Vietnam in the 1960s and 1970s, many have resettled in the United States.

When maintaining a nomadic way of life in the mountainous regions of Southeast Asia, jewelry, dress and other easily portable items became essential social and cultural markers among the various Hmong groups, with a family's rank and wealth demonstrated by the materials and complexity of their clothing (**3**). Girls learn from their mothers how to spin and dye yarns, weave cloth, embroider and produce appliqué patterns when they are very young. Over the years they develop a body of clothing as a trousseau, with their abilities contributing to their desirability as marriage partners.

Women produce textiles in the times between farming and other household tasks. Hemp and cotton are coloured with indigo, natural or synthetic dyes and elaborately decorated with cross-stitch embroidery, appliqué, batik-resist patterns, beads and coins (**1**). While darker colours prevailed in the late 19th and early 20th centuries, more recently bright colours have become popular, and embroidery and strips of printed floral cloth from China have been replacing the more difficult technique of appliqué. Even though techniques and materials are simpler, and jeans and t-shirts are more prevalent, the traditional style of textiles retains its social significance. Special clothes, including bags, with substantial decoration are worn during festivals (**2**), and items of clothing for babies are decorated with protective patterns.

1. Skirt

As an item of clothing made by a woman for her daughter's dowry, this skirt displays traditional techniques, including indigo dyeing, batik patterning, cross-stitch embroidery and pleating. The embroidery band is in orange, red and white, while the white batik designs, comprising geometric shapes, concentric lines, and designs resembling cross-stitches, are thickly distributed across the central section. Skirts were worn with leggings, jacket, sash and apron.

1900 to mid-1920s
Hmong peoples, northern Thailand
Cotton
Length 55 cm, width 42 cm
Donated by J. Cater, As 1984,16.1

2. Money bag

The Hmong used small, square bags to hold money. This example's design is typical, with pom-poms around a square embroidered and appliquéd panel, as well as glass beads and tassels. The embroidery includes chain, satin and running stitches.

Mid-20th century
Thailand
Cotton, wool, glass
Length 21 cm, width 17 cm
As1983,09.35

3. Jacket

As the Hmong have spread across the highland regions of mainland Southeast Asia, different groups have developed varying designs. This jacket from northern Vietnam displays very thin strips of coloured fabric appliqué interspersed with wider bands of embroidery. The floral and geometric patterns are less stylized than those found on Hmong clothing from Thailand.

20th century
Northern Vietnam
Cotton
Length 42 cm, width 148 cm
As1995,28.4

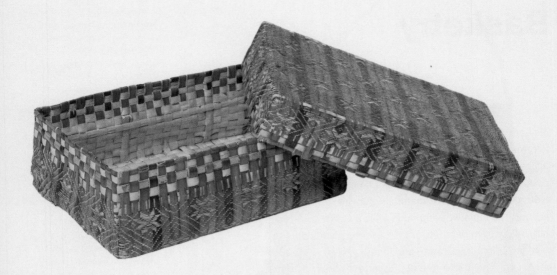

1. Box

Although the basketry looks complex, this box is made of plain chequerwork interlacing in red, brown and natural colours. The patterning has been created by cutting the fibre strips on the outside of the lid and base into narrow lengths and interweaving them to create eight-point star motifs surrounded by white diagonal lines. These resemble the patterns commonly found on Tai textiles from northern Thailand, Laos, Shan State in Myanmar and Sipsong Panna in southwestern China.

Mid-19th century
Thailand
Rattan
Height 9 cm, width 26.5 cm
As2004,03.1.a–b

2. Steamer (*paung-o*)

Soaked in lacquer to strengthen the materials against rot, this *paung-o*, made of coiled rattan or bamboo bound together, would have been used to steam packets of food wrapped in leaves. The upper curve and lip of the steamer resemble earthenware pots commonly used for cooking and to hold water in many parts of Southeast Asia.

Mid-20th century
Myanmar
Bamboo or rattan, lacquer
Height 18 cm, diameter 22 cm
Donated by Ralph and Ruth Isaacs, 1998,0723.44

Basketry

Basketry forms a major part of the material culture of Southeast Asia, and such objects are still used extensively for functional purposes and in rituals and ceremonies. It is sometimes also used as a base for other materials, such as lacquer. The main weaving material is plant fibre, particularly from bamboo, grasses, various types of palm including sago, rattan and lontar, and pandanus, a palm-like tree (**2**). Either the fibres of these plants are separated into strands or whole leaves are used for the weaving process. While loom weaving is associated with women physically and symbolically in Southeast Asia, both men and women produce basketry by hand, though women predominate; basketry can be an important secondary occupation for women. If the objects are for use locally, then usually the materials are sourced in the immediate region. Regional trade in raw materials supports larger-scale production. In many small-scale communities, basketry is a way of demonstrating skill within gender roles and therefore marriageability. Among the Uut Danum of Borneo, oral literature describes their ways of life:

> Gathered like a flock of rhinoceros hornbills, you were sitting on mats made of *Lajan* leaves ... each one plaiting a different design...
> (Couderc 2012, 304)

Basketry is used for many things, from walls of houses to mats, hats, shoes, toys, coverings, agricultural and hunting equipment including fish nets and traps, and domestic, commercial and ceremonial containers (**5**, **6**). Basketry covered with foil was even used to make television satellite dishes in the second half of the 20th century. While many functional objects are not decorated,

3. Carrying basket
Southeast Asians developed techniques that made use of elements moving in several directions, as seen in the openwork of this carrying basket composed of three strands – a horizontal element and two others that move obliquely, one to the left and the other to the right. The fineness of the strips and the loose weave indicate that the basket was not used for heavy goods. The carrying straps are made of bark.

19th century
Malay peninsula
Cane, bark
Height 54.5 cm, width 40 cm
Donated by the Sultan of Perak,
As 1902,0715.51

4. Basket (*selop*)

Baskets like this one were attached to belts to carry rice seeds while sowing, and they were also used as containers for betel equipment. This example has oblique twill patterns. There is a band of twining around the rim, and the carrying rope is also twined. While women wove the bodies of baskets, often men made the rims and attached the two together.

Late 19th century
Baram River District, Sarawak, Borneo
Cane
Height 23.8 cm, width 21.3 cm
As1904,0416.17

5. Mat (*tikar burit*)

Mats were generally important among Borneo communities for sitting and sleeping, as well as for wrapping belongings. They would have been provided for a guest to sit on as a mark of hospitality. Most mats were plain, with patterned ones used on special occasions. This example was made with an oblique twill weave in black and natural colours with curvilinear patterns (representing plants and associated with fertility) that were popular among some Borneo communities. The piece is edged with red fabric. Red, black and natural or white are part of a Southeast Asian symbolic aesthetic dating back to ancient times.

Early 20th century
Northern Borneo
Rattan, cotton
Length 71.2 cm, width 51 cm
Donated by George Woolley,
As1925,1118.23

6. Backpack (*bango*)

Bango hairy backpacks are still used by the Ifugao for hunting and in connection with ceremonial activities to protect against disasters. This example is made of twilled split rattan on a wooden base, with the loose tufts of fibres protecting the contents during tropical rains.

Late 19th–early 20th century
Ifugao peoples, Luzon, Philippines
Rattan, bejuco
Height 40 cm, width 40.5 cm
As1914,0414.29

some ceremonial pieces are distinguished by the use of coloured fibres, often red or black, or by specific weaves, which can be related to textile techniques (**1**). Sometimes basketry patterns were named and have stories associated with them. Among the Murut of Borneo, a four-cornered, looping pattern is called *nagulalang*. The name is derived from a word about going on a headhunting raid. The story tells of a man who asked his wife to make a basketry pattern, but she was unable to do so. After being accused of being incompetent, she challenged him to prove he was better at men's jobs. He then completed a successful headhunting raid, and once she had the head, she wove the pattern easily (Woolley 1929, 302).

There are numerous production methods, including coiling, plaiting with varying numbers of elements, twill work, wickerwork and mad weave. Coiling involves the wrapping of a spiralling core element (**2**, **8**). Plaiting involves the equal participation of the various elements moving over and under each other (**11**). The most basic plaiting method is chequerwork, in which horizontal and vertical fibres alternately pass over and under each other, sometimes on an oblique angle.

It is a technique produced across Southeast Asia (**1**). Another regional technique is three-strand plaited basketry that involves interlacing fibres diagonally across horizontal and vertical ones to produce hexagonal openings (**3**, **4**). Popular on Borneo and in western Indonesia, twill work involves passing fibres over and under two or more strands (**4**, **5**). Twill work can also be made on the bias. Often used for functional objects, wickerwork has a stiff structure interwoven by flexible fibres, resulting in rigid objects that retain their shape while in use (**7**). Similarly, twining has a stiff structure over which the weft fibres are twisted, but it displays a greater density of weave than wickerwork. A technique called mad weave (*anyam gila*), because of its complexity, is unique to Southeast Asia and involves three pairs of fibres interlaced to form rhombic shapes (**9**). Often more than one technique is used in making a single piece with form and size determined by function (**10**).

Currently, manufactured products are making inroads into basketry traditions, but basketry objects, some now made of woven plastic and other recycled materials, still play a prominent role in Southeast Asia.

7. Carrying basket
This basket is made of rigid bamboo vertical slats, through which strips of bamboo have been woven using the wickerwork technique. The base is made of wood with bamboo at each corner, and the rim is lashed on to ensure the piece holds its circular shape. The accompanying braided bamboo strap, called a tumpline, was used across the top of the head, rather than the shoulders.

Early 1990s
Ifugao peoples, Kiangan, Luzon, Philippines
Bamboo, rattan
Height 63 cm, diameter 43.5 cm
As 1996,04.34.a–b

8. Covered box

The structure of this low, circular, covered box was created by coiling rattan strips and binding them together with flexible bamboo fibres in a decorative pattern.

Mid-19th century
Talaud Islands, Indonesia
Rattan, bamboo
Height 12.3 cm, diameter 22 cm
Donated by A. Meyer,
As,+.1272.a–b

9. Container

Wrapping baskets with imported cloth was a popular production method in the Maluku region. Here the body has been covered with a block-printed cloth, while the lid has been separately covered with red and black material. Although the basket is made of coiled fibres, the lid was created with mad weave (*anyam gila*) that was twisted into a sculptural form with attached coloured cotton yarns, glass beads and shells. Animal-like shapes also made of mad weave have been added around the lower part of the lid.

Mid-19th century
Kei Islands, Maluku, Indonesia
Fibre, cotton
Height 47.5 cm, width 24.5 cm
As 1891,0815.37.a–b

10. Basket

Basketry begins with the
weaving of the base, and
sometimes more than one
weaving method is used on a
single piece. On this basket the
twill weave of the interior base
merges into the sides made with
single fibre strands that cross
pairs of strands at right angles,
a variation on a plain weave.

1960s
Ruhuwa, Seram, Indonesia
Bamboo, rattan
Height 12.8 cm, width 66.1 cm,
depth 65.1 cm
Donated by Roy Ellen,
As 1972,01.127

11. Openwork basket for yarn

Used to hold cotton yarn
during the weaving process,
this two-part basket with
a carrying handle was made
with interlacing elements
and looping paired strands in
a format commonly used on
Sulawesi. The rims where the
upper and lower halves meet
have been strengthened by
a wrapped rattan coil.

Mid-20th century
Barupu, Sulawesi, Indonesia
Fibre
Height 13.25 cm, width 20.25 cm
As 1987,01.53.a–b

Timeline

1896–98	Philippine revolution against Spain
1906	Ho Chi Minh founds Young Men's Buddhist Association in Myanmar
1917–45	École des Arts Cambodgiens
1925	Establishment of the Vietnamese revolutionary youth league
1925–45	École des Beaux-Arts de L'Indochine
1930	Saya San rebellion against British control in Myanmar
1932	Thailand becomes a constitutional monarchy
1941–45	Pacific theatre of the Second World War
1942–45	Japan controls much of Southeast Asia
1946	Philippines becomes independent from the United States
1948	Myanmar becomes independent from Britain
1949	Indonesia becomes independent from the Netherlands
1950	Kalimantan ceded to Indonesia by Dutch
	Indonesian Arts Academy opens
1953	Cambodia and Laos become independent
Mid-20th century	Post-independence development of national dress, such as the *peci* hat and shoulder sashes in Indonesia and a sarong and jacket popularized by Queen Sirikit of Thailand
	Christian Evangelicalism expands in the island region
1957	After a struggle with the government, Central Kalimantan established as a new province in Indonesian Borneo run by and for Dayak peoples
	Malaya becomes independent from Britain
1959–84	Brunei self rule until granted full independence
1960s	Increasing influence of the Middle East in Islamic Southeast Asia
1960s–1970s	Hmong flee the fighting in Laos, arriving in refugee camps in Thailand; many are resettled in the United States
1962	Military coup under General Ne Win ushers in the 'Burmese path to socialism' and isolates Myanmar; expulsion of Indians from Myanmar; companies nationalized
1963	Formation of Malaysia, comprising the Malay peninsula, Singapore, Sarawak and north Borneo
1965	General Suharto comes to power in Indonesia; pogroms against the Chinese
	Singapore separates from Malaysia
1969	Death of Ho Chi Minh
1972	Ferdinand Marcos places the Philippines under martial law
1975	Vietnam reunites the northern and southern halves of the country after more than twenty years of warfare
1975–79	The Khmer Rouge dominate Cambodia, killing up to half the population
1980	Indonesia officially recognizes Dayak religion
1980s onwards	Huge growth of tourism in Southeast Asia
1985	Hun Sen comes to power in Cambodia
1990s	Sales of Southeast Asian modern and contemporary art start at large auction houses
1997	Economic downturn in the region
2002	East Timor becomes independent
2021	Military coup in Myanmar reverses the political and economic developments of the previous decade

7 The 20th and 21st centuries

1. Plate with an image of Gandhi and a Tamil inscription
Engaging in trading and money-lending, Indian communities, particularly Tamils, in Myanmar expanded during the colonial period. This plate is decorated with the *shwezawa* technique, in which gold leaf is fixed to a lacquer surface to create a pattern. The image of Gandhi is an example of how Myanmar artists in different media tailored their productions for specific customers. The Tamil inscription reads: 'Freedom is our birthright. Do not give room for those who try to say or do otherwise. Truth will triumph.'

1930s–1940s
Myanmar
Bamboo, lacquer, gold
Diameter 18 cm
Donated by Henry Noltie,
2001,0209.2

At the start of the 20th century, colonial powers were firmly in control of most of Southeast Asia, but resistance movements, such as the Philippine revolution of 1896 and the Saya San rebellion of 1930 in Myanmar, and nationalist organisations, such as the Young Men's Buddhist Association in Myanmar founded in 1906 and the Vietnamese revolutionary youth league established by Ho Chi Minh in 1925, started to emerge. The Japanese invasion and the Second World War in Southeast Asia from 1941 to 1945 caused devastation, but made independence from European colonial powers possible politically. In some instances, independence occurred without military action, but in others, such as Indonesia and Vietnam, the struggles were protracted and bloody.

In the 1940s, Myanmar, the Philippines and Indonesia acquired independence, the latter after four years fighting the Dutch. Cambodia and Laos were granted partial independence in the 1940s, and both acquired full independence in 1953. Laos became a kingdom again, but it was short-lived as civil war led to the Pathet Lao, a communist group, gaining control, which they hold to this day, in 1975. Cambodia's civil war, supported on opposite sides by North Vietnam and the United States and South Vietnam, ended in 1975 when the ideologically communist Khmer Rouge gained control, instigating four years of devastation. They were only removed when a unified Vietnam, after fighting a protracted war with France and the

2. *Kendi* ritual water vessel
Long-necked water vessels were made in silver and brass for ritual and ceremonial purposes in many parts of island Southeast Asia, including among the Muslim Minangkabau people living in the highlands of central Sumatra. Made from sheet brass soldered together, this *kendi* is decorated with floral and geometric forms particular to Sumatra and similar to those found in wood-carving. They were produced with chasing and repoussé techniques, in which the design is respectively pushed in from the outside or pushed out from the inside with hammers and chisels.

20th century
Minangkabau peoples, Sumatra, Indonesia
Brass
Height 31 cm
2005,0507.1

United States from the 1950s until 1975, invaded. Malaysia became independent in 1957, with Sabah and Sarawak on Borneo added in 1963, and it was also briefly joined by Singapore from 1963 to 1965. The last two countries to obtain independence were Brunei in 1984 and East Timor in 2002. Although Portugal left East Timor in 1975, it was occupied by Indonesia, resulting in a conflict that ended only in 1999.

Having in many cases absorbed Western ideas of rigid ethnic categories, and because of the perceived need to forge unified national identities, the new governments often ignored the voices and imagery of minority groups. This contributed to the emergence of separatist movements, including those of Muslims in the south of Thailand and the Philippines, and the Karen and Kachin in Myanmar. In some instances, Indian and Chinese communities that had expanded under colonialism were expelled or attacked (1). Indians, mostly Tamils, were expelled from Myanmar in 1962, and the Chinese were attacked during the communist purge in Indonesia in 1965. Perceived threats to national unity also contributed to the emergence of military dictatorships under General Suharto in Indonesia in 1965, General Ne Win in Myanmar in 1962 (who closed off the country to the world and set it on the 'Burmese path to socialism') and Ferdinand Marcos in 1972 in the Philippines. The Thai military has also taken control of the country on several occasions since the mid-20th century, most recently

3. Sinah Rang Bala, Carrying basket (*uyut*)

Carrying baskets were used as backpacks by many groups on Borneo to collect food and forest products, and to carry personal possessions. This example has lettering woven into the basket which says 'God bless you all' around the upper edge and 'The truth of God' around the lower, integrating beliefs with everyday practices. Many Borneo societies converted to Christianity in the 19th and 20th centuries, and since the mid-20th century Evangelicalism has developed a growing following in the island region.

c. 1970
Long Peluan, Sarawak, Borneo
Rattan, nylon
Height 47.1 cm
As1988,22.53

under General Prayuth Chan-ocha in 2014. Also supported by the military, Hun Sen has been in power in Cambodia since 1985. Most recently, Myanmar's military, the Tatmadaw, overturned democratic elections in a February 2021 coup.

In the development of nationalist movements and in the post-war period, art was marshalled as propaganda to bolster morale and to construct ideas of unity, using imagery ranging from scenes of plenty to representations of historical figures and monuments, in addition to well-known cultural elements. Students who graduated from European-established art schools, such as the École des Beaux-Arts de L'Indochine (1925–45), the École des Arts Cambodgiens (1917–45) and Silpakorn University, Thailand, founded in 1943, were instrumental in the development of national modern art movements. At these schools, artists were initially trained in Western techniques, materials and ideas to represent landscapes and scenes of daily life. Soon locally sponsored schools opened, such as the Indonesian Arts Academy in 1950, and repertoires enlarged and became more experimental. More recently, artists' groups and collectives, such as The Artists Village in Singapore, Stiev Selapak in Cambodia and 98B Collaboratory in the Philippines, have been providing support for artists, critically assessing artistic concepts and assumptions, and expanding art-making across disciplines.

As conflicts slowed or ceased in the late 20th century, art became important in other ways. The burgeoning trade in antiquities from the 1960s and 1970s led to the trafficking of looted objects and a large industry producing fakes. The destruction of archaeological and historic sites through uncontrolled digging and removal of statuary and architectural elements became a major problem, of which the most publicized is the material taken from Cambodia.

International, and later regional and local, tourism prompted the extensive production of souvenirs in homes, small workshops and large factories, including replicas of earlier art forms and minority groups' textiles. Local individuals and groups have also promoted a re-engagement with traditional cultural practices, particularly among minority communities. More recently, training in traditional art forms from dance to textiles, metalwork and painting has been revived at universities and educational centres. Southeast Asian art became more prominent in global markets with customers including local collectors. Sotheby's held its first biannual sale of Southeast Asian modern and contemporary art in Singapore in 1996, while Christie's started its sales in 2004.

As religious beliefs and practices have changed, new imagery and art forms have been adopted and adapted. In the 20th and 21st centuries, shamans, healers and wizards have continued to play a role among many groups. As societies have shifted towards globalized modernity, some traditional accoutrements – hand-written manuals, and hand-made staffs and coats, for example – have fallen out of use, while others still play important roles in ritual (2) or are made in new forms or with new materials. Objects associated with Buddhism, Islam and Christianity combine the local and the global. Links with the Middle East have prompted changes in mosque form and dress; Buddhist paintings utilize modern imagery and techniques in illustrations of old stories; and Christian ideas and symbols are incorporated into everyday objects (3). Technology too has been harnessed to support older activities, as well as contribute to social, political and religious innovations. In the art being produced today, past and present intertwine to create modern Southeast Asia.

7 | 1 War and refugees

There are numerous physical reminders of the wars that have convulsed Southeast Asia during the 20th and 21st centuries. During the Second World War, the Japanese controlled most of the region from 1942 to 1945 and issued local currency in Myanmar, the Philippines, Malaya and Indonesia (**3**). While the transition to independence was relatively smooth in Myanmar and the Philippines after the war, the Indonesians, led by Sukarno, had to fight the Dutch until 1949, despite declaring independence in August 1945. As the conflict between Vietnam and the United States escalated in the 1960s (**4**), Cambodia and Laos were drawn into the war when the United States bombed them in an attempt to destroy Vietnamese military and supply routes, exacerbating internal political disputes. At a tremendous cost in lives, the north Vietnamese reunited the country in 1975, leading to the vast exodus of south Vietnamese. Communist success in Laos and the victory of the extreme Marxist group, the Khmer Rouge, in Cambodia also led to the displacement of people in the second half of the 1970s, many of whom fled to Thailand, Malaysia and Indonesia (**1**). Numerous refugee camps were established, many of which still exist today, since other conflicts in the region, such as the long-running wars between minority groups and the military in Myanmar, continue to cause people to flee their homes. East Timor, which was colonized by the Portuguese, rather than the Dutch, until 1975, was not part of independent Indonesia, and fought the invading Indonesian army from 1975 to 1999, becoming officially independent in 2002. War materiel still litters many parts of Southeast Asia; unexploded ordinance causes casualties even in the 21st century, but the detritus also provides raw materials for new purposes (**2**).

1. Woven and embroidered story cloth (detail)

Laos was drawn into the war between the Vietnamese and the Americans, and many Hmong people who had fought on the side of the United States fled the country in the mid-1970s when the communist Pathet Lao gained control. Story cloths were an invention of the 1970s, when Hmong women in refugee camps were encouraged to make textiles to support their families. These cloths told of life before, during and after the war, and narrated Hmong legends. This one shows soldiers with weaponry and in battle, as well as people leaving their homes with their possessions and livestock.

Late 1970s–early 1980s
Hmong peoples, Thailand
Polyester, cotton
Height 142 cm, width 172 cm
As 1983,09.28

2. Torque

In Southeast Asia, jewelry and ornamentation on clothing can be a way of storing a family's wealth; they also indicate status and attract suitors for unwed women. Although torques are traditionally silver, this one was made of aluminium from the fuselage of an aeroplane downed during the war between Vietnam and the United States. Increasing poverty in many areas has caused silver to be replaced by silver-coloured metals.

1960s
Northern Thailand
Aluminium
Width 20.5 cm
Donated by Andrew Turton,
2018,3034.39

3. Five-*rupiah* Japanese occupation banknote

When Japan defeated the Europeans and Americans in Southeast Asia in the Second World War, the myth of white superiority was destroyed, reshaping intercultural relationships and paving the way for the end of colonialism in the region. Despite proclamations of an 'Asian Co-Prosperity Sphere', however, the Japanese did not share power with local leaders, becoming another colonizer. Japanese-issued currency combined local imagery – here a traditional Karo Batak house on the front and a Minangkabau woman wearing a traditional headcloth on the reverse – with Japanese text. The issuing government is identified as the Imperial Japanese Government in Roman letters and Japanese *kanji*.

1942–45
Imperial Japanese Government, Indonesia
Paper
Width 15 cm, height 7 cm
1980,1212.4

4. Van Da and Nguyen Thu, *Con Co*

North Vietnamese artists produced numerous images of combat and life behind the lines during the war with the French and Americans. The United States controversially began using defoliants, including napalm and Agent Orange, in 1962 to tackle Vietnamese guerilla-style warfare. These toxic chemicals killed everything living in the landscape, leaving, as well as preserving for decades, charred remains like the trees at Con Co seen in this drawing. The chemicals have also caused numerous birth defects.

1965
Vietnam
Charcoal on paper
Height 27.5 cm, width 39 cm
Donated by the British Museum Friends, 1999,0630,0.12

7 | 2 Modern currency

In struggling for independence from the colonial powers and in the establishment of modern nation states, the production and design of currency in Southeast Asia became strongly politicized, often functioning effectively as propaganda. Since independence, local designers have replaced foreign ones, although in most instances Southeast Asian governments use such international currency firms as De La Rue and Giesecke & Devrient for banknote printing, or draw on their expertise in establishing printing works, as Myanmar did in the early 1970s.

Many banknote designs display national heroes and major figures in independence movements, including Aung San in Myanmar, José Rizal in the Philippines, Sukarno in Indonesia and Ho Chi Minh in Vietnam (**1**, **3**, **5**). Immediately after the Second World War, Indonesia had three currencies – Japanese occupation notes, Netherlands East Indies guilders and the *rupiahs* issued by the Indonesian government. The first president of independent Indonesia, Sukarno, described revolution as like an erupting volcano – initially damaging, but eventually productive – and a volcano was pictured on banknotes issued during the Dutch–Indonesian war (1945–49) (**4**). Imagery drawing upon local cultural elements and ancient civilizations, such as Myanmar's mythical lion, the *chinthe*, or historic monuments in Thailand or Cambodia, presented the idea of unified, stable nations with one history or religion (**2**). This was a view that became increasingly important to governments during the various conflicts experienced after independence, including separatist movements by minority groups, such as on the heavily Muslim island of Mindanao in the southern Philippines and the Karen in Myanmar. Within regimes that underwent communist revolutions, imagery was presented in a socialist-realist style (**1**, **2**, **3**). The Marxist Khmer Rouge issued coins and banknotes briefly before abolishing money altogether during their control of Cambodia from 1975 to 1979 (**2**). In a unified Vietnam, portrayals of agriculturalists, workers and factories on banknotes emphasized the goals of the government (**1**).

1. 2000 *dong* banknote
The front of this banknote portrays Ho Chi Minh, who directed the Vietnamese independence movement and led the country from the early 1940s until his death in 1969. The reverse depicts women working in a textile factory to convey a positive image of industrialization and labour, and in combination with other banknotes of different denominations, it would show the variety of work available.

1988
State Bank of Vietnam
Paper
Width 13.3 cm, height 6.5 cm
2007,4125.17

2. Five *riel* banknote

The Khmer Rouge in Cambodia
issued their own currency,
featuring agrarian and military
imagery and such architectural
masterpieces as the 12th-
century Angkor Wat, before
eliminating money. They radically
reorganized society by forcing
city dwellers to move to the
countryside in order to farm
grossly mismanaged collectives,
triggering a famine that, along
with other causes, killed
from 1.5 million to 3 million
Cambodians, about a quarter
to a half of the population,
between 1975 and 1979.

1975
Banque Nationale du Cambodge
Paper
Width 12 cm, height 5.7 cm
2017,4036.4

3. Forty-five *kyat* banknote

In 1987, the Socialist Republic of
the Union of Burma government
cancelled 25, 35 and 75 *kyat*
notes as legal tender, and
45 and 90 *kyat* notes (based
on General Ne Win's lucky
number 9) were issued instead.
In Myanmar, astrology and
numerology have been important
to establish when to start
enterprises, such as embarking
on a journey, commissioning a
monastery or building a house,
but in this instance the currency
alteration obliterated most
people's savings. This banknote
depicts U Po Hla Gyi, a leader
in the independence movement
against the British (front), and
oil fields and workers (reverse).

1987
Issued by Union Bank of Burma
Paper
Width 15.6 cm, height 7.5 cm
Donated by T. Richard Blurton,
2006,0805.9

4. One *rupiah* banknote

In August 1945 Sukarno
declared Indonesia's
independence from the
Netherlands, but it was not until
December 1949, after hard
fighting, that Indonesia became
autonomous. Under the slogan
'Unity in diversity', modern
Indonesia combined politically
the numerous cultures that were
once the Dutch East Indies.
Among many of these peoples,
mountains played an important
symbolic role, including as a
locus of spiritual power, and
images of volcanoes were
illustrated on both sides of
this one *rupiah* banknote
issued in 1945.

October 1945
Government of Indonesia
Paper
Width 13.9 cm, height 6.5 cm
1980,0378.589

5. Two *peso* banknote

This two *peso* banknote
shows an image of José Rizal
(1861–1896), a writer who
called for political reforms and
was executed by the Spanish
after the start of the Philippine
rebellion in 1896. The United
States assumed colonial control
of the Philippines after the brief
Spanish-American war in 1898.
Early examples of Philippine
banknotes were modelled after
green American dollars, but
shortly after independence
in 1946, more colourful local
designs were introduced.

1949
Banco Central, Philippines
Paper
Width 16 cm, height 6.7 cm
1977,0802.10

7 | 3 Islamic trends

Brunei Darussalam and the Federation of Malaysia (which comprises the Malay peninsula and two states on Borneo, Sabah and Sarawak) have both had Islam as the official state religion since their independence from the British in 1984 and 1963, respectively. Although Indonesia has the largest number of Muslim citizens of any state, it is a secular country. Islam in Southeast Asia became more conservative as prosperity brought opportunities to go on the hajj pilgrimage to Mecca in Saudi Arabia and students travelled to study in the Middle East in the 1960s. Southeast Asia became more closely connected with the global Islamic community (*umma*), with Arabs viewed as religiously correct owing to their association with the birthplace of Islam. Oil-rich Middle Eastern countries and individuals have also promoted conservative Islamic views through business, educational and cultural investments. Anwar Ibrahim (b. 1947) institutionalized the call for greater Islamification (*dakwah*) in Malaysia in the early 1980s. Upon independence, Brunei's Sultan Hassanal Bolkiah (r. 1967–present) styled his position as defender of the faith through the Malay Muslim Monarchy state ideology, and Brunei formally adopted Islamic *sharia* law in 2014.

The growing Islamic movements of the late 20th century had an impact upon cultural expressions in Southeast Asia. Women increasingly wore body-obscuring clothing and headscarves, although these were generally made of local batik and colourful cloths rather than black fabric. Textile hangings were embroidered with extracts from the Qur'an and the profession of faith in the Southeast Asian *songket* technique (**1**). Local art forms were Islamicized in the 19th and early 20th centuries, as in the case of the semi-divine clown Semar from Java (**2**). External funding has also promoted the construction of mosques in a Middle Eastern style (**3**).

1. Wall hanging with Qur'anic text

Using the *songket* technique (see pp. 224–25), weavers in Pandai Sikek in the early 2000s began producing wall hangings with religious texts to be framed and hung in homes. The technique is associated with rank and prestige, so is considered appropriate for the first verse of the Surah Al-Fatihah (first chapter) of the Qur'an written in Arabic script, as seen here. The text praises and gives thanks to God, as well as asking for mercy and guidance.

2016
Pandai Sikek, Sumatra, Indonesia
Cotton and metal thread
Height 51 cm, width 69 cm
2016,3065.4

2. Rastika, Reverse glass painting of the semi-divine clown Semar

Semar is a semi-divine being from Indonesian mythology and the primary clown (*punakawan*) of Javanese shadow theatre. Although shadow theatre mostly enacts local versions of the Mahabharata and Ramayana epics, over time Islamic concepts and beliefs have been incorporated. In one shadow play, Semar travels on the hajj to Mecca. Although usually wearing a chequered cloth indicating his divinity, Semar is here composed of Arabic calligraphy of the Muslim declaration of belief in God and the acceptance of Muhammad as His prophet. Reverse glass painting developed in Indonesia only in the 19th century.

Early 1990s
West Java, Indonesia
Pigment on glass
Height 70 cm, width 49.5 cm
2016,3020.2

3. Postcard of the Sultan Mosque in Singapore

The first mosque in Singapore was constructed by Sultan Hussain Shah of Johor in 1826 in traditional Southeast Asian style with a two-tiered pyramidal roof. By 1924, it was too small for the growing Muslim community, and it was rebuilt by Denis Santry of the architectural firm Swan & Maclaren in a Middle Eastern and Indian style with minarets and domes (shown here). It is a popular tourist site and in 1975 was declared a national monument.

Malayan Color Views Company
1960s
Singapore
Printing inks on paper
Height 9 cm, width 13.8 cm
EPH-ME.1760

1. Painting on cloth

A popular tourist destination since the early 20th century, Bali adapted art forms rapidly to suit foreign tastes. The ruler of Ubud, local artists and Western ones promoted the representation of Balinese life, festivals and the landscape on paper in the 1930s. This was in part a response to Western artistic imagery. The production of such pictures became standardized over time and expanded to painting on cloth, as here. These images combine figures full of movement with busy landscapes of decorative, repetitive foliage, in contrast to traditional painting.

1970s–early 1980s
Ubud, Bali, Indonesia
Pigment on cotton
Length 39 cm, width 32 cm
As 1984,13.20

2. Batik painting of Vishnu

The god Vishnu in the form of a shadow puppet riding on his mount, the mythical bird Garuda, is the subject of this batik painting. As tourism to Southeast Asia increased in the 1960s, Javanese batik paintings became increasingly popular and are now common products available in a full range of qualities. They are produced on cotton or synthetic cloth using a combination of implements, including the traditional *canting* spouted cup. The process of waxing, dyeing, re-waxing and re-dyeing until the desired effect is achieved remains unchanged. Replica batiks are now also printed in factories.

1970s–early 1980s
Java, Indonesia
Cotton
Length 61 cm, width 45 cm
As 1984,13.24

Tourism and commercialization

Until the early 1980s, Southeast Asia primarily engaged with international economies through the export of agricultural and natural products, as had been the tradition for more than two millennia, although a tourism industry had been developing since transportation technology began improving in the late 19th century. The Irrawaddy Flotilla Company Ltd operated passenger and cargo transport services along the Irrawaddy River in Myanmar between 1865 and the 1942, and in the 1930s Bali, Java and Sumatra were marketed by the Netherland Indies tourism information bureau as 'wonder isles of colour'. In the 1980s, however, tourism grew exponentially. Regional tourism, such as from Hong Kong, Taiwan, Japan, South Korea and later China, and tourism within the Association of Southeast Asian Nations (ASEAN), also became a major part of the boom. Local tourism, including religious pilgrimages and visits to national and historical monuments, expanded greatly due to the growing prosperity of Southeast Asians. Individual countries' marketing efforts to attract tourists were successful, such as the Visit Thailand Year 1987, and ASEAN countries worked to promote the region jointly with Visit ASEAN Year 1992. Numerous Southeast Asians came to depend financially on tourism. This is not to say that the industry experienced continuous growth, as the 1997 financial crisis, the 2003 SARS epidemic, the 2004 tsunami, various terrorist incidents in the early 2000s and lately the Covid-19 pandemic have all caused serious downturns in tourism, resulting in financial catastrophe for many.

Tourism has impacted the production of arts and crafts in Southeast Asia. Host areas in some instances modified and adapted cultural expression to suit touristic needs, and this in turn could become part of the cultural mainstream. Theatrical performances at Javanese courts that were traditionally accompanied by food were transformed into performances with receptions. There are school trips to Borobudur and Prambanan for Indonesian children to understand the past and reify national identity. Pilgrimage has always been part of Buddhism, and tour companies cater for people visiting famous stupas, temples and Buddha images in Myanmar and Thailand. Objects are made for these local tourists, including religious items in traditional and contemporary formats for home shrines (**5, 6**). While goods made for a tourist market are often simpler than traditional crafts, they can also represent practices adapted for a new market (**1**), as well as industrialized production. New shapes, such as picture frames, and new art forms, such as batik painting (**2**), became common, and tourism also stimulated the further manufacture of models and miniatures (see pp. 120–23). Photography resulted in the production of visiting cards and postcards depicting local sites and peoples. Initially encouraged by Christian missionaries, such minority groups as the Hmong and Karen in northern Thailand produced their textiles as shirts and trousers for sale to tourists (**3**). One result is that tourism has become connected with issues of identity as minority groups and their art forms have become commoditized. Workshops making souvenirs in mass quantities, sometimes on assembly lines, have proliferated along with sales venues and export companies, forming a major part of the tourist economy. Ceramic production in old and new forms for export and local consumption remains a major industry in Vietnam and Thailand (**4**).

3. Sgaw Karen waistcoat

This waistcoat is made of embroidered and brocaded cotton, with a diamond patterning based on designs known from at least the 19th century. The production of Karen textiles in Western forms, like this waistcoat, has been in evidence for more than a century, as they were made as gifts for colonial officials and missionary families. With the displacement of Karen communities into refugee camps in Thailand during the ongoing war with the Myanmar state, making textiles became a source of income, and in the 1980s and 1990s numerous workshops were established.

Mid-20th century
Sgaw Karen peoples, Thailand
Cotton
Length 59 cm, width 58 cm
(at hem)
As1981,21.28

4. Blue-and-white and celadon bowl

Ceramics form a large part of the Vietnamese economy, and exports are worth hundreds of millions of dollars annually. The ceramics industry has drawn on old decorative types, such as celadon glazes and underglaze painting, and has also developed new designs to suit international markets. This bowl innovatively combines celadon and blue-and-white decoration.

1995–96
Vietnam
Porcelain
Diameter 18.3 cm, height 9 cm
Donated by Bich Tyler,
1996,0510.19

5. Popular print of the Phra Chinarat Buddha image

Pilgrimage is important in Buddhism, and people acquire religious souvenirs, such as posters to hang in homes, shrines, restaurants and other public spaces, as a reminder of the Buddha and his teachings. Many depict famous statues of the Buddha and important pilgrimage sites; here, it is the Phra Chinarat Buddha at the Phra Si Rattana Mahathat temple founded in 1357. The inscription gives the name of the Buddha, the monastery and the province. It also states that 'Loving-kindness (*metta*) is the support of the world', encouraging compassionate behaviour.

Siam Gallery Company Ltd
1990
Bangkok, Thailand
Printing inks on paper
Height 53 cm, width 38.5 cm
1991,1022,0.27

6. U Hla Maung, Replicas of the Phaung Daw Oo Buddha images

U Hla Maung produces replica Buddha images in large quantities for sale to pilgrims. The highly revered Buddha images at the Phaung Daw Oo monastery in Myanmar have had so much gold leaf applied to them that they have lost their original shape, and it is these new, rounded forms that are copied using lacquered and gilded clay mixed with ashes and flowers that were offered to the Buddhas. The images are set into metal *palin* – thrones – decorated with the animals representing the days of the week, important elements of astrology in Myanmar.

2017
Lae Char, Shan State, Myanmar
Fired clay, gold leaf, lacquer, metal
Heights from 4.2–8.5 cm
Donated by Gillian and Ron Graham, 2017,3086.1.a–j

7 | 4 Technology, innovation and revivals

While Western tourists seek to experience 'traditional' culture when visiting Southeast Asia, the assumptions that the region is either mired in the past or is changing beyond recognition are not necessarily accurate. Some cultural knowledge of traditional techniques has been lost, but Southeast Asians have also adapted and developed new forms that demonstrate both active interaction with the modern world and retention of earlier social customs and activities. Technology has enabled religion to reach a wide audience in homes and other venues, for example when Qur'an-reading contests are broadcast on the radio and the internet in Malaysia or when the sermons of Buddhist monks are made available via compact discs or through social media (**1**). Comic books are used to convey older stories, as when Thailand's King Bhumibol Adulyadej (r. 1946–2016) published a version of the Buddhist Mahajanaka Jataka in 1996. As discussed in Chapter 5, many theatrical types are no longer as popular as they once were, but artists are using modern instruments to accompany performances, developing such innovative forms as *Wayang Hip Hop* that mixes new and old (**2**), and creating contemporary stories. Other artists actively work to revive older forms, giving them a modern twist (**3**), to ensure that they do not get forgotten.

1. Compact disc with Buddhist sermons

This compact disc has recordings of five sermons delivered by the five monks pictured on it. In Myanmar, monks' sermons are often recorded on CDs and DVDs, to be sold in markets, from street stalls, and at religious sites. Sermons are also available to download from websites. They develop connections between devotees and specific monks, and enable monks to broadcast their ideas widely.

2013–14
Myanmar
Plastic and paper
Diameter 11.9 cm
2014,3026.1

2. Catur Kuncoro, *Wayang Hip Hop* puppet of Semar and a microphone

The clown Semar from traditional Javanese shadow theatre is presented here as a character in *Wayang Hip Hop*, a theatrical form created in 2010 by puppeteer Catur Kuncoro that mixes Javanese hip hop songs with comic sketches about contemporary topics. Although this Semar wears modern clothes and stylish sports shoes and uses 3-D glasses and a microphone, his body shape and facial features instantly identify him.

2015–16
Yogyakarta, Java, Indonesia
Hide, horn, bamboo
Height 81.4 cm (clown), height 51.7 cm (microphone)
2016,3035.1, 2016,3035.5

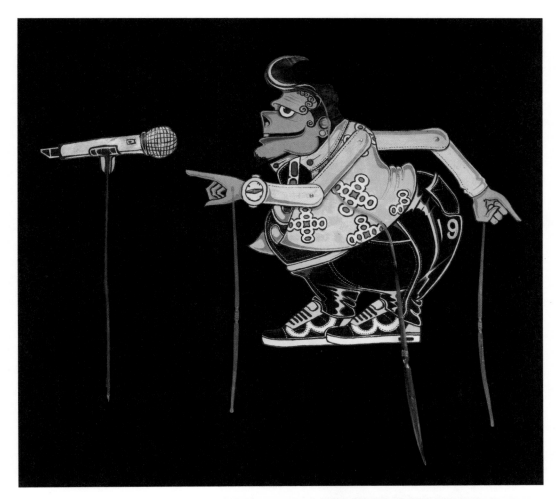

3. Bin Song, Mouth harp (*angkuoch daek*)

Unusually made of iron, this *angkuoch daek* is a revival of a type of musical instrument that is rarely used in Cambodia today. Most *angkuoch* are made from bamboo, but in this instance, the maker, Bin Song, experimented with a new material, creating an innovative variation of the earlier form.

2020
Cambodia
Iron
Length 12 cm, width 2.3 cm
Donated by the Endangered Material Knowledge Programme,
2020,3017.1

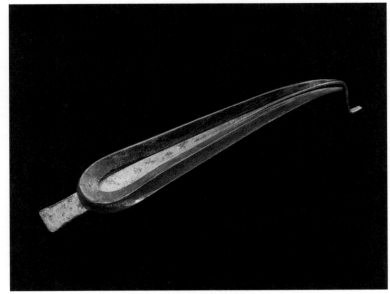

7 | 5 Contemporary art

Over the course of the 19th and 20th centuries, Southeast Asian artists adapted and transformed Western media and techniques, merging them with the personal and the local to express themselves. Although modern and contemporary art has been viewed separately from traditional forms, the two are inextricably intertwined as artists use new methods to reinterpret and explore their world. Vietnam, the Philippines, Thailand and Indonesia have had highly active contemporary art scenes since the 1980s and 1990s. Myanmar has only started to develop one as it emerged from isolation and eased censorship in the 2000s. Some artists, such as Min Wae Aung from Myanmar, focus on detailed, realistic works (**2**), while others, such as José Joya and Fernando Zóbal de Ayala, pioneered and encouraged abstraction in the Philippines (**3**). Artists from Southeast Asia in the diaspora, many displaced by the wars and atrocities of the 20th century, provide an international perspective on the region, and their work often engages with both regional and global socio-political issues, as seen in the work of Vietnamese American Tiffany Chung (**1**).

1. Tiffany Chung, *UNHCR Red Dot Series tracking the Syrian Humanitarian Crisis April–Dec 2012* (9th of 9 drawings)
Tiffany Chung was born in Vietnam in 1969, but her family left for the United States in 1975 at the end of the war. She relocated to Ho Chi Minh City in 2000. In 2007 she began overlaying information gleaned from archival material, news, treaties, memories and interviews on maps to explore political traumas, displacement and migration, and conflict in different parts of the globe. In the process of creating maps, Chung combines the

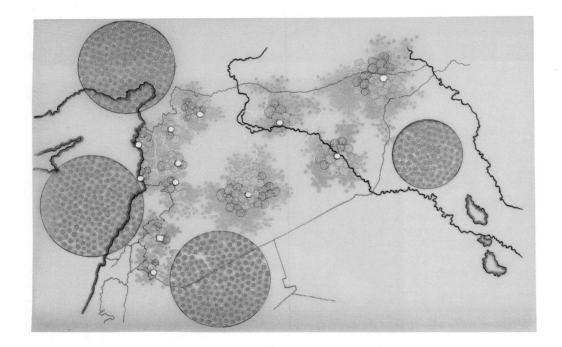

international and the local, exposing the impact of political ideologies on personal experiences by representing the decline or disappearance of urban areas.

2014–15
Vietnam
Oil and ink on vellum and paper
Height 21 cm, width 30 cm
Donated by the UK Government, 2020,3018.9

2. Min Wae Aung, *Novice with Dog*

Born in 1960 in Danubyu, Myanmar, shortly before the military coup that isolated the country, Min Wae Aung first worked as a commercial graphic artist after graduating from the State School of Fine Arts in Yangon (Rangoon). After travelling to the United States and Japan in 1993 and 1994, he developed a realistic aesthetic featuring central images in spaces of solid colours, and he became one of the first Myanmar artists to develop an international reputation. His works display a strong relationship with Buddhism. Based on a photograph, this drawing was commissioned from him in 2000.

2000
Myanmar
Pencil on paper
Height 30.3 cm, width 37.8 cm
Donated by B. D. G. Leviton Foundation, 2017,3083.1

3. José Joya, *Composition Study*

José Joya (1931–1995) was a versatile artist working as a painter, printmaker, mixed-media artist and ceramicist who led the development of abstract expressionism in the Philippines and was a recipient of the National Artist awards. Joya argued that in creating art, the artist is communicating in concrete forms. His work was characterized by bold lines and

imagery, seen in this print as the juxtapositioning of circles and squares and the strong outlines of the shapes.

1967
Philippines
Lithographic print
Height 37.5 cm, width 28 cm
Donated by John Addis, 1984,0203,0.66

Selected bibliography

The publications referenced here do not comprehensively cover the topic, but instead represent a selection of works consulted in the preparation of this book. They are intended as an aid to further reading.

General sources

Baker, Chris & Phongpaichit, Pasuk, 2009, *A History of Thailand*, Bangkok.

Bennett, James (ed.), 2006, *Crescent Moon: Islamic Art and Civilisation in Southeast Asia*, Adelaide.

Bonnefoy, Yves, 1993, *Asian Mythologies*, Chicago.

Brown, Roxanna M., 1988, *The Ceramics of South-East Asia: Their Dating and Identification*, Kuala Lumpur.

Cribb, Joe, et al., 1999, *The Coin Atlas: A Comprehensive View of the Coins of the World throughout History*, New York.

Dallapiccola, Anna L. & Verghese, Anila (eds), 2017, *India and Southeast Asia: Cultural Discourses*, Mumbai.

Girard-Geslan, Maud, et al., 1994, *Art of Southeast Asia*, Paris.

Guise, Lucien de, 2005, *The Message and the Monsoon: Islamic Art of Southeast Asia*, Kuala Lumpur.

Hall, K., 2011, *A History of Early Southeast Asia: Maritime Trade and Societal Development*, Lanham, MD.

Kerlogue, Fiona, 2004, *Arts of Southeast Asia*, London.

Lieberman, Victor B., 2003 and 2009, *Strange Parallels: Southeast Asia in Global Context, c. 800–1830*, Vols 1–2, Cambridge.

Miksic, John, 2010, *The A to Z of Ancient Southeast Asia*, Toronto.

Miksic, John & Goh, Geok Yian, 2017, *Ancient Southeast Asia*, New York.

Nguyen-Long, Kerry, 2013, *The Arts of Viet Nam, 1009–1945*, Ha Noi.

Osborne, Milton, 2016, *Southeast Asia: An Introductory History*, Sydney.

Reid, Anthony, 1992, 'Southeast Asia: A Region and a Crossroad', in *Cultures at Crossroads: Southeast Asian Textiles from the Australian National Gallery*, Canberra, pp. 8–17.

Scott, Rosemary & Guy, John (eds), 1994, *South East Asia and China: Art, Interaction and Commerce*, London.

Sumner, Christina, 2001, *Arts of Southeast Asia from the Powerhouse Museum Collection*, Sydney.

Tarling, Nicholas (ed.), 1992, *Cambridge History of Southeast Asia*, Vols 1 & 2, Cambridge.

Wolters, O. W., 1999, *History, Culture, and Region in Southeast Asian Perspectives*, revised edition, Ithaca, NY.

Zwalf, W. (ed.), 1985, *Buddhism: Art and Faith*, London.

Chapter 1

Bacus, Elisabeth A., 2004, 'The archaeology of the Philippine Archipelago', in Ian Glover & Peter Bellwood (eds), *Southeast Asia: From Prehistory to History*, New York, pp. 257–81.

Bellina, Bérénice, et al. (eds), 2010, *50 Years of Archaeology in Southeast Asia: Essays in Honour of Ian Glover*, Bangkok.

Bellwood, Peter, 1985, *Prehistory of the Indo-Malaysian Archipelago*, Canberra.

Bellwood, Peter, 2017, *First Islanders: Prehistory and Human Migration in Island Southeast Asia*, Hoboken, NJ.

Borell, Brigitte, Bellina, Bérénice & Boonyarit, Chaisuwan, 2014, 'Contacts between the Upper Thai-Malay Peninsula and the Mediterranean World', in Nicolas Revire & Stephen A. Murphy (eds) *Before Siam: Essays in Art and Archaeology*, Bangkok, pp. 98–117.

Calo, Ambra, 2008, 'Heger I Bronze Drums and the Relationships between Dian and Dong Son Cultures', in Elisabeth A. Bacus, Ian C. Glover & Peter D. Sharrock (eds), *Interpreting Southeast Asia's Past: Monument, Image and Text*, Singapore, pp. 208–24.

Calo, Ambra, 2014, *Trails of Bronze Drums across Early Southeast Asia*, Singapore.

Carter, Alison, 2016, 'The Production and Exchange of Glass and Stone Beads in Southeast Asia from 500 BCE to the Early Second Millennium CE: An Assessment of the Work of Peter Francis in Light of Recent Research', *Archaeological Research in Asia* 6, pp. 16–29.

Carter, Alison, Abraham, Shinu Anna & Kelly, Gwendolyn O., 2016, 'Updating *Asia's Maritime Bead Trade*: An Introduction', *Archaeological Research in Asia* 6, pp. 1–3.

Dussubieux, Laure & Gratuze, Bernard, 2010, 'Glass in Southeast Asia', in Bérénice Bellina, et al. (eds), *50 Years of Archaeology in Southeast Asia: Essays in Honour of Ian Glover*, Bangkok, pp. 247–59.

Glover, Ian, 1976, 'Ulu Leang Cave, Maros: A Preliminary Sequence of post-Pleistocene Cultural Development in South Sulawesi', *Archipel* 11, pp. 113–54.

Glover, Ian, 1981, 'Leang Burung 2: An Upper Palaeolithic Rock Shelter in South Sulawesi, Indonesia', *Modern Quaternary Res. SE Asia* 6, pp. 1–38.

Glover, Ian, 1999, 'The Archaeological Past of Island Southeast Asia', in Jean Paul Barbier (ed.), *Messages in Stone: Statues and Sculptures from Tribal Indonesia in the Collections of the Barbier-Mueller Museum*, Geneva, pp. 17–34.

Glover, Ian, 2010, 'Bronze Drums, Urns, and Bells in the Early Metal Age of Southeast Asia', in Louise Allison Cort & Paul Jett (eds), *Gods of Angkor: Bronzes from the National Museum of Cambodia*, Washington, DC, pp. 18–29.

Glover, Ian & Bellwood, Peter, 2004, *Southeast Asia: From Prehistory to History*, New York.

Glover, Ian, Hughes-Brock, Helen & Henderson, Julian (eds), 2003, *Ornaments from the Past, Bead Studies after Beck: A Book on Glass and Semiprecious Stone Beads in History and Archaeology for Archaeologists, Jewellery Historians and Collectors*, London.

Glover, Ian, Suchitta, Pornchai & Villiers, John (eds), 1992, *Early Metallurgy, Trade and Urban Centres in Thailand and Southeast Asia*, Bangkok.

Higham, Charles, 1989, *The Archaeology of Mainland Southeast Asia*, Cambridge.

Higham, Charles, 1996, *The Bronze Age of Southeast Asia*, Cambridge.

Higham, Charles, 2002, *Early Cultures of Mainland Southeast Asia*, Bangkok.

Karlström, Anna & Källén, Anna (eds), 2003, *Fishbones and Glittering Emblems: Southeast Asian Archaeology 2002*, Uppsala.

Klokke, Marijke & Degroot, Véronique (eds), 2013, *Unearthing Southeast Asia's Past: Selected Papers from the 12th International Conference of the European Association of Southeast Asian Archaeologists*, Vol. 1, Singapore.

Miksic, John, 2018, 'Archaeology, Pottery and Malay Culture', *Passage*, pp. 14–15.

Moore, Elizabeth H., 2007, *Early Landscapes of Myanmar*, Bangkok.

O'Connor, Sue, 2015, 'Rethinking the Neolithic in Island Southeast Asia, with Particular Reference to the Archaeology of Timor-Leste and Sulawesi', *Archipel* 90, pp. 15–47.

Olsen, Sandra & Glover, Ian, 2004, 'The Bone Industry of Ulu Leang 1 and Leang Burung 1 Rockshelters, Sulawesi, Indonesia, in its Regional Context', *Modern Quaternary Res. SE Asia* 18, pp. 273–99.

Peacock, B. A. V., 1959, 'A Short Description of Malayan Prehistoric Pottery', *Asian Perspectives* 3, pp. 121–56.

Tan, Noel Hidalgo, 2014, 'Rock Art Research in Southeast Asia: A Synthesis', *Arts* 3, 1, pp. 73–104.

Theunissen, Robert, 2003, *Agate and Carnelian Beads and the Dynamics of Social Complexity in Iron Age Mainland Southeast Asia*, PhD thesis, University of New England, Australia.

Chapter 2

Anonymous, 2003, *Vietnamese Antiquities*, Hanoi.

Aung-Thwin, Michael, 1987, 'Heaven, Earth, and the Supernatural World: Dimensions of the Exemplary Center in Burmese History', in Bardwell Smith & Holly Baker Reynolds (eds), *The City as a Sacred Center: Essays in Six Asian Contexts*, Leiden, pp. 88–102.

Barnes, Ruth, 1997, *Indian Block-Printed Textiles in Egypt: The Newberry Collection in the Ashmolean Museum, Oxford*, 2 vols, Oxford.

Bautze-Picron, Claudine, 2002, 'The Biography of the Buddha in Indian Art: How and When?' in Andreas Schüle (ed.), *Biography as a Religious and Cultural Text*, Berlin, pp. 197–239.

Bautze-Picron, Claudine, 2015, 'Textiles from Bengal in Pagan (Myanmar) from the Late Eleventh Century and Onwards', in Mokammal H. Bhuiyan (ed.), *Studies in South Asian Heritage: Essays in Memory of M. Harunur Rashid*, Dhaka, pp. 19–29.

Borell, Brigitte, 2017a, 'Gold Coins from Khlong Thom', *Journal of the Siam Society*, 107, 1, pp. 151–77.

Borell, Brigitte, 2017b, 'Gold Coins from Khlong Thom', *Journal of the Siam Society*, 107, 2, pp. 155–58.

Brown, Robert L., 1990, 'God on Earth: The Walking Buddha in the Art of South and Southeast Asia', *Artibus Asiae* 50, 1, 2, pp. 73–107.

Brown, Robert L., 1991, 'Ganesa in Southeast Asian Art: Indian Connections and Indigenous Developments', in Robert L. Brown (ed.), *Ganesh: Studies of an Asian God*, Albany, pp. 171–233.

Brown, Robert L., 1992, 'Indian Art Transformed: The Earliest Sculptural Styles of Southeast Asia', in Ellen M. Raven & Karel R. van Kooij (eds), *Panels of the VIIth World Sanskrit Conference* 10, *Indian Art and Archaeology*, Leiden, pp. 40–53.

Brown, Robert L., 2008, 'The Act of Naming Avalokiteśvara in Ancient Southeast Asia', in Elisabeth A. Bacus, Ian C. Glover & Peter D. Sharrock (eds), *Interpreting Southeast Asia's Past: Monument, Image and Text*, Singapore, pp. 263–74.

Brown, Robert L., 2011, 'The Importance of Gupta-period Sculpture in Southeast Asian Art History', in Pierre-Yves Manguin, A. Mani & Geoff Wade, *Early Interactions between South and Southeast Asia: Reflections on Cross-cultural Exchange*, Singapore, pp. 317–31.

Chandler, David P., 1993, *A History of Cambodia*, Chiang Mai.

Chutiwongs, Nandana, 1999, 'Early Buddhist Sculpture of Thailand: Circa sixth–thirteenth century', in Robert L. Brown (ed.), *Art from Thailand*, Mumbai, pp. 19–33.

Cort, Louise, 2000, 'Khmer Stoneware Ceramics', in Louise Allison Cort, Massumeh Farhad & Ann C. Gunter (eds), *Asian Traditions in Clay: The Hauge Gifts*, Washington DC, pp. 91–149.

Diskul, M. C. Subhadradis, et al., 1980, *The Art of Śrīvijaya*, Singapore.

Feener, R. Michael, et al., 2021, 'Islamisation and the Formation of Vernacular Muslim Material Culture in 15th-century Northern Sumatra', *Indonesia and the Malay World* 49, pp. 1–41.

Fontein, Jan, 1990, *The Sculpture of Indonesia*, Washington, DC.

Frédéric, Louis, 1994, *Borobudur*, New York.

Galloway, Charlotte, 2002, 'Relationships Between Buddhist Texts and Images of the Enlightenment During the Early Bagan Period', in Alexandra Green & T. Richard Blurton (eds), *Burma: Art and Archaeology*, London, pp. 45–54.

Galloway, Charlotte, 2010, 'Ways of Seeing a Pyu, Mon and Dvaravati Artistic Continuum', *Bulletin of the Indo-Pacific Prehistory Association* 30, pp. 70–78.

Galloway, Charlotte, 2013, 'Buddhist Narrative Imagery during the Eleventh Century at Pagan, Burma: Reviewing Origins and Purpose', in Alexandra Green (ed.), *Rethinking Visual Narratives from Asia: Intercultural and Comparative Perspectives*, Hong Kong, pp. 159–74.

Giteau, Madeleine, 1976, *The Civilization of Angkor*, New York.

Glover, Ian, 2010, 'The Dvaravati Gap: Linking Prehistory and History in Early Thailand', *Bulletin of the Indo-Pacific Prehistory Association* 30, pp. 79–86.

Griffiths, Arlo, 2014, 'Written Traces of the Buddhist Past: Mantras and Dharanis in Indonesian Inscriptions', *Bulletin of the School of Oriental and African Studies* 77, 1, pp. 137–94.

Guillon, Emmanuel, 2001, *Cham Art: Treasures from the Dà Nang Museum, Vietnam*, London.

Gutman, Pamela, 2001, *Burma's Lost Kingdoms: Splendours of Arakan*, Bangkok.

Guy, John, 2014, (ed.), *Lost Kingdoms: Hindu-Buddhist Sculpture of Early Southeast Asia*, New Haven, CT.

Harris, P., 2007, *Zhou Daguan: A Record of Cambodia, the Land and its People*, Bangkok.

Harrison-Hall, Jessica, 2002, 'Vietnamese Ceramics in the British Museum', *Apollo: The International Magazine of Arts* 489, pp. 3–11.

Higham, Charles, 2001, *The Civilisation of Angkor*, London.

Jarrige, Jean-François & Maud Girard-Geslan, 1999, *Indonesian Gold: Treasures from the National Museum, Jakarta*, South Brisbane.

Jessup, Helen Ibbitson & Zéphir, Thierry (eds), 1997, *Millennium of Glory: Sculpture of Angkor and Ancient Cambodia*, Washington, DC.

Kinney, Ann R., 2003, *Worshipping Siva and Buddha: The Temple Art of East Java*, Honolulu.

Klokke, Marijke J., 1994, 'The Iconography of the So-called Portrait Statues in Late East Javanese Art', in Marijke J. Klokke & Pauline Lunsingh Scheurleer (eds), *Ancient Indonesian Sculpture*, Leiden.

Klokke, Marijke J. & Scheurleer, Pauline Lunsingh (eds), 1994, *Ancient Indonesian Sculpture*, Leiden.

Krahl, Regina, Guy, John, Wilson, J. Keith & Raby, Julian (eds), 2010, *Shipwrecked: Tang Treasures and Monsoon Winds*, Washington, DC.

Lambourn, Elizabeth, 2004, 'Carving and Communities: Marble Carving for Muslim Patrons at Khambhāt and around the Indian Ocean Rim, Late Thirteenth–Mid-Fifteenth Centuries', *Ars Orientalis* 34, pp. 99–133.

Lambourn, Elizabeth, 2008, 'Tombstones, Texts, and Typologies: Seeing Sources for the Early History of Islam in Southeast Asia', *Journal of the Economic and Social History of the Orient* 51, 2, pp. 252–86.

Lammerts, D. Christian (ed.), 2017, *Buddhist Dynamics in Premodern and Early Modern Southeast Asia*, Singapore.

Lankton, James W., Dussubieux, Laure & Rehren, Thilo, 2008, 'A Study of Mid-First Millenium CE Southeast Asian Specialized Glass Beadmaking Traditions', in Elisabeth A. Bacus, Ian C. Glover & Peter D. Sharrock (eds), *Interpreting Southeast Asia's Past: Monument, Image and Text*, Singapore, pp. 335–56.

Luce, G. H., 1969, *Old Burma Early Pagan*, Vols 1–3, Locust Valley, NY.

Mabbett, I. W., 1983, 'The Symbolism of Mount Meru', *History of Religions* 23, 1, pp. 64–83.

Mabbett, Ian & Chandler, David, 1995, *The Khmers*, Oxford.

Mahlo, Dietrich, 2012, *The Early Coins of Myanmar (Burma): Messengers from the Past*, Bangkok.

Manguin, Pierre-Yves, 1991, 'The Merchant and the King: Political Myths of Southeast Asian Coastal Polities', *Indonesia* 51, pp. 41–54.

Manguin, Pierre-Yves, Mani, A. & Wade, Geoff, 2011, *Early Interactions between South and Southeast Asia: Reflections on Cross-cultural Exchange*, Singapore.

Miksic, John, 1990a, *Borobudur: Golden Tales of the Buddhas*, Boston.

Miksic, John, 1990b, *Old Javanese Gold*, Singapore.

Mitchiner, Michael, 1998, *The History and Coinage of Southeast Asia until the Fifteenth Century*, London.

Moore, Elizabeth H., 2007, *Early Landscapes of Myanmar*, Bangkok.

Murphy, Stephen A., 2018, 'Revisiting the Bujang Valley: A Southeast Asian Entrepôt Complex on the Maritime Trade Route', *Journal of the Royal Asiatic Society* 28, 2, pp. 355–89.

Nguyen, Van Huy and Kendall, Laurel (eds), 2003, *Vietnam: Journeys of Body, Mind, and Spirit*, Berkeley, CA.

Postma, Antoon, 1992, 'The Laguna Copper-Plate Inscription: Text and Commentary', *Philippine Studies* 40, 2, pp. 183–203.

Reichle, Natasha, 2007, *Violence and Serenity: Late Buddhist Sculpture from Indonesia*, Honolulu.

Revire, Nicolas & Murphy, Stephen A. (eds), 2014, *Before Siam: Essays in Art and Archaeology*, Bangkok.

Romain, Julie, 2011, 'Indian Architecture in the "Sanskrit Cosmopolis": The Temples of the Dieng Plateau', in Pierre-Yves Manguin, A. Mani & Geoff Wade (eds), *Early Interactions between South and Southeast Asia: Reflections on Cross-cultural Exchange*, Singapore, pp. 299–316.

Scheurleer, Pauline Lunsingh & Klokke, Marijke J., 1988, *Divine Bronze: Ancient Indonesian Bronzes from AD 600 to 1600*, Leiden.

Sen, Tansen, 2009, 'The Military Campaigns of Rajendra Chola and the Chola-Srivijaya-China Triangle', in Herman Kulke, K. Kesavapany & Vijay Sakuja (eds), *Nagapattinam to Suvarnadwipa: Reflections on the Chola Naval Expeditions to Southeast Asia*, Singapore.

Skilling, Peter, 2008, 'Buddhist Sealings in Thailand and Southeast Asia: Iconography, Function, and Ritual Context', in Elisabeth A. Bacus, Ian C. Glover & Peter D. Sharrock (eds), *Interpreting Southeast Asia's Past: Monument, Image and Text*, Singapore, pp. 248–62.

Szczepanowska, H. & Ploeger, R., 2019, 'The Chemical Analysis of Southeast Asian Lacquers Collected from Forests and Workshops in Vietnam, Cambodia, and Myanmar', *Journal of Cultural Heritage* 40, pp. 215–25.

Tan, Heidi (ed.), 2012, *Enlightened Ways: The Many Streams of Buddhist Art in Thailand*, Singapore.

Wade, Geoff, 2010, 'Early Muslim Expansion in Southeast Asia, Eighth to Fifteenth Centuries', in David O. Morgan & Anthony Reid, *The New Cambridge History of Islam*, Vol. 3, pp. 366–408.

Wade, Geoff, 2014, 'Beyond the Southern Borders: Southeast Asia in Chinese Texts to the Ninth Century', in John Guy (ed.), *Lost Kingdoms: Hindu-Buddhist Sculpture of Early Southeast Asia*, New Haven and London, pp. 25–31.

Wicks, Robert S., 1992, *Money, Markets, and Trade in Early Southeast Asia: The Development of Indigenous Monetary Systems to AD 1400*, Ithaca, NY.

Wolters, O. W., 1969, *Early Indonesian Commerce: A Study of the Origins of Srivijaya*, Ithaca, NY.

Wolters, O. W., 1970, *The Fall of Srivijaya in Malay History*, Ithaca, NY.

Woodward, H., 1995, 'Thailand and Cambodia: The Thirteenth and Fourteenth Centuries. Studies and Reflections on Asian Art History and Archaeology', in Khaisri Sri-Aroon, et al. (eds), *Essays in Honour of H.S.H. Professor Subhadradis Diskul*, Bangkok, pp. 335–42.

Woodward, Hiram W., Jr., 1997, *The Sacred Sculpture of Thailand*, Baltimore.

Chapters 3 to 6

Adams, Kathleen M. & Gillogly, Kathleen A., 2011, *Everyday Life in Southeast Asia*, Bloomington, IN.

Andaya, Barbara Watson, 2003a, 'Aspects of Warfare in Premodern Southeast Asia', *Journal of the Economic and Social History of the Orient* 46, 2, pp. 139–42.

Andaya, Barbara Watson, 2003b, 'History, Headhunting and Gender in Monsoon Asia: Comparative and Longitudinal Views', *South East Asia Research* 12, 1, pp. 13–52.

Andaya, Barbara Watson & Andaya, Leonard Y., 2015, *A History of Early Modern Southeast Asia, 1400–1830*, Cambridge.

Appleton, Naomi, 2010, *Jātaka Stories in Theravada Buddhism: Narrating the Bodhisatta Path*, Aldershot and Burlington, VA.

Appleton, Naomi, Shaw, Sarah & Unebe, Toshiya, 2013, *Illuminating the Life of the Buddha: An Illustrated Chanting Book from Eighteenth-Century Siam*, Oxford.

Baker, C. & Pasuk Phongpaichit, 2009, *A History of Thailand*, Bangkok

Barbier, Jean Paul & Newton, Douglas (eds), 1988, *Islands and Ancestors: Indigenous Styles of Southeast Asia*, Munich.

Barley, Nigel & Sandaruppa, Stanislaus, 1991, *The Toraja Ricebarn*, London.

Barnes, Ruth, 1993, 'South-East Asian Basketry', *Journal of Museum Ethnography* 4, pp. 83–102.

Barnes, Ruth, 2006, 'Indian Textiles for Island Taste: The Trade to Eastern Indonesia', in Rosemary Crill (ed.), *Textiles from India: The Global Trade*, Calcutta, pp. 99–116.

Barnes, Ruth & Kahlenberg, Mary Hunt, 2010, *Five Centuries of Indonesian Textiles: The Mary Hunt Kahlenberg Collection*, Munich.

Beemer, Bryce, 2009, 'Southeast Asian Slavery and Slave-Gathering Warfare as a Vector for Cultural Transmission: The Case of Burma and Thailand', *The Historian* 71, 3, pp. 481–506.

Bell, Edward N., 1907, *A Monograph: Iron and Steel Work in Burma*, Rangoon.

Bennett, James (ed.), 2011, *Beneath the Winds: Masterpieces of Southeast Asian Art from the Art Gallery of South Australia*, Adelaide.

Bjork, Katharine, 1998, 'The Link that Kept the Philippines Spanish: Mexican Merchant Interests and the Manila Trade, 1571–1815', *Journal of World History* 9, 1, pp. 25–50.

Blurton, T. Richard, 1999, '"Looking very gay and bright": Burmese Textiles in the British Museum', *Apollo: The International Magazine of Arts* 453, pp. 38–42.

Boisselier, Jean, 1976, *Thai Painting*, Tokyo.

Brandon, James R., 2009, *Theatre in Southeast Asia*, Cambridge, MA.

Brinkgreve, Francine, 2016, *Lamak: Ritual Objects in Bali*, Oxfordshire.

Brinkgreve, Francine & Sulistianingsih, Retno (eds), 2009, *Sumatra: Crossroads of Cultures*, Leiden.

Brown, C. C., 1953, 'Sejarah Melayu or "Malay Annals", a translation of Raffles Ms 18', *Journal of the Malayan Branch of the Royal Asiatic Society* 25, 2 and 3

Brown, Roxanna, 2009, *The Ming Gap and Shipwreck Ceramics in Southeast Asia: Towards a Chronology of Thai Trade Ware*, Bangkok.

Brownrigg, Henry, 1992, *Betel Cutters from the Samuel Eilenberg Collection*, Stuttgart.

Casal, Father Gabriel, et al. (eds), 1981, *The People and Art of the Philippines*, Los Angeles, CA.

Cate, Sandra & Lefferts, Leedom, 2012, 'Becoming Active/Active Becoming: Prince Vessantara Scrolls and the Creation of a Moral Community', in Julius Bautista (ed.), *The Spirit of Things: Materiality and Religious Diversity in Southeast Asia*, Ithaca, NY, pp. 165–82.

Césard, Nicolas, 2013, 'Heirlooms and Marriage Payments: Transmission and Circulation of Prestige Jars in Borneo', *Indonesia and the Malay World* 42, 122, pp. 1–26.

Chalermpow, Paritta, 1981, *A popular drama in its social context: nang talung shadow puppet theatre of South Thailand*, PhD dissertation, University of Cambridge.

Chandavij, Natthapatra & Pramualaratana, Promporn, 1998, *Thai Puppets and Khon Masks*, Bangkok.

Charney, Michael W., 2004, *Southeast Asian Warfare, 1300–1900*, Leiden.

Charney, Michael W., 2018, 'Warfare in Premodern Southeast Asia', in *Oxford Research Encyclopedia, Asian History*, Oxford.

Charney, Michael W. & Wellen, Kathryn (eds), 2018, *Warring Societies of Pre-Colonial Southeast Asia: Local Cultures of Conflict within a Regional Context*, Copenhagen.

Ché-Ross, Raimy, 2012, 'Malay Silverware', *Arts of Asia* 42, 1, pp. 68–83.

Chin, Edmond, 1991, *Gilding the Phoenix: The Straits Chinese and Their Jewellery*, Singapore.

Chiu, Angela, 2017, *The Buddha in Lanna: Art, Lineage, Power, and Place in Northern Thailand*, Honolulu.

Ch'ng, David, 1986, 'Malay Silver', *Arts of Asia* 16, 2, pp. 102–9.

Chong, Alan (ed.), 2016, *Christianity in Asia: Sacred Art and Visual Splendour*, Singapore.

Chutiwongs, Nandana, 1995, 'The Role of Narrative Sculpture and Painting in Thailand', in K. R. van Kooij & H. van der Veere (eds), *Function and Meaning in Buddhist Art*, Groningen, pp. 167–78.

Clayre, Beatrice & Nicholson, Julia, 1999, 'Melanau Sickness Images in the Pitt Rivers Museum', *Sarawak Museum Journal* 54, pp. 105–42.

Cohn, Bernard S., 1996, *Colonialism and its Forms of Knowledge: The British in India*, Princeton, NJ.

Conway, Susan, 2001, 'Power Dressing: Female Court Dress and Marital Alliances in Lan Na, the Shan States, and Siam', *Orientations* 32, 4, pp. 42–49.

Conway, Susan, 2006, *The Shan: Culture, Art and Crafts*, Bangkok.

Cort, Louise Allison & Lefferts, Leedom, 2010–11, 'Pots and How They are Made in Mainland Southeast Asia', *Transactions of the Oriental Ceramic Society* 75, pp. 1–16.

Couderc, Pascal, 2012, 'Cultural and Literary Aspects of Uut Danum Patterned Plaiting', in Bernard Sellato (ed.), *Plaited Arts from the Borneo Rainforest*, Copenhagen, pp. 294–312.

Cribb, Joe, 1999, *Magic Coins of Java, Bali and the Malay Peninsula: A Catalogue Based on the Raffles Collection of Coin-Shaped Charms from Java in the British Museum*, London.

Crosby, Kate, 2013, *Theravada Buddhism: Continuity, Diversity and Identity*, Chichester.

Dell, Elizabeth & Dudley, Sandra (eds), 2003, *Textiles from Burma: Featuring the James Henry Green Collection*, Brighton.

Dixon, Charlotte, 2018, *Sailing the Monsoon Winds in Miniature: Model Boats as Evidence for Boat Building Technologies, Cultures, and Collecting*, PhD thesis, University of Southampton.

Djajasoebrata, Alit, 1999, *Shadow Theatre in Java: The Puppets, Performance and Repertoire*, Amsterdam.

Dubin, Lois Sherr, 2009, *The Worldwide History of Beads*, London.

Dudley, Sandra, 2008, 'Karenic Textiles', in Alexandra Green (ed.), *Eclectic Collecting: Art from Burma in the Denison Museum*, Singapore, pp. 19–48.

Eiseman, Fred, 1990, *Bali: Sekala and Niskala: Essays on Religion, Ritual, and Art*, Hong Kong.

Eiseman, Fred & Eiseman, Margaret, 1988, *Woodcarvings of Bali*, Singapore.

Endres, Kirsten W. & Lauser, Andrea (eds), 2011, *Engaging the Spirit World: Popular Beliefs and Practices in Modern Southeast Asia*, New York.

Feldman, Jerome (ed.), 1985, *The Eloquent Dead: Ancestral Sculpture of Indonesia and Southeast Asia*, Los Angeles, CA.

Fischer, Joseph, et al., 1994, *The Folk Art of Java*, Kuala Lumpur.

Fong Peng Khuan, 2012, 'Malay Brassware', *Arts of Asia* 42, 1, pp. 120–27.

Forbes, Henry O., 1885, *A Naturalist's Wanderings in the Eastern Archipelago: A Narrative of Travel and Exploration from 1878 to 1883*, New York.

Forge, Anthony, 1993, 'Balinese Painting: Revival or Reaction', in John Clark (ed), *Modernity in Asian Art*, Broadway, Australia.

Fowler, John, 1988, 'Classical Wayang Painting of Bali', *Orientations* 19, 1, pp. 47-57.

Fraser, David W. & Fraser, Barbara G., 2005, *Mantles of Merit: Chin Textiles from Myanmar, India and Bangladesh*, Bangkok.

Fraser-Lu, Sylvia, 1981a, 'Buddha Images from Burma: Sculptured in Stone, Part 1', *Arts of Asia* 11, 1, pp. 72–82.

Fraser-Lu, Sylvia, 1981b, 'Buddha Images from Burma: Bronze and Related Metals, Part 2', *Arts of Asia* 11, 2, pp. 62–72.

Fraser-Lu, Sylvia, 1981c, 'Buddha Images from Burma: Wood and Lacquer, Part 3', *Arts of Asia* 11, 3, pp. 129–36.

Fraser-Lu, Sylvia, 1982, 'Kalagas: Burmese Wall Hangings and Related Embroideries', *Arts of Asia* 12, 4, pp. 73–82.

Fraser-Lu, Sylvia, 1988, *Handwoven Textiles of Southeast Asia*, Singapore.

Fraser-Lu, Sylvia, 1989, *Silverware of South-East Asia*, Singapore.

Fraser-Lu, Sylvia, 1994, *Burmese Crafts: Past and Present*, Kuala Lumpur.

Fraser-Lu, Sylvia, 2000, *Burmese Lacquerware*, Bangkok.

Fraser-Lu, Sylvia & Stadtner, Donald M., 2015, *Buddhist Art of Myanmar*, New Haven, CT.

Fujimoto, Helen, 1988, *The South Indian Muslim Community and the Evolution of the Jawi Peranakan in Penang up to 1948*, Tokyo.

Gallop, Annabel Teh, 1995, *Early Views of Indonesia: Drawings from the British Library*, London.

Gallop, A. T., 2004, 'An Achenese Style of Manuscript Illumination', *Archipel* 68, pp. 193–240.

Gallop, A. T., 2007, 'The Art of the Qur'an in Southeast Asia', in Fahmida Suleman (ed.), *Word of God, Art of Man: The Qur'an and its Creative Expressions: Selected Proceedings from the International Colloquium, London, 18–21 October 2003*, Oxford, pp. 191–204.

Gallop, A. T., 2012, 'The Art of the Malay Qur'an', *Arts of Asia* 42, 1, pp. 84–95.

Galloway, Charlotte, 2001, 'An Introduction to the Buddha Images of Burma,' *TAASA Review* 10, 2, pp. 8–10.

Gavin, Traude, 2004, *Iban Ritual Textiles*, Singapore.

Ginsburg, Henry, 2000, *Thai Art and Culture: Historic Manuscripts from Western Collections*, Chiang Mai.

Ginsburg, Henry, 2005, 'Ayutthaya Painting', in Forrest McGill (ed.), *The Kingdom of Siam: The Art of Central Thailand, 1350–1800*, San Francisco, CA, pp. 95–110.

Ginsburg, Henry & Chakrabonse, Narisa, 2020, '*Phra Bot*: Thai Buddhist Paintings on Cloth', *Arts of Asia* 50, 1, pp. 142–50.

Gittinger, M., 1989, *To Speak with Cloth: Studies in Indonesian Textiles*, Los Angeles, CA.

Gommans, Jos & Leider, Jacques (eds), 2002, *The Maritime Frontier of Burma: Exploring Political, Cultural, and Commercial Interactions in the Indian Ocean World*, Amsterdam.

Green, Alexandra (ed.), 2008, *Eclectic Collecting: Art from Burma in the Denison Museum*, Singapore.

Green, Alexandra, 2011, 'From Gold Leaf to Buddhist Hagiographies: Contact with Regions to the East Seen in Late Burmese Murals,' *Journal of Burma Studies* 15, 2, pp. 305–58.

Green, Alexandra, 2015, 'Space and Place in a Burmese Cosmology Manuscript at the British Museum', in Justin McDaniel & Lynn Ransom (eds), *From Mulberry Leaves to Silk Scrolls: New Approaches to the Study of Asian Manuscript Traditions*, The Lawrence J. Schoenberg Studies in Manuscript Culture, Vol. 1, Philadelphia, PA, pp. 42–69.

Green, Alexandra, 2018, 'Pattern of Use and Reuse: South Asian Trade Textiles and Burmese Wall Paintings,' in Anna Dallapiccola & Anila Verghese (eds), *India and Southeast Asia: Cultural Discourses*, Mumbai, pp. 459–84.

Green, Alexandra & Blurton, T. Richard (eds), 2002, *Burma: Art and Archaeology*, London.

Green, Gillian, 2003, *Traditional Textiles of Cambodia: Cultural Threads and Material Heritage*, Bangkok.

Griffiths, A., Acri, Andrea & Creese, H. M. (eds), 2010, *From Lanka Eastwards: The Ramayana in the Literature and Visual Arts of Indonesia*, Leiden.

Groneman, Isaäc. 2009, *The Javanese Kris*, Leiden.

Guha-Thakurta, Tapati, 2004, *Monuments, Objects, Histories: Institutions of Art in Colonial and Postcolonial India*, New York.

Guy, John, 1998, *Woven Cargoes: Indian Textiles in the East*, London.

Håbu, Anne & Rooney, Dawn F. (eds), 2013, *Royal Porcelain from Siam: Unpacking the Ring Collection*, Oslo.

Hales, Robert, 2013, *Islamic and Oriental Arms and Armour: A Lifetime's Passion*, Farnham Common, UK.

Hamilton, Roy W. & Barrkman, Joanna (eds), 2014, *Textiles of Timor: Island in the Woven Sea*, Los Angeles, CA.

Hauser-Schäublin, Brigitta, Nabholz-Kartaschoff, Marie-Louise & Ramseyer, Urs, 1991, *Balinese Textiles*, London.

Hemmet, Christine, 1996, *Nang Talung: The Shadow Theatre of South Thailand*, Amsterdam.

Heppell, Michael, 2005, *Iban Art: Sexual Selection and Severed Heads*, Amsterdam.

Herbert, Patricia M., 1992, *The Life of the Buddha*, London.

Herbert, Patricia, 1999, 'Burmese Court Manuscripts,' in Donald Stadtner (ed.), *The Art of Burma: New Studies*, Bombay, pp. 89–102.

Herbert, Patricia, 2002, 'Burmese Cosmological Manuscripts', in Alexandra Green & T. Richard Blurton (eds), *Burma: Art and Archaeology*, London, pp. 77–98.

Herbert, Patricia, 2006, 'Myanmar Manuscript Art', in Teruko Saito & U Thaw Kaung (eds), *Enriching the Past: Preservation, Conservation and Study of Myanmar Manuscripts*, Tokyo, pp. 23–41.

Heringa, Rens, 2010, 'Upland Tribe, Coastal Village, and Inland Court: Revised Parameters for Batik Research', in Ruth Barnes & Mary Hunt Kahlenberg (eds), *Five Centuries of Indonesian Textiles: The Mary Hunt Kahlenberg Collection*, Munich, pp. 121–31.

Heringa, Rens & Veldhuisen, Harmen C., 1996, *Fabric of Enchantment: Batik from the North Coast of Java*, Los Angeles, CA.

Ho Wing Meng, 1987, *Straits Chinese Beadwork and Embroidery*, Singapore.

Hobart, Angela, 1987, *Dancing Shadows of Bali: Theatre and Myth*, London.

Hobart, Angela, Ramseyer, Urs & Leeman, Albert, 1996, *The Peoples of Bali*, Oxford.

Honda, Hiromu & Shimazu, Noriki, 1997, *The Beauty of Fired Clay: Ceramics from Burma, Cambodia, Laos, and Thailand*, Oxford.

Howard, Michael C., 1999, *Textiles of the Hill Tribes of Burma*, Bangkok.

Isaacs, Ralph & Blurton, T. Richard, 2000, *Visions from the Golden Land: Burma and the Art of Lacquer*, London.

Janowski, Monica, 1998, 'Beads, Prestige and Life among the Kelabit of Sarawak, East Malaysia', in Lidia Sciama & Joanne Eicher (eds), *Beads: Gender, Making and Meaning*, Oxford, pp. 213–46.

Janowski, Monica, 2014, *Tuked Rini, Cosmic Traveller: Life and Legend in the Heart of Borneo*, Copenhagen.

Janowski, Monica, 2020, 'Stones Alive! An Exploration of the Relationship between Humans and Stone in Southeast Asia', *Bijdragen Tot De Taal-, Land- En Volkenkunde* 176, pp. 105–46.

Jessup, Helen Ibbitson, 1990, *Court Arts of Indonesia*, New York.

Johnson, Irving Chan, 2012, *The Buddha on Mecca's Verandah: Encounters, Mobilities, and Histories Along the Malaysian-Thai Border*, Seattle.

Jory, Patrick, 2002, 'The *Vessantara Jataka*, *Barami*, and the *Bodhisatta*-Kings: The Origin and Spread of a Premodern Thai Concept of Power', *Crossroads: An Interdisciplinary Journal of Southeast Asian Studies* 16, 1, pp. 152–94.

Jose, R. T., 2004, 'Image', in R. T. Jose & R. N. Villegas (eds), *Power + Faith + Image: Philippine Art in Ivory from the 16th to the 19th Century*, Philippines, pp. 97–133.

Kahlenberg, Mary Hunt, 2006, 'Who Influenced Whom? The Indian Textile Trade to Sumatra and Java', in Rosemary Crill (ed.), *Textiles from India: The Global Trade*, Kolkata, pp. 135–52.

Kaiser, Thomas, Lefferts, Leedom, & Wernsdorfer, Martina, 2017, *Devotion: Image, Recitation, and Celebration of the Vessantara Epic in Northeast Thailand*, Stuttgart.

Keeler, Ward, 1992, *Javanese Shadow Puppets*, Oxford.

Kerlogue, F., 2001, 'Islamic Talismans: The Calligraphy Batiks', in Itie van Hout (ed.), *Batik: Drawn in Wax: 200 Years of Batik Art from Indonesia in the Tropenmuseum Collection*, Amsterdam, pp. 124–35.

Khazeni, A., 2019, 'Indo-Persian Travel Writing at the Ends of the Mughal World', *Past and Present* 243, 1, pp. 141–74.

King, Victor T., 1993, *The Peoples of Borneo*, Oxford.

Koentjaraningrat, 1985, *Javanese Culture*, Singapore.

Lammerts, Christian, 2010, 'Notes on Burmese Manuscripts: Text and Images', *Journal of Burma Studies* 14, pp. 229–53.

Lee, Peter, 2014, *Sarong Kebaya: Peranakan Fashion in an Interconnected World, 1500–1950*, Singapore.

Lefferts, Leedom, Cate, Sandra & Tossa, Wajuppa, 2012, *Buddhist Storytelling in Thailand and Laos*, Singapore.

Lewis, Paul & Lewis, Elaine, 1998, *Peoples of the Golden Triangle*, London.

Lieberman, Victor B., 1978, 'Ethnic Politics in Eighteenth-Century Burma', *Modern Asian Studies* 12, 3, pp. 455–82.

Lopetcharat, Somkiart, 2000, *Lao Buddha: The Image and Its History*, Bangkok.

Maxwell, Robyn, 1990, *Textiles of Southeast Asia: Tradition, Trade and Transformation*, Hong Kong.

Maxwell, Robyn, 2010, *Life, Death, and Magic. 2000 Years of Southeast Asian Ancestral Art*, Canberra.

Mackenzie Private 16, 'Copy of an Historical Account of the Island of Great Java by François Van Boeckholtz'. British Library.

McGill, Forrest (ed.), 2005, *The Kingdom of Siam: The Art of Central Thailand, 1350–1800*, San Francisco, CA.

McGill, Forrest (ed.), 2009, *Emerald Cities: Arts of Siam and Burma 1775–1950*, San Francisco, CA.

McGill, Forrest (ed.), 2016, *The Rama Epic: Hero, Heroine, Ally, Foe*, San Francisco, CA.

Miksic, John (ed.), 2003, *Earthenware in Southeast Asia*, Singapore.

Morris, Stephen, 1991, *The Oya Melanau*, Kuching, Sarawak, Malaysia.

Munan, Heidi, 2005, *Beads of Borneo*, Kuala Lumpur.

Munan, Heidi, 2012, 'Hornbill Wood Carvings', *Arts of Asia* 42, 1, pp. 106–13.

Murphy, Stephen A. (ed.), 2016, *Cities and Kings: Ancient Treasures from Myanmar*, Singapore.

Murphy, Stephen A., Wang, Naomi & Green, Alexandra (eds), 2019, *Raffles in Southeast Asia: Revisiting the Scholar and Statesman*, Singapore.

Nguyen-Long, Kerry, 2002, 'Lacquer Artists of Vietnam', *Arts of Asia* 39, 1, pp. 27–39.

Niessen, Sandra, 2009, *Legacy in Cloth: Batak Textiles of Indonesia*, Leiden.

Novellino, Dario, 2006, 'Weaving Traditions from Island Southeast Asia: Historical Context and Ethnobotanical Knowledge', *Proceedings of the IVth International Congress of Ethnobotany*, pp. 307–16.

Peacock, A. C. S. & Gallop, Annabel Teh, 2015, 'Islam, Trade and Politics Across the Indian Ocean: Imagination and Reality', *Proceedings of the British Academy* 200, pp. 1–23.

Pollock, Polly, 1993, 'Basketry: Tradition and Change', *Journal of Museum Ethnography*, December, pp. 1–24.

Pourret, Jess G., 2002, *The Yao: the Mien and Mun Yao in China, Vietnam, Laos and Thailand*, London.

Prapatthing, Songsri (ed.), 1993, *Thai Minor Arts*, Bangkok.

Rafee, Yaup Mohd, et al., 2017, 'Bilum: A Cultural Object of the Pagan Melanau', *Journal of Engineering and Applied Sciences* 12, pp. 6968–73.

Ramseyer, Urs, 2002, *The Art and Culture of Bali*, Basel.

Reid, Anthony, 1988, *Southeast Asia in the Age of Commerce, 1450–1680*, New Haven, CT.

Richards, Thomas, 1993, *The Imperial Archive: Knowledge and the Fantasy of Empire*, London.

Richman, Paula, 1991, *Many Rāmāyaṇas: The Diversity of a Narrative Tradition in South Asia*, Berkeley, CA.

Richter, Anne, 2000, *The Jewelry of Southeast Asia*, London.

Ricklefs, M. C., Voorhoeve, P. & Gallop, A. T., 2014, *Indonesian Manuscripts in Great Britain. New Edition with Addenda et Corrigenda*, Jakarta.

Rogers, Susan, 1985, *Power and Gold: Jewelry from Indonesia, Malaysia, and the Philippines*, Geneva.

Rooney, Dawn F., 1993, *Betel Chewing Traditions in South-East Asia*, Kuala Lumpur.

Ross, Lauri Margot, 2016, *The Encoded Cirebon Mask: Materiality, Flow, and Meaning along Java's Islamic Northwest Coast*, Leiden.

Sadan, Mandy, 2008, 'Kachin Textiles', in Alexandra Green (ed.), *Eclectic Collecting: Art from Burma in the Denison Museum*, Singapore, pp. 75–96.

San San May & Igunma, Jana (2018), *Buddhism Illuminated: Manuscript Art from Southeast Asia*, London.

Schefold, Reimar (ed.), 2013, *Eyes of the Ancestors: the Arts of Island Southeast Asia*, New Haven, CT.

Schober, Juliane, 1980, 'On Burmese Horoscopes', *The South East Asian Review* 5, 1, pp. 43–56.

Scott, P., 2019, *Vietnamese Lacquer Painting: Between Materiality and History*. Online: https://www.nationalgallery.sg/magazine/vietnamese-lacquer-painting-between-materiality-and-history [Accessed 28 July 2021].

SEAMEO-SPAFA, 2015, *100 Everyday Objects from Southeast Asia and Korea*, Bangkok.

Sellato, Bernard (ed.), 2012, *Plaited Arts from the Borneo Rainforest*, Copenhagen.

Shaw, J. C., 1989, *Northern Thai Ceramics*, Chiang Mai.

Sibeth, Achim, 1991, *The Batak: Peoples of the Island of Sumatra*, London.

Singer, Noel, 1989, 'The Ramayana at the Burmese Court', *Arts of Asia* 19, 6, pp. 90–103.

Singer, Noel F., 2002, 'Myanmar Lacquer and Gold Leaf: From the Earliest Times to the 18th Century,' *Arts of Asia* 32, 1, pp. 40–52.

Singh, Saran, 1986, *The Encyclopaedia of the Coins of Malaysia, Singapore, and Brunei*, Kuala Lumpur.

Skeat, W. W. & Blagden C. O., 1906, *The Pagan Races of the Malay Peninsula*, 2 vols, London.

Skilling, Peter, 2006, '*Pata (Phra Bot)*: Buddhist Cloth Painting of Thailand', in François Lagirarde & Paritta Chalermpow Koanantakool (eds), *Buddhist Legacies in Mainland Southeast Asia*, Paris and Bangkok, pp. 223–76.

Skilling, Peter, 2013, 'Rhetoric of Reward, Ideologies of Inducement: Why Produce Buddhist "Art"?' in David Park, Kuenga Wangmo & Sharon Cather (eds), *Art of Merit: Studies in Buddhist Art and its Conservation*, London, pp. 27–37.

Skilling, Peter, 2007, 'For Merit and Nirvana: The Production of Art in the Bangkok Period', *Arts Asiatiques* 62, pp. 76–94.

Sng, Jeffery, et al. (eds), 2011, *Bencharong and Chinaware in the Court of Siam: The Surat Osathanugrah Collection*, Bangkok.

Stratton, Carol, 2004, *Buddhist Sculpture of Northern Thailand*, Chiang Mai.

Sumarsam, 1992, *Gamelan: Cultural Interaction and Musical Development in Central Java*. Chicago, IL.

Surakiat, Pamaree, 2006, *The Changing Nature of Conflict between Burma and Siam as Seen from the Growth and Development of Burmese States from the 16th to the 19th Centuries*, Singapore.

Suanda, Endo, 1985, 'Cirebonese Topeng and Wayang of the Present Day', *Asian Music* 16, 2, pp. 84–120.

Sweeney, Amin, 1972, *Malay Shadow Puppets*, London.

Sweeney, Amin, 1972, *The Ramayana and the Malay Shadow-Play*, Malaysia.

Sweeney, Amin, 1974, 'The Rama Repertoire in the Kelantan Shadow Play: A Preliminary Report', in Mohd Taib Osman (ed), *Traditional Drama and Music of Southeast Asia, Kuala Lumpur*, pp. 5–18.

Taylor, Paul M., Aragon, Lorraine V. & Rice, Annamarie L. (eds), 1991, *Beyond the Java Sea: Art of Indonesia's Outer Islands*, New York.

Than Htun (Dedaye), 2013, *Lacquerware Journeys: The Untold Story of Burmese Lacquer*, Bangkok.

Thaw Kaung, 2002, 'The *Ramayana* Drama in Myanmar', *Journal of the Siam Society* 90, 1, pp. 137–48.

Thompson, Ashley, 2017, 'Hiding the Female Sex: A Sustained Cultural Dialogue between India and Southeast Asia', in A. Dallapiccola & A. Verghese (eds), *Cultural Dialogues between India and Southeast Asia from the 7th and the 16th century*, Mumbai, pp. 125–44.

Tiffin, Sarah, 2006, *Southeast Asia in Ruins: Art and Empire in the Early 19th Century*, Singapore.

Tingley, Nancy, 2003, *Doris Duke: The Southeast Asian Art Collection*, New York.

Totton, Mary-Louise, 2005, 'Cosmopolitan Tastes and Indigenous Designs – Virtual Cloth in a Javanese *candi*,' in Ruth Barnes (ed.), *Textiles in Indian Ocean Societies*, London, pp. 110–29.

Totton, Mary-Louise, 2009, *Wearing Wealth and Styling Identity: Tapis from Lampung, South Sumatra, Indonesia*, Hanover, NH.

Truong, Philippe, 2007, *The Elephant and the Lotus: Vietnamese Ceramics in the Museum of Fine Arts, Boston*, Boston.

Trusted, Marjorie, 2009, 'Propaganda and Luxury: Small-Scale Baroque Sculptures in Viceregal America and the Philippines', in Donna Pierce, et al. (eds), *Asia and Spanish America: Trans-Pacific Artistic and Cultural Exchange, 1500–1850*, Denver, CO, pp. 151–63.

Vandergeest, Peter and Chalermpow-Koanantakool, Paritta, 1993, 'The Southern Thai Shadowplay Tradition in Historical Context', *Journal of Southeast Asian Studies* 24, 2, pp. 307–29.

van Hout, Itie (ed.), 2001, *Batik: Drawn in Wax*, Amsterdam.

Vickers, Adrian, 2012, *Balinese Art: Paintings and Drawings of Bali 1800–2010*, Tokyo.

Vickers, Adrian, 2016, *Balinese Painting and Sculpture from the Krzysztof Musial Collection*, Clarendon, VT.

Waterson, Roxana, 1990, *The Living House: An Anthropology of Architecture in South-East Asia*, Oxford.

Wichienkeeo, Aroonrut, 2006, 'Buddha Images from Lan Na (Northern Thailand): A Study from Palm-leaf Texts and Inscriptions', in François Lagirarde & Paritta Chalermpow Koanantakool (eds), *Buddhist Legacies in Mainland Southeast Asia*, Paris and Bangkok, pp. 33–52.

Woolley, G. C., 1929, 'Some Notes On Murut Basketwork and Patterns', *Journal of the Malayan Branch of the Royal Asiatic Society* 10, 1, pp. 291–302.

Wright, Barbara Ann Stein, 1980, *Wayang Siam: An Ethnographic Study of the Malay Shadow Play of Kelantan*, PhD thesis, Yale University, New Haven, CT.

Yahya, Farouk, 2016, *Magic and Divination in Malay Illustrated Manuscripts*, Leiden.

Chapter 7

Anderson, Benedict, 1991, *Imagined Communities: Reflections on the Origin and Spread of Nationalism*, London.

Bruntz, Courtney & Schedneck, Brooke, 2020, *Buddhist Tourism in Asia*, Honolulu.

Cribb, Robert, 1981, 'Political Dimensions of the Currency Question 1945–1947', *Indonesia* 31, pp. 113–36.

Dewhurst, Kurt C. & MacDowell, Marsha (eds), 1983, *Michigan Hmong Arts: Textiles in Transition*, Lansing, MI.

Geertz, Hildred, 1994, *Images of Power: Balinese Paintings Made for Gregory Bateson and Margaret Mead*, Honolulu.

Harrison, David & Hitchcock, Michael (eds), 2005, *The Politics of World Heritage: Negotiating Tourism and Conservation*, Buffalo, NY.

Harrison-Hall, Jessica, 2002, *Vietnam Behind the Lines: Images from the War 1965–1975*, London.

Hitchcock, Michael, King, Victor T. & Parnwell, Mike (eds), 2009, *Tourism in Southeast Asia: Challenges and New Directions*, Leiden.

Hockenhull, Tom, 2020, 'Peasants, Produce and Tractors: Farming Scenes on Communist Banknotes', *International Bank Note Society Journal* 59, 2, pp. 26–39.

Joya, José & Benesa, Leonidas V., 1981, *José Joya: A 30-year Retrospective*, Manila.

Ma Thanegi, 2000, *The Native Tourist: In Search of Turtle Eggs*, Yangon.

O'Neill, Hugh, 1994, 'South-East Asia', in M. Frishman and H. Khan (eds), *The Mosque: History, Architectural Development and Regional Diversity*, London, pp. 225–41.

Picard, Michel (ed.), 1997, *Tourism, Ethnicity, and the State in Asian and Pacific Societies*, Honolulu.

Riddell, P., 2001, *Islam and the Malay-Indonesian World: Transmission and Responses*, Honolulu.

Sabapathy, T. K., 2011, 'Developing Regionalist Perspectives in Southeast Asian Art Historiography (1996)', in Melissa Chiu & Benjamin Genocchio (eds), *Contemporary Art in Asia: A Critical Reader*, Cambridge, MA, pp. 47–61.

Taylor, Nora A., 1997, 'Orientalism/Occidentalism: The Founding of the l'École des Beaux-Arts d'Indochine and the Politics of Painting in Colonial Vietnam 1925–45', *Crossroads* 11, 2, pp. 1–33.

Taylor, Nora A. & Ly, Boreth (eds), 2012, *Modern and Contemporary Southeast Asian Art: An Anthology*, Ithaca, NY.

Taylor, Paul Michael (ed.), 1994, *Fragile Traditions: Indonesian Art in Jeopardy*, Honolulu.

Websites

Anonymous, 2000, *Heilbrunn Timeline of Art History*, New York, https://www.metmuseum.org/toah/chronology/#!?geo=ss [accessed 1 August 2021].

Artoftheancestors.com [accessed 14 August 2021]

British Library blog post, 24 March 2014, *An Illuminated Qur'an manuscript from Aceh*, https://britishlibrary.typepad.co.uk/asian-and-african/2014/03/an-illuminated-quran-manuscript-from-aceh.html [accessed 14 August 2021].

British Library blog post, 28 November 2016, *Batak Manuscripts in the British Library*, https://blogs.bl.uk/asian-and-african/2016/11/batak-manuscripts-in-the-british-library.html [accessed 14 August 2021].

British Library blog post, 22 August 2019, *Monastic ordination in Theravada Buddhism*, https://blogs.bl.uk/asian-and-african/2019/08/monastic-ordination-in-theravada-buddhism.html [accessed 14 August 2021].

British Library blog post, 4 February 2021, *Qur'an manuscripts from Southeast Asia in the British Library*, https://blogs.bl.uk/asian-and-african/2021/02/quran-manuscripts-from-southeast-asia-in-the-british-library.html [accessed 14 August 2021].

British Library blog post, 14 June 2021, *Three Qur'an Manuscripts from Aceh in the British Library*, https://blogs.bl.uk/asian-and-african/2021/06/three-quran-manuscripts-from-aceh-in-the-british-library.html [accessed 14 August 2021].

Min Wae Aung images at Karin Weber Gallery: https://www.karinwebergallery.com/artists/min-wae-aung/ [accessed 17 August 2021].

Nationaal Museum van Wereldculturen, *The Great Pustaha*, https://artsandculture.google.com/story/GAVBQ-bzRQMA8A?hl=fr [accessed 25 August 2020].

Smithsonian Southeast Asian ceramics information: https://asia.si.edu/collections-area/southeast-asian/southeast-asia-objects/southeast-asian-art-ceramics/ and https://archive.asia.si.edu/publications/seaceramics/default.php [accessed 15 August 2021].

Tattoo pattern block and equipment: http://web.prm.ox.ac.uk/bodyarts/index.php/permanent-body-arts/tattooing/168-tattoo-pattern-block-and-equipment.html [accessed 15 August 2021].

Tiffany Chung: Vietnam, Past is Prologue: https://americanart.si.edu/exhibitions/chung [accessed 17 August 2021].

Tiffany Chung (biography and works): http://www.trfineart.com/artist/tiffany-chung/#artist-works [accessed 17 August 2021].

Acknowledgments

The objects in this volume represent only a tiny fraction of the art forms found in highly diverse Southeast Asia, and likewise, they are only a small part of the numerous Southeast Asian collections at the British Museum. The diversity of objects, cultures and countries means that I am indebted to many colleagues and friends who gave generously of their time and expertise to assist me. I am very grateful to Theresa McCullough, Fiona Kerlogue and Leonard Andaya who read the volume cover to cover, and to Angela Chiu and Ashley Thompson who read large sections, for their invaluable comments, suggestions and advice. Monica Janowski took me under her wing for the sections on Borneo, as it was an entirely new topic for me. Joe Cribb did the same for Southeast Asian coinage, and Annabel Gallop assisted me with the Islamic sections. I am also very grateful to the many others who contributed by commenting on chapters, sections and topics, or provided information and translations, including Michael Backman, Nigel Barley, Ruth Barnes, Ambra Calo, Barbie Campbell Cole, Sau Fong Chan, Michael Charney, David Clinnick, Pamela Cross, Charlotte Dixon, R. Michael Feener, Barbara and David Fraser, Traude Gavin, Gillian Green, Alfred Haft, Jessica Harrison-Hall, Michael Hitchcock, Tom Hockenhull, Irving Chan Johnson, Cristina Juan, Zeina Klink-Hoppe, James Lankton, Peter Lee, Leedom Lefferts, Pauline Lunsingh Scheurleer, Valerie Mashman, Forrest McGill, Edmund McKinnon, Stephen Murphy, Sandra Niessen, Kerry Nguyen-Long, Chris Reid, Marion Pastor Roches, Tyler Rollins, Geoffrey Saba, Noel Hidalgo Tan, Nora Taylor, Aprille Tijam, Mary-Louise Totton, Adrian Vickers, Helen Wang, Mei Xin Wang, Naomi Wang, Pim Westerkamp and Michael Willis.

Many people at the British Museum and Thames & Hudson generously shared their time, skills and knowledge in working with me to produce this book. Without them, this volume would not have been possible. On the publishing side, I was wonderfully supported by Claudia Bloch, Bethany Holmes and Laura Meachem at the British Museum, and by Philip Watson, Melissa Mellor, and Susanna Ingram at Thames & Hudson. Carolyn Jones and Ben Plumridge edited the volume with eagle eyes for which I am very grateful. Peter Dawson developed a wonderful design and accommodated my requests for minute adjustments with great patience. The museum's photographic department was heroic in dealing with a very large body of material that had not been photographed. I am very grateful to Joanna Fernandes in particular for managing the task, as well as conducting photography. Many thanks are also due to photographers David Agar, Stephen Dodd, Kevin Lovelock, Saul Peckham, Michael Row, Bradley Timms and John Williams. The Asia, Prints and Drawings, Coins and Medals, and Textile collections teams transported a seemingly endless stream of objects to conservation and photography and back again. My heartfelt thanks go to Gavin Bell, Paul Chirnside, Henry Flynn, Amanda Gregory, Jim Peters, Simon Prentice, Stephanie Richardson, Chloe Windsor, Helen Wolfe, Stella Yeung and Enrico Zanoni. Imogen Laing and Benjamin Watts are due particular thanks. Rachel Berridge, Eliza Doherty, Kyoko Kusunoki, Alex Owen, Monique Pullan, Carla Russo and Stephanie Vasiliou in the Conservation department generously accommodated work on numerous objects, despite their busy schedules. I am also very appreciative of the encouragement offered by Richard Blurton, Hugo Chapman, J. D. Hill and particularly Jane Portal.

Finally, I would like to thank my family for their unwavering support and patience. Needless to say, all errors remain my own.

Credits

Index

First published in the United Kingdom in 2023 by Thames & Hudson Ltd, 181A High Holborn, London WC1V 7QX, in collaboration with the British Museum

First published in the United States of America in 2023 by Thames & Hudson Inc., 500 Fifth Avenue, New York, New York 10110

Southeast Asia: A History in Objects © 2023 The Trustees of the British Museum/Thames & Hudson Ltd, London

Series design concept and layout by Peter Dawson, www.gradedesign.com

British Library Cataloguing-in-Publication Data
A catalogue record for this book is available from the British Library

Library of Congress Control Number 2022939653

ISBN 978-0-500-48087-8

Printed and bound in Slovenia by DZS Grafik

For more information about the Museum and its collection, please visit
britishmuseum.org

Be the first to know about our new releases, exclusive content and author events by visiting
thamesandhudson.com
thamesandhudsonusa.com
thamesandhudson.com.au